CW00666332

CONVERSING WITH CHAOS IN GRAECO-ROMAN ANTIQUITY

Ancient Environments

Series Editors
Anna Collar, Esther Eidinow and Katharina Lorenz

The Ancient Environments series explores the worlds of living and non-living things, examining how they have shaped, and been shaped by, ancient human societies and cultures. Ranging across the Mediterranean from 3500 BCE to 750 CE, and grounded in case studies and relevant evidence, its volumes use interdisciplinary theories and methods to investigate ancient ecological experiences and illuminate the development and reception of environmental concepts. The series provides a deeper understanding of how and why, over time and place, people have understood and lived in their environments. Through this approach, we can reflect on our responses to contemporary ecological challenges.

Also available in the series

Mountain Dialogues from Antiquity to Modernity, edited by Dawn Hollis and Jason König

Ovid's Metamorphoses and the Environmental Imagination, edited by Francesca Martelli and Giulia Sissa

Seafaring and Mobility in the Late Antique Mediterranean, edited by Antti Lampinen and Emilia Mataix Ferrándiz

The Spirited Horse: Equid–Human Relations in the Bronze Age Near East, by Laerke Recht

Trees in Ancient Rome: Growing an Empire in the Late Republic and Early Principate, by Andrew Fox

CONVERSING WITH CHAOS IN GRAECO-ROMAN ANTIQUITY

WRITING AND READING ENVIRONMENTAL DISORDER IN ANCIENT TEXTS

Edited by Esther Eidinow and Christopher Schliephake

BLOOMSBURY ACADEMIC

NEW YORK · LONDON · OXFORD · NEW DELHI · SYDNEY

BLOOMSBURY ACADEMIC
Bloomsbury Publishing Plc
50 Bedford Square, London, WC1B 3DP, UK
1385 Broadway, New York, NY 10018, USA
29 Earlsfort Terrace, Dublin 2, Ireland

BLOOMSBURY, BLOOMSBURY ACADEMIC and the Diana logo are trademarks of
Bloomsbury Publishing Plc

First published in Great Britain 2025

Copyright © Esther Eidinow and Christopher Schliephake, 2025

Esther Eidinow and Christopher Schliephake have asserted their right under the Copyright,
Designs and Patents Act, 1988, to be identified as Editors of this work.

Cover design: Terry Woodley
Cover image: Black-figured bowl (*dinos*) and stand, signed by Sophilos as painter
© The Trustees of the British Museum

Bloomsbury Publishing Plc does not have any control over, or responsibility for, any
third-party websites referred to or in this book. All internet addresses given in this
book were correct at the time of going to press. The author and publisher regret
any inconvenience caused if addresses have changed or sites have ceased
to exist, but can accept no responsibility for any such changes.

A catalogue record for this book is available from the British Library.

A catalog record for this book is available from the Library of Congress.

ISBN: HB: 978-1-3503-4419-8
       ePDF: 978-1-3503-4420-4
       eBook: 978-1-3503-4421-1

Series: Ancient Environments

Typeset by RefineCatch Limited, Bungay, Suffolk

To find out more about our authors and books visit www.bloomsbury.com
and sign up for our newsletters.

CONTENTS

Contents

Part IV Change

CONTRIBUTORS

Leonardo Cazzadori (PhD Stanford) collaborates with the University of Padova (Italy). His interests include Greek didactic poetry, ancient science and ideas about the environment in Antiquity.

Maria Combatti, having earned a doctorate in Classics at Columbia University, is now enrolled at Nanterre University in France to get a teaching certificate in French Literature and Classics. Her publications include an article on Euripides' *Helen* published in *Helios*.

Esther Eidinow is Professor of Ancient History at the University of Bristol. She researches and publishes on ancient Greek culture, especially religion and magic. She is co-editor of *Ancient Environments* (Bloomsbury) and was Primary Investigator of the Virtual Reality Oracle project (vroracle.co.uk).

Marco Formisano teaches Latin literature at Ghent University. He is the editor of *sera tela. Studies in Late Antique Literature and Its Reception* (Bloomsbury) and PI of the research project 'Coming After. Late Antique Ecopoetics', funded by FWO.

Jason König is Professor of Classics at the University of St Andrews. His publications include *The Folds of Olympus: Mountains in Ancient Greek and Roman Culture* (2022) and (jointly with Dawn Hollis) *Mountain Dialogues from Antiquity to Modernity* (Bloomsbury, 2021).

Simona Martorana is an Alexander von Humboldt Research Fellow (Kiel/Hamburg). Her work combines philological readings of ancient texts with modern theoretical approaches, including gender, ecocriticism and medical humanities. Her first monograph is *Seeking the Mothers in Ovid's Heroides* (2024).

Christopher Schliephake is Senior Lecturer in ancient history at the University of Augsburg. His research focuses on environmental history, the history of knowledge and ecocritical approaches to ancient literature.

Aaron M. Seider is Dean of Faculty and Professor of Classics at the College of the Holy Cross. His interests include the landscapes of the ancient Mediterranean; gender in Antiquity and its reception; and the construction of memory in Roman culture.

M. D. Usher is Lyman-Roberts Professor of Classical Languages and Literature at the University of Vermont. His books include *Plato's Pigs* (2020) and four volumes in the *Ancient Wisdom for Modern Readers* series.

Michiel van Veldhuizen (PhD Brown University, 2019) is an Assistant Professor in the Department of Classical Studies at the University of North Carolina at Greensboro.

He works at the intersection of ancient Greek religion, intellectual history and ecocriticism.

Krešimir Vuković (DPhil, Oxford University) is Researcher at Charles University, Prague. He has held research posts at the University of Venice, British School at Rome and LMU, Munich. His publications include *Wolves of Rome: The Lupercalia from Roman and Comparative Perspectives*.

Eris B. Williams Reed is a researcher at Wellcome Collection and was Senior Teaching Fellow at the University of Warwick. Her research includes environments and communities at the 'edges' of the Roman Empire and their entanglement in diachronic colonial narratives.

PREFACE

While our intention in writing this preface was to provide a neutral introduction that could stand for the whole series, recent events are too dramatic and relevant to ignore. As we launch the series, and write this text, we are (hopefully) emerging from the ravages of the 2020 Covid-19 pandemic. Along with the climate crisis, this experience has increased awareness of human reliance and impact on the environments we occupy, dramatically emphasised human inability to control nature, and reinforced perceptions that the environment is the most pressing political and social issue of our time. It confirms our belief that the time is right to situate our current (abnormal?) relationship with nature within an examination of human interactions with the environment over the *longue durée*—a belief that has given rise to this series.

Ancient Environments sets out to explore (from a variety of perspectives) different constructions of the 'environment' and understandings of humankind's place within it, across and around the Mediterranean from 3500 BCE–750 CE. By 'environment' we mean the worlds of living and non-living things in which human societies and cultures exist and with which they interact. The series focuses on the *co-construction* of humans and the natural world. It examines not only human-led interactions with the environment (e.g., the implications of trade or diet), but also those that foreground earth systems and specific environmental phenomena; it investigates both physical entities and events and ancient, imagined environments and alternate realities. The initial and primary focus of this series is the ancient world, but by explicitly exploring, evaluating and contextualising past human societies and cultures in dialogue with their environments, it also aims to illuminate the development and reception of environmental ideas and concepts, and to provoke a deeper understanding of more long-term and widespread environmental dynamics.

The geographical remit of this series includes not only the cultures of the Mediterranean and Near East, but also those of southern Europe, North Africa including Egypt, northern Europe, the Balkans and the shores of the Black Sea. We believe that encompassing this broader geographical extent supports a more dynamic, cross-disciplinary and comparative approach – enabling the series to transcend traditional boundaries in scholarship. Its temporal range is also far-reaching: it begins with the Neolithic (a dynamic date range, depending on location in the Near East/Europe) because it marks a distinct change in the ways in which human beings interacted with their environment. We have chosen *c.* 750 CE as our end date because it captures the broadest understanding of the end of Late Antiquity in the Central Mediterranean area, marking the rise of the Carolingians in the West, and the fall of the Umayyad Caliphate in the East.

Our series coincides with, and is inspired by, a particular focus on 'the environmental turn' in studies of the ancient world, as well as across humanities more generally. This focus is currently provoking a reassessment of approaches that have tended to focus solely on people and their actions, prompting scholars to reflect instead (or alongside) on the key role of the environments in which their historical subjects lived, and which shaped and were shaped by them. By extending beyond the chronological and geographical boundaries that often define—and limit—understanding of the meaning of 'antiquity', we intend that this series should encourage and enable broader participation from within and beyond relevant academic disciplines. This series will, we hope, not only advance the investigation of ancient ecological experiences, but also stimulate reflection on responses to contemporary ecological challenges.

The editors would like to express heartfelt thanks to Alice Wright at Bloomsbury Press who first conceived of the idea and suggested it to Esther, and who has done so much to develop it, and to Georgina Leighton, in particular for her work in launching the series. We are extremely grateful to the members of the Series Board, who have provided such wonderful encouragement and support, and to our authors (current and future) who have entrusted their work to this 'home'. We have chosen the 'Mistress of Animals' or *Potnia Theron*, a figure found in Near Eastern, Minoan, Mycenean, Greek and Etruscan art over thousands of years, as the motif for the series.

Anna Collar
Esther Eidinow
Katharina Lorenz

ABBREVIATIONS

For ancient sources, etc. the contributors have used the list of abbreviations found in Hornblower, S., Spawforth, A., and Eidinow, E. 2012. *The Oxford Classical Dictionary*. Oxford (4th edn); this is also available online.

Ael. Arist. *HL*	Aelius Aristides, *Hieroi logoi*
Ael. Arist. *Orat.*	Aelius Aristides, *Orationes*
App. Tib.	*Appendix Tibulliana*
Claud. *De raptu Proserpinae*	Claudius Claudianus, *De raptu Proserpinae*
Plut. *De E*	Plutarch, *De E apud Delphos*
Plut. *Publ.*	Plutarch, *Publicola*
Sen. *Ag.*	Seneca, *Agamemnon*
Sen. *HF*	Seneca, *Hercules Furens*
Sen. *Oed.*	Seneca, *Oedipus*
Sen. *Pha.*	Seneca, *Phaedra*
Sen. *Thy.*	Seneca, *Thyestes*
Serv. *Aen.*	Servius Honoratus, *Commentarii in Vergilii Aeneidos libros*
OCIANA	M. C. A. Macdonald, A. Al-Manser, and M. de Carmen Hidalgo-Chacón Diez, eds. *Online Corpus of the Inscriptions of Ancient North Arabia*, 2017. Available online: http://krcfm.orient.ox.ac.uk/fmi/webd/ociana (last accessed: 21/3/2024)
OLD	*Oxford Latin Dictionary*, 2nd edn, Oxford, 2012.
Varro, *de vir. Ill.*	Varro, *De viris illustribus*
Wadd.	W. H. Waddington, *Inscriptions grecques et latines de la Syrie*, Paris, 1870.

INTRODUCTION: READING AND WRITING ENVIRONMENTAL DISORDER IN ANCIENT TEXTS

Esther Eidinow and Christopher Schliephake

The origins of this volume lie in a panel that we, the editors, brought together for the International Environmental Humanities Conference hosted by KTH Environmental Humanities Laboratory, in Sweden, in August 2020. We assembled the panel with the intention of drawing attention to work on the environment in the ancient world, setting out to address the sense that (at that time) the premodern world only played a marginal role in the paradigm of the 'Environmental Humanities'. We chose the topic of 'Conversing with Chaos', in order to challenge the prevailing view that, in Antiquity, the cosmos was generally understood to be stable and harmonious and under mortal control. In doing so, we were drawing on the multiple meanings of the term, in both ancient and modern, popular and specialist contexts: we start from the ancient Greek concept of *Chaos*, the first progenitor, followed by Earth, in Hesiod's *Theogony*.[1] And, in turn, this account of the creation of the environment – in both its poetic evocation of sheer multiplicity and diversity, and its explicit attempts at systematization – speaks to us of other, later uses of the term: on the one hand, as a common descriptor of an overwhelming experience of instability and lack of order; and, on the other hand, of the scientific definition of chaos, in which a system that appears random may in fact be viewed as exhibiting deterministic behaviour.[2]

We were soon confronted by the reality of such a system:[3] it scarcely needs to be said that the Conference plans were severely disrupted by the Covid-19 pandemic. In those dreadful times, we found that our topic had come to life: our arguments about the ancient world – that ancient experience encompassed the idea that humankind can be viewed as just one agent among many non-human agents, and that our environments are anything but under mortal control – were given a terrifying reality. The irony of this collision of topic and circumstances gave our current endeavours a real sense of urgency. Thanks to the resilience and good will of our panel members, we are grateful to be able to say that we were able to rearrange the original panel into three very stimulating online workshops, held over the period of December 2020 to June 2021; and, indeed, the Humanities Conference itself was also finally held online a year later than its original date.

In the essays that emerged from that context, which are presented in this volume, the overall title of 'Conversing with Chaos' retains its relevance. Each of them explores this theme in different ways, some explicitly, some touching on the topic more implicitly. They investigate the experience of the interaction of humans with the environment, as reflected in ancient evidence; they consider the role of the human in the formation of perspectives about the world around us; they inquire into the role of non-humans, and the deprioritization of human agency. The theme of agency, and related topics of affordances, ecophobia, gender and temporality are key concerns of the essays in this volume, and, in this introduction, we explore those areas, before turning to the essays themselves to show how these different themes occur and interconnect. But, first, we offer an overview of the context of scholarship, in particular the long-held understanding of ancient views of the 'environment', which is gradually changing, and which the essays in this volume aim to address. As this indicates, this means engaging with the semantics and use of language used to describe the environment – including that term and others, such as 'landscape' and 'nature' – and of the role of human culture, including language, in shaping the world around us.

The context of scholarship: Beyond *Kosmos*

At the dawn of the industrial era, Friedrich Schiller wrote one of his most famous essays. In 'On Naive and Sentimental Poetry', he declared that poets are 'by their definition, the guardians of nature'.[4] In this foundational text of modern literary theory and 'prototype', as Greg Garrard puts it, 'of ecocritical theory',[5] Schiller embeds a diachronic element. He distinguishes between 'ancient' and 'modern' styles of writing: whereas ancient literature tends to be, according to Schiller, characterized by concreteness and sensuous immediacy, modern writing, begins where nature ends, with a greater degree of reflective distance and imaginative freedom. According to Schiller, the culture of ancient poets like Homer was still largely integrated into nature, that is to say the ancients were not alienated from it.[6] In consequence, the ancients paid comparatively little attention to the beauties of the natural world in their writings, while authors in later eras would increasingly make natural sceneries, elements and wild landscapes integral parts of their literary creations – quite in proportion to the way nature disappeared from their everyday lives. As Kate Rigby neatly sums up Schiller's observation: 'Nature becomes thematic in literature only when it becomes problematic in reality'.[7]

   It has often been noted that Schiller's text not only had a profound impact on German Romanticism, but has also left its mark on European and British attitudes towards the general relationship between literature, art and nature.[8] In *Kosmos*, Alexander von Humboldt too paid homage to Schiller. Von Humboldt, who had a classical education, admitted that there was a lot to admire about Schiller's general comments. But he also had a few problems with them: he had his doubts as to whether Schiller's comments could really be said to encompass all of Antiquity, and he thought that Schiller's Greco-centrism hardly did justice to the diversity of ancient culture. Be that as it may, von Humboldt held that a feeling for nature, a sentimental treatment of it, was only a sort of embellishment in ancient Greek literary culture that he characterizes as clearly anthropocentric. Studying the archaic and classical texts the ancient tradition had to offer, von Humboldt looked in vain for the kind of 'nature writing' ('Naturbeschreibung') that he found in later epochs of literary history. If prolonged descriptions of landscapes only appear as embellishments, it is, however, not because the ancients were wholly unaware of the beauties of the natural world, von Humboldt writes, but rather because they did not share in modern sentiments of having to somehow put their perceptions of the inanimate nature into words. Rather, the ancient Greeks were interested in human thoughts and actions (not so much in sentiments), and their literary genres reflect this tendency: there simply was not any room for nature writing in the modern – and one may add, romanticized – sense of Humboldt's time.[9]

Alexander von Humboldt was no literary theorist, of course. He was one of the seminal figures of his own day and age and his global exploration travelogues were scientific records as well as cultural, literary and pictorial narratives.[10] Written on the basis of a collaborative exchange with transnational networks of scholars and assembling the available cosmological, geographical, biological and geological knowledge of his time, *Kosmos* was a major undertaking as much as it was a literary event. Von Humboldt championed a proto-ecological, unified view of the world as a chain of causes and effects, where no single fact could be considered in isolation. This is also the reason why it would be wrong to view his excursions into ancient literature as a merely self-contained episode of aesthetic reflection. Rather, they have to be seen as central to his overall project of looking at the cultural roots of contemplating the natural world. This can also be seen in how he rendered ancient environments in general: Greek culture had, according to von Humboldt, a unique opportunity to witness first-hand the elemental interactions at work in nature and this was reflected in how they wrote about the non-human world.[11]

As Laura Dassow Walls has argued, 'For Humboldt, landscapes are languages – and vice versa. (. . .) He saw spatial patterns of distribution and change pointing back in an unbroken continuum through human history to the deep geological (. . .) past.'[12] For Humboldt, natural history and cultural history were inextricably intertwined. Nature and culture were thus seen as interactive processes: human culture is influenced by the landscape as well as effecting change on it. This is also why Humboldt chose the Greek term *kosmos* as title for his multivolume book: for although the physical universe exists apart from such anthropogenic influence, it is only through cultural mediation and reflection that it can be said to be beautiful or ordered in human terms. And that is why imaginative literature features so prominently in *Kosmos*: von Humboldt was convinced that ancient texts help reveal the natural as well as cultural layers embedded within landscapes. The Greeks may not have shared the romanticizing outlook that von Humboldt saw at work in the literature of his own time, but he nonetheless perceived ancient literature as a cultural response to the landscapes in which it was set.

In discussions involving both ecology and aesthetics, the relationship between order and chaos has been a recurring theme.[13] Both Schiller and von Humboldt stand in a long tradition of classical aesthetics, observable at least since the Renaissance, which emphasized balance, order and beauty as properties of the natural world. In the latter half of the twentieth century, harmonious perspectives were gradually supplanted by concepts of chance, contingency and recurrent catastrophes, highlighting the chaotic unpredictability inherent in natural processes. The traditional environmental discourse advocating for the restoration of a presumed pre-existing balance of nature clashed with modern chaos-theoretical interpretations of ecology.[14] These newer perspectives reject the idea of an independent, self-adaptive natural balance altogether, asserting that '"nature" is already, in itself, turbulent, imbalanced'.[15] As the essays in our volume show, this insight is not as modern as it may seem. Rather, ancient writers repeatedly expressed the unforeseeable and disturbing 'agency' of the non-human world, finding highly creative and aesthetically challenging ways to reflect on the interplay between humans and the wider, disorderly cosmos. Against this background, tracing modern ways of writing about 'nature' shows two things: first, that the environmental humanities and ecocriticism, as the literary strand of this interdisciplinary field, reach far back in time. Secondly, ancient culture and literature were, in the formative years of environmental criticism, central to the formulation and reflection of many of key concepts and ideas – from Schiller's remarks on naïve and sentimental poetry all the way to von Humboldt's *Kosmos*. At the same time, two general views expressed by Schiller and von Humboldt, namely that the ancients did not pay a lot of attention to the beauties and, one may add, to the ambiguities of the natural world and that Greco-Roman culture was anthropocentric, remain, to this day, common tropes in environmental studies.[16] The essays in this volume suggest that these views are in need of a re-assessment, including a re-assessment of what counts as an environmental text.

From the early 1990s onwards, 'nature writing' has functioned as a major focus of environmental studies in the humanities.[17] The term itself is most often associated with a more 'specific genre of nonfiction prose in English that blends lyricism or other literary qualities with scientific facts or observations of nature, typically also incorporating personal reflection or philosophical interpretation'.[18] The term has met with criticism, because traditional definitions seem limited in that they focus on wild or pastoral landscapes, ignoring urban and suburban environments, and because they seem to disproportionately feature the privileged as people who are able to enjoy these settings in their retreat from social life. Among other things, newer approaches aim for a re-conceptualization of how 'nature' might be understood, looking for more inclusive definitions of the concept that highlight the interconnection and interdependence between humans and non-humans. Especially promising is work, as Karla Armbruster has argued, 'that focuses on cultures outside those that produced the nature writing tradition – cultures that potentially offer not only diverse literary traditions but also different concepts of nature and perspectives on human relationships to the environment'.[19]

Studying the literature of nature across culture can also lead to a better understanding of how such literature relates to human attitudes and behaviours.[20] Moreover, a comparative approach will show that the nature writing tradition spans not only centuries, but also continents. And for how elastic certain generic expectations and conceptions become when we turn away from Western Romanticism and its cultural descendants and open ourselves up to different environmental worldviews. We can see this specifically in how the relatively recent discipline of ecocriticism has evolved: As Timothy Clark observes in a recent study, 'Thirty years ago, ecocriticism was an infant tendency mainly visible in American studies, celebrating a national tradition of environmentalist nonfiction and British Romantic poetry. Now ecocriticism is a global academic phenomenon, studying multiple texts in innumerable regions.' Clark goes on to cite ecocritical overviews of literature from different continents, illustrating 'the newly global cosmopolitan discourse and intellectual movement' that ecocriticism has inspired.[21]

Ecocriticism has indeed undergone significant changes over the last two decades that have brought about a 'substantial extension and diversification of the epistemic scope, scale and interdisciplinary range of the ecocritical project'.[22] Once defined as 'the study of the relationship between literature and the physical environment',[23] ecocriticism has branched out into other cultural domains and also epochs of human history. What is increasingly at stake 'is the study of the relationship of the human and the non-human, throughout human cultural history and entailing critical analysis of the term "human" itself'.[24] Ecocriticism is therefore not solely a 'cross-cultural', but also a 'cross-historical' undertaking that studies the way that diverse historical traditions have rendered the myriad interrelationships between human societies and their respective surroundings.[25] As the co-editors of a recent 'Global History of Literature and the Environment' formulate, ecocritical approaches to ancient cultures make palpable how these writings 'continued to express preliterate traditions of interaction with the natural world while at the same time responding to historical conditions and challenges such as the expansion of cities and agricultural systems'.[26]

Although no ecocritic would probably contest this claim, it is interesting to note that almost none of the many handbooks that have appeared over the last decade or so include a chapter on the classical tradition.[27] On the one hand, this has to do with the regional beginnings of the field in the context of the Western Literature Association of America. On the other hand, this may be traced to the initial focus on Romanticism (see above). So far, only a handful of texts from the ancient world have been granted a place amongst the 'ecocritical canon'. One introduction into the field lists a diverse range of works ranging from 'Mesopotamian and biblical texts' over the '*Ramayana*, Euripides' *Bacchae*, Ovid's *Metamorphoses*, the Mayan Popol Vuh, the ancient Chinese poetry pf Li Po, the work of Japanese poets Chomei and Basho, and, of course, the European pastoral'.[28] There seems to be a tension between the rather recent 'environmentalist attention to literature' and the fact that 'rich traditions in all major cultures have focused on the human place in the natural world'.[29]

If ancient literature is mostly absent from traditional textbooks on ecocriticism, it has to do with certain generic expectations that are far too narrow in that they exclude all but the most clearly ecologically orientated work. It would, of course, also be problematic if we included any of the vast array of literary works in which nature figures at all.[30] Lawrence Buell sounded this note of caution in his landmark 1995 study *The Environmental Imagination* where he argued that, in light of the environmental crisis, a re-evaluation of the criteria by which the traditional nature writing-canon was drawn up would be in order. He suggests that to count as nature writing, a text should show the non-human environment a presence in its own right, suggesting that human history is implicated in natural history and that the human interest is not understood to be the only legitimate interest. Buell prefers the term 'environment' instead of 'nature', because it draws our attention to the fact that we are always dealing with a 'fusion of "natural" and "constructed" elements' whenever we speak of our surroundings.[31] Others, however, point to the problem inherent in the term 'environment' in that it 'presupposes a topology of centre and surroundings that implicitly prioritizes human agency and interests'.[32]

Embedded in these criticisms is a problematization of the term 'nature' quite characteristic of many strands within the environmental humanities. What especially deconstructivist and poststructuralist philosophy in the vein of Jacque Derrida has shown is that there never existed an unmediated category of 'Nature', with nature understood as a metaphysical construct.[33] In recent years, various attempts have been made to find alternatives to 'nature' within ecologically oriented literary and cultural studies.[34] Yet, 'the general question that remains to be addressed here is', as Kate Rigby puts it, 'that of the relationship between such writing and the more-than-human others, places and histories to which it bids us turn. We must also acknowledge at the very least that our constructions are never entirely free, but always also constrained by a more-than-human material reality that precedes whatever we might make of it.' Rigby suggests that such writing be considered as embodying what she refers to as a 'literary practice of response': as such, we can say that writing is relational in that it can be seen to react to the non-human world, 'while becoming in turn the locus of a new call, to and upon the reader'. Yet, as Rigby also notes, since writing is inextricably bound up with a specific human communicative context, 'the particular mode of written response will vary in accordance with a range of cultural, social, situational and generic contingencies'.[35]

It is these particular modes of written response, these different types of sociocultural frameworks, and generic contingencies that can be analysed for different epochs and eras. Arguably, it is only when we do this that it will become possible to open up the scholarly analysis of so-called 'nature-writing' and, indeed, ecocriticism to a study of the premodern world. If we reframe the term 'nature writing' and understand it not as the portrayal of an idyllic or a pastoral 'Nature', but rather when we perceive the practice of writing as, in Rigby's words, 'a literary practice of response' to the non-human, or more-than-human,[36] then it becomes possible to detach our own reading from certain generic expectations. It is by looking at this literary response that we can catch a glimpse of the way in which ancient writers related to the non-human world.

Within scholarship on the ancient world, approaches are certainly changing. Building on past research that has explored the environment and nature, and related topics, there is now a burgeoning variety of work that takes an ecocritical approach, and/or foregrounds the themes, theories and analytical approaches of the environmental humanities.[37] Recognizing the importance of this new field, the structures of the discipline are also reshaping to include it, supporting the teaching of environmental histories, and offering scholars opportunities in which to discuss and publish their research.[38] Building on these developments, this volume suggests that the ecocritical/environmental perspective on ancient sources is an essential step, not only because it opens a new field of research, but also because it changes all fields. With this volume, the editors and contributors hope to contribute further to developing this field of research, supporting the role it plays not only in offering insights into the ancient world, but also in further enhancing and elaborating perspectives and understandings of human relationships with their environment over time and place.

Themes of the chapters

This volume starts from a reconsideration of the idea that ancient perceptions of the non-human world rested on the profound belief in universal order and therefore paid little attention to variety, irregularity and change. For while it is true that early Mesopotamian and Greek myths explained natural phenomena and attributed an exceptional place within creation to humankind, these mythological stories (and the narratives they inspired over the course of Antiquity) also present us with a world teeming with multiple agencies (encompassing human as well as natural and especially divine forces), undermining or even challenging humankind's sense of control. Against this background, our contributors explore how ancient texts about the ancient environment offer a strong, intricate relationship to their surroundings, not merely as settings for other events, but as an integral part of their innermost fabric; and not merely as reinforcing existing social categories, but as problematizing them, and/or undermining them. In that context, we hope these essays may be seen not only as contributing to ecocriticism more generally, but also as participating in specific themes of that field, including, for example, discussions of ecophobia, which highlight humankind's 'irrational fear of the natural world and its entities, and groundless hatred for the unpredictable climactic and natural patterns around us (for instance, earthquakes, volcano eruptions, flooding, hurricanes), as well as anxiety produced by doomsday scenarios'.[39] We also thoroughly endorse the view put forward by Greta Gaard in her comments on the role of feminism in the development of ecocriticism, and suggest also that they encompass the role of Antiquity in the development of human attitudes to the environment: 'Our failure to accurately and inclusively describe the past will surely limit our capacity to envision potential maps for viable futures.'[40]

Two recent themes of ecocriticism are particularly relevant for the essays in this volume. The first lies in Iovino and Opperman's emphasis on how material ecocriticism draws attention to the ways in which the environment itself (ancient or otherwise) may be read, its interactions with its own entities and with humankind, 'producing configurations of meanings and discourses that we can interpret as stories.'[41] While recognizing the challenge that material ecocriticism presents, as it attempts to reset our intellectual boundaries, nevertheless, we also underline its potency for challenging our conception of ancient views of the non-human world. There are several dimensions to this approach that are relevant for this volume.

One is the sense of an agentic, communicative nature that refutes human exceptionalism. A key theme of all these essays is the investigation of the ways in which ancient environments were socio-culturally constructed as living entities, comprising a network of actors, both human and non-human. Moreover, as recent work on the non-secular

Anthropocene has argued, and many of the essays in this volume demonstrate, this network can also be expanded to include the more-than-human or supernatural.[42] Whether these entities were anthropomorphized or not (and ancient cultures offer a spectrum of personification), human agents were understood as enmeshed in a network of relations with a range of visible and invisible forces. These essays explore those relations, offering insights into the ways in which environments/the entities which they were perceived to comprise were gendered or attributed with specific traits/characteristics. As these analyses reveal, these entities were perceived to participate in the hierarchies and power structures of human communities – be those epistemological, ontological, ethical – in different ways. They were seen, on the one hand, as respondent (even vulnerable) to human activity and decision-making; and, on the other hand, as able to take the initiative, to make choices, to generate action. As this suggests, if we perceive the environment as comprising many different potential agents, not only human, but also non-human and more-than-human, then that radically changes our comprehension of the field in which we operate – the 'affordances' of our surroundings.[43]

The essays in this volume reveal how – across many different sources – that perspective can be found in the ancient world, problematizing the 'nature'-'culture'-dyad, and drawing humankind into confrontation with the fundamental uncontrollability of the (ancient) environment – and the experience of uncertainty and disruption, even chaos, and, perhaps, of disaster, that results. They also show that the unpredictable 'agency' of the non-human world was oftentimes framed in religious terms, by attributing to divine powers the capacity to act in or through 'nature'. Such attributions were never self-explanatory, but displayed a high degree of ambivalence: could humans be certain that what they perceived in 'nature' was truly the expression of a divine capacity to act or to react to what humans were doing? Or were they dealing with processes that were completely independent of sociocultural systems of meaning? These essays portray ancient understandings of a sentient, agentic, feeling world, of which humankind is but one entity.

In this context, we should also pay some attention to another dimension of this first theme, that is, the range of ways in which humankind represents those understandings. From myths and philosophical treatises to epigraphic evidence and archaeological remains, these essays bring us to reflect on the role of (different kinds of) narratives in the articulation, creation and negotiation of environmental knowledge (as opposed to or in conjunction with other narrative/discursive forms of world-making); and, some of the different ways in which this knowledge is expressed by and shapes the interactions of humankind and environment. Among the evidence explored in this volume, we find: complex conceptions of the role of gender in ecology expressed through foundation myths (Vuković); notions of blame for natural disasters emerging from both textual and visual sources (Veldhuizen). Ancient theatrical texts dramatize the decentring of humankind and challenge the conception that we can direct natural phenomena (Combatti and Martorana). The Delphic maxims urge humankind to live within socio-ecological bounds (Usher); and Vergil's *Aeneid* offers warnings about presuming control over your surroundings (Seider). Plutarch raises questions about material (and embodied) changes in the environment (Schliephake); and Thucydides' battle scenes resonate with insights about the experiences of darkness (Eidinow). Finally, suggestions for how to grieve ecological loss is found in evidence as diverse as desert inscriptions and philosophical and rhetorical texts (Williams Reed and König).

And this brings us to the second theme of recent scholarship that underpins the explorations of these essays: the role of affect. Recent work in the environmental humanities has highlighted the role of affect as a response to the current climate crisis; and here we take on the argument made by Bladow and Ladino, in choosing to identify 'affect' rather than 'emotion' in this context, as offering a broader, more inclusive category,[44] emphasizing the ways in which affect is 'ecological "by nature"' operating 'at the confluence of environments, texts and bodies – including non-human and inanimate bodies.'[45] This insight is supported, and elaborated, by the essays in this volume, which, across the different texts they examine, whether or not they focus explicitly on feeling, illustrate how the stories that humankind tells about its environments are pervaded with affect – often, although not always, a sense of dislike or fear; often, although not always, in interaction with more-than-human entities. These insights bring us back to – and help to extend our comprehension of – the theme of ecophobia, and how it may be explored in this different cultural context.

Part of the environmental uncertainty (and the implicit sense of disorder in it) had to do with the unpredictability of non-human forces: in Antiquity there was a rich semantics connected to signs in nature that would allow humans to predict certain events (such as the harvest or an imminent catastrophe), but, as the essays show, the attempt at understanding the semantics of the natural world were often futile or entailed the danger of misunderstanding/misinterpretation. The environmental knowledge negotiated in a lot of the texts analysed in the volume is not so much a testament to the conviction that humans would ever be in complete control of their environments, or would entirely understand them; it rather displays a great degree of ignorance, or at least the inability to find explanations for what was happening in 'nature'. The texts grapple with the need to express what could be known of the non-human world, while also coming to terms with the fact that human systems of meaning were inadequate to fully explain or understand this world and the experience of 'chaos' that this can bring.

What were the literary strategies/motifs that ancient authors used to both reflect on the limits of environmental knowledge and to illustrate the entanglements that existed between humans and their surroundings? One aspect that is highlighted in many of the readings presented here is an embodied perspective that presents humans as standing in an intricate relationship to the non-human elements in their lifeworld. With this comes a sense of vulnerability to the dangers and risks; and one of the central features of the ancient texts in our volume from an environmental vantage point is a full exposure/expression of this awareness of vulnerability. The texts often present humans as reacting to changes in the world surrounding them, changes that they were probably unable to fully explain or comprehend, but that could be somatically felt – and that they tried to express in a semantics that would express their experiences and emotions. Feelings of grief and loss, in particular, and also of disorientation loom large in the texts explored in the book. The ancient authors did not only try to express their feelings, but attempted to respond to the interconnections across bodies/matter in a way that would allow their recipients to reflect on what was being communicated. Many of the texts explored reveal the modes/possibilities of expression of emotions for non-human objects or landscapes, and the translation of environmental experience into human discourse (in ways that would sometimes undermine familiar cultural notions of human supremacy or power/imperialism, and showcase the different temporalities at work in human discourses on the environment, from cyclical conceptions of the time structure of 'nature' to the disorder [and linearity] brought about by human history).

We have organized these essays under four sub-headings, drawing attention to particular themes they share; but these are, of course, just one perspective on their contents, and, reflecting a key approach of this volume, we encourage a plurality of viewpoints. Our sub-headings: 'Control', 'Connection', 'Contact' and 'Change' foreground some significant ideas across the volume itself. The essays in the section 'Control' each address how humans attempt, but inevitably fail, to dominate the environment. In 'Perilous Environs: The Rustic World in Aratus and Nicander', Leonardo Cazzadori considers didactic poetry of the Hellenistic age and its presentation of the environment as one that entangles humans with other entities of nature, in imperfect balance. This requires farmers to pay 'anxious thoughtfulness' to their surroundings and remain attentive to the uncertainty and unpredictability of their lifeworld. As the chapter argues, the analysed poems do not so much offer a detached view of 'nature', but rather present their readers with an affective literary ecology that both draws on mythological motifs and the practical knowledge of farmers that serve as focalizers for the authors. The idea that humankind must pay careful attention to its environment surfaces again in Aaron Seider's examination of the theme of environmental mastery in Vergil's *Aeneid*, 'Shared Suffering and Cyclical Destruction: Failures of Environmental Control in the *Aeneid*'. Seider draws on ecocriticism that conceptualizes the relationship between human beings and the environment as one characterized by reciprocal influence and shifting constructions, exploring how the Trojans' attempts to found a city result in horrific environmental transformations. By highlighting the environmental dimension of the *Aeneid*, the reading not only illustrates how its characters interact with the natural world surrounding them, but also explores how the text problematizes the lack of environmental understanding on the part of the Romans, thus subverting Rome's imperial self-representation. Finally, in the last essay in this section, 'Chaos and *Kosmos*: An Ecocritical Reading of Seneca's *Thyestes*', Simona Martorana brings to bear posthuman ecocriticism on Seneca's *Thyestes* to argue that the play demonstrates how 'Nature' – unintelligible to human perspectives – cannot be made to respond to human demands. Instead, the ambivalence of natural forces in the *Thyestes* challenges the idea of (hu)man's sense of control and subverts the anthropocentric notion of material as well as interpretative mastery over the non-human.

In the section 'Connection', we have included essays that analyse how ancient writers interrogate the relations or potential relations between different entities, and foreground the idea of the human-non-human-more-than-human network. The first essay, 'The Interspecies and Trans-Corporeal Mesh in Euripides' *Bacchae*' by Maria Combatti adopts a non-human-centred focus to examine the more-than-human power of Dionysos and how it spreads throughout the environment – including across human bodies, animals, plants and material entities – in Euripides' *Bacchae*. By bringing the intricate entanglement of humans and non-humans centre stage, the drama undermines the cultural categories that sees them as separate entities. Rather, the essay invites an understanding of Dionysus' agency as a transformative force that acts in the environment and that has a power that can easily subvert social and normative standards. Building on the notion of the environment and its affordances, in 'The Relationality of Darkness in Thucydides', Esther Eidinow explores how meaning and experience interact to convey the embodied experiences of colour terms, specifically, *skoteinos* and *skotos*, terms that can be translated as 'darkness', and used by Thucydides to evoke the experience of a night battle; she argues that words, too, are part of the environmental network. She thereby illustrates the rich meaning of ancient literary representations of the environment and how they related cognitive, emotional and embodied experiences – encompassing both human, non-human and more-than-human elements – with myriad dangers for all actors involved. Finally, in 'The Only Constant Is Change: The Environmental Dimension of Plutarch's *De defectu oraculorum*' Christopher Schliephake discusses a text from the early second century CE that explores the apparent decline of oracles around the Mediterranean world. By highlighting the material dimensions of Delphi, particularly the soil and the associated inspiring vapours that emanate from below, and by reflecting on how they relate to the (human) body, Plutarch's dialogue shows remarkable parallels to recent approaches in the environmental humanities that have illustrated the interrelationship between cultural imagination and material agency. By showing how Plutarch's text embeds these arguments within a religious framework, the essay underlines the particular ancient twist on this discussion.

The essays in 'Contact' all ask how humans have attempted to communicate with the entities in these networks. Encompassing very different forms of evidence, in a broad range of locations, they offer case studies that reveal how communities anthropomorphize particular forces as gods to whom they attribute specific actions and responses and with whom they try to communicate. In 'Poseidon's Mode of Action: Divine Agency and the Helike Disaster', Michiel Veldhuizen looks to the ancient Greek town of Helike, destroyed by earthquake and tsunami in the fourth century BCE, to explore the role of Poseidon as an agent of disaster. Exploring the semantics and sociocultural views that led to the attribution of divine agency in the natural environment, the chapter argues that Poseidon's agency becomes manifest in the way he intervenes in the landscape, especially in his ability to uproot and in making visible what was invisible and vice versa. Thereby, the essay illustrates how the ancient disaster discourse was religiously framed and how language rendered the god's mode of action. Moving from the destruction of cities to their creation, in 'River, Agency and Gender: An Ecocritical Reading of the Myths of the Tiber', Krešimir Vuković turns to the myths of the foundation of Rome. He focuses on the role of the river, Tiber, and surrounding landscape, the Tiber Island, to highlight the ecological knowledge that these stories convey – along with insights into social, religious, political and gender concerns. As the chapter argues, the mythological narratives did not simply present the river as an integral part of the landscape that made up the static background of Rome's history. Rather, the analysed texts imagined the Tiber as an agent in its own right, with a highly ambivalent status that combined both life-giving as well as destructive elements. And from contemplation of rivers, we move to life in the desert: Eris Williams Reed's essay on 'Ecological Grief and the Safaitic Inscriptions of Ancient North Arabia' offers us profound insights into lived experience of environmental change among nomadic pastoralists of the Harrah desert, in the first to third centuries CE. Drawing on the concept of ecological grief, the reading shows how the authors framed their anxieties in the face of unpredictable desert environments. In doing so, it seeks to generate new ways of thinking about the lived experience of environmental change in the ancient world and to expand our understanding of human–environmental interactions in Antiquity by inviting a comparative methodology for analysing how people across cultures and history have perceived and made sense of natural processes.

Finally, while we hope that all the essays in this volume will prompt reflection on contemporary issues, the essays in 'Change' each explicitly raise the question of how reflecting on ecological perspectives in the ancient world can inform our approaches in the modern world. König's essay 'Ecological Grief in Aelius Aristides and Philostratus' revisits ancient reactions to the earthquake that destroyed the city of Smyrna in 178 CE. The analysis pits these against the recent theoretical notion of ecological grief in order to outline the tension between continuity and discontinuity in ancient and modern representations of emotional expressions as regards non-human environments. One key difference to modern presentations of disaster is the apparent lack of focus on human suffering; as the reading suggests, this has to do with the rhetorical character of the analysed texts. Formisano's essay 'An Allegory of the Anthropocene: Environmental and Textual Disorder in Claudian's *De raptu Proserpinae*' offers an ecocritical reading of a Latin epic poem. Highlighting the poem's incompleteness as a structural as well as distinctive narrative feature of the text, the analysis shows how the description of broken and unstable landscapes serves as main motifs that, at the same time, challenge or undermine any sense of human control or understanding. As the chapter proposes, the formal and narrative features of *De raptu Proserpinae* powerfully resonate with the environmental imagination in the Anthropocene. Usher's essay 'The Environmental Ethics of Delphi: Back-filling Latour's *Facing Gaia*' argues that ancient thought (as it was encoded in ritual and myth) still has a great deal to offer and can be a means of fostering environmental awareness today. Revisiting Delphi, the essay reads two maxims associated with it – 'nothing in excess' and 'know thyself' – from an environmental vantage point. The reading highlights the traditional folk wisdom encapsulated in these phrases and interprets them as a cultural expression of the need to live within socio-ecological bounds. By looking at a range of ancient texts, the essay brings the sources in close dialogue with Latour's notion of 'Facing Gaia' and shows how we can re-frame environmental ethics with an ancient model in mind.

Most of the essays in this volume were written during experiences of the pandemic (and we write this, knowing that those experiences have continued for many people); we are all living during a time of environmental crisis. For some, the latter fact in particular, may mean that a volume about the ancient world and the ancient experience of the environment feels irrelevant. Nevertheless, we offer this in the belief that consideration of the experiences and perspectives of another culture can provide us with some opportunity to reflect on our own. The editors of and contributors to this volume believe that the time is right to situate our current relationship with our environment within an examination that spans the *longue durée,* offering an exploration, evaluation and a contextualization of past human societies and cultures in dialogue with their experience of their environments – and what it means to converse with *Chaos*, in all its manifestations. As scholars of the ancient world, the authors in this volume aim to bring a further perspective for those working in their disciplines, helping to broaden and deepen shared understandings of the lived experience of our ancient subjects. These essays, we hope, will challenge our comprehension of ancient understandings of the environment, and prompt questions about both the similarities and the many differences between our ancient subjects and modern perspectives (in all their pluralities). In addition, beyond our own field, we hope that the ecocritical perspectives on this range of ancient sources can support a re-assessment of modern environmental theory concerning the ancient world: that it will help both to strengthen what we believe is a key role for classical studies in the environmental humanities, and to support a re-assessment of modern environmental theory. And, finally, we hope it will find resonance with contemporary readership in broader circles, such that comprehension of humankind's relationship with the environment can be enriched by and seek out further historical perspectives.

Notes

1. Hes. *Theog.* 116, 123.
2. The well known 'Butterfly Effect' also known as 'sensitive dependence on initial conditions' indicates one of the key tenets of chaos theory – that an apparently very minor change in the initial conditions of an a determinstic, non-linear system may produce major consequences. For further information on chaos theory, see Gleick 1987.
3. Jones and Strigul 2021.
4. Schiller 1985: 191.
5. Garrard 2012: 49.
6. Schiller 1985: 180–5.
7. Rigby 2015: 358.
8. This is a complex story that we can hardly do justice to in this framework. For a comprehensive account see Rigby 2004. Cf. also Schliephake 2020.
9. Cf. von Humboldt 1847: 6–9.
10. On the context of von Humboldt's work see Walls 2017: 194–7, also Zapf 2017: 275–7.
11. For von Humboldt 1847: 8 and 11, Greek religion with its myths and nature deities was one cultural area where the nonhuman world featured prominently.
12. Walls 2017: 195.
13. Heide Scott illustrated this in her 2014 work titled *Chaos and Cosmos*. In this study, she contends that chaos and balance have simultaneously served as paradigms for comprehending

'nature' and ecosystems in Romantic and Victorian literature. Scott demonstrates that the interdisciplinary evolution of these concepts was influenced not only by scientific models but also by poetic representations of ecological processes, revealing a complex interplay between scientific and artistic perspectives.

14. On this cf. Zapf 2016b: 139–46.

15. Žižek 1991: 38.

16. Cf. Clark 2019: 13 and 129 on some metaphysical implications of Aristotelian thought. See also Platt on the literary pastoral 2018: 220. For a re-assessment of an 'ancient ecocriticism' and its potential see, in general, Iovino 2016.

17. See the prominence given to the term in Glotfelty and Fromm 1996.

18. Armbruster 2016: 156.

19. Armbruster 2016: 157.

20. Karen Thornber's 2012 study of East Asian literature, *Ecoambiguity*, is a good example in this context. In her book, Thornber questions conventional images of Asian ecological harmony, citing literary references pointing to ecological abuse that go back for centuries, as she also analyses the multifaceted relationships between humans and nature.

21. Clark 2019: 137.

22. Zapf 2016a: 1.

23. Glotfelty 1996: xix.

24. Garrard 2012: 5.

25. Westling and Parham 2017: 9.

26. Westling and Parham 2017: 2.

27. Garrard 2014, Zapf 2016a.

28. Westling 2014: 2.

29. Westling 2014: 2.

30. Garrard 2012: 58.

31. Buell 1995: 7–8.

32. Rigby 2015: 363.

33. Cf. Derrida 1997.

34. As already noted, Buell prefers the term 'environment', the posthuman philosophers Latour (1993) and Haraway (2007) speak of 'nature-cultures' or 'culture-natures' to highlight the constant forms of hybridization involved in environmental interaction, while there is, of course, also Ernst Haeckel's coinage of 'ecology', implying an endeavour to understand the multiple interrelationships between living entities in the 'whole household' of the earth in its varied regions in a manner that does not centralize humankind – 'ecology' has indeed become a bridging concept between the sciences and the humanities, where terms like 'cultural ecology' or 'literary ecology' feature prominently.

35. Rigby 2015: 364.

36. David Abram (1996), along with other thinkers in environmental philosophy and ecopsychology, introduced the concept 'more-than-human' to emphasize the complexity and interconnectedness of the natural world beyond just human perception and understanding. While the term 'nonhuman' refers to entities that are not human and that were, as a result, often considered as passive objects to be studied, used, or dominated by humans, the term 'more-than-human' goes beyond the simple categorization of entities as either human or

nonhuman. It suggests that these entities possess qualities, agencies, and ways of being that exceed human understanding and perception. This perspective challenges the anthropocentric view that places humans at the centre of the universe and emphasizes the importance of recognizing and respecting the autonomy and integrity of nonhuman entities.

37. A few recent examples include: Hunt 2016, Hawes 2017, Korhonen and Ruonakoski 2017, Felton 2018, Bosak-Schroeder 2020, Hollis and König 2022, Sissa and Martelli 2023. Cf. also Schliephake 2022 with a brief overview.

38. See the series *Ancient Environments*, published by Bloomsbury.

39. Iovino and Opperman in their call for papers for the volume *Material Ecocriticism*, and cited in approval in Estok 2013: 74.

40. Gaard 2010: 660.

41. Iovino and Oppermann 2014: 7.

42. E.g. Bubandt 2018.

43. Gibson 1979: 127: The idea of 'affordances' concerns how, when we perceive our environment, we perceive 'action possibilities', that is, what the environment 'offers the animal, what it provides or furnishes, either for good or ill' in terms of pragmatic action (rather than information that requires decoding).

44. Bladow and Ladino 2018: 5.

45. Bladow and Ladino 2018: 8.

PART I
CONTROL

CHAPTER 1
PERILOUS ENVIRONS: THE RUSTIC WORLD IN ARATUS AND NICANDER
Leonardo Cazzadori

Hellenistic writers are known for emphatically and dramatically representing nature.[1] The early Romantics suggested that Hellenistic people perceived themselves as more removed from the natural world, unlike Homer, and this prompted them to depict the natural world so attentively.[2] This was for them a negative consequence, not a strength, of this epoch. Friedrich Schlegel, in the essay *Von den Schulen der griechischen Poesie* (1794), calls the Hellenistic period 'artificial' and 'corrupt'. But recent scholarship has seen the potential in these later texts. In particular, the work of Mark Payne has aimed at reconsidering Hellenistic poets as interpreters of the natural world.[3] Hellenistic poetry does not offer a theory about the world that surrounds human life; it rather features different forms of insight into the environment. Payne, with respect to the didactic poets of this period, rightly speaks of 'an occasion for perspectivism'.[4]

Didactic poetry of the Hellenistic period is keen on thematizing the natural world. It presents (in verses) various forms of specialized knowledge, which assist humans with their daily activities, such as farming, fishing, hunting, cooking, travelling, finding remedies against bites of dangerous animals, looking for time pointers in the sky, and so forth. Describing and mentioning aspects of nature and the environment in these poems is dependent on the idea that this type of information will be useful to the reader.[5] Didactic poetry, indeed, does not convey a theory of the environment. But the environment is an essential component for the topics of this poetry.[6] Indeed, this poetry does not provide any theory about the cosmos. I wish, however, to point out in this essay that there are some common features in two influential didactic poets of the Hellenistic epoch,[7] Aratus and Nicander. Both poets conjure one specific type of environment, namely the countryside world. In their work, we find a shared view of how human and non-human beings are entangled in this rustic world, which looks neither too wild nor too domesticized by humans but is exactly a space in-between.

Sections 1 and 2 of this essay argue that Aratus and Nicander present us with a complex view on the countryside environment, which is central in their poems. Both poets share some optimistic ideas about the rustic world, which offers plenty of resources that are vital for humankind. But, throughout the poems, one notices that humans inhabit this world with some accompanying tension. Imbalance, danger and risk due to unpredictability mark these rustic environs and make them perilous. Aratus and Nicander represent the countryside not as a reality ruled exclusively by order, but with room for the chaotic; not only this, but they also provide some justification for this view, as section 3 will argue.

The rustic world in Aratus

Aratus of Soli wrote the poem *Phaenomena* in about the first half of the third century BCE.[8] He was active in Greece, especially in the city of Athens and in Northern Greece, in the city of Pella, at the court of king Antigonus Gonatas.[9] The title of the poem, *Phaenomena*, is intriguing. On the one hand, it is a technical word that refers to celestial phenomena, such as stars and constellations, and Aratus might use it in this sense since the first half of the poem deals exactly with these topics. The poet, on the other hand, seems to extend the meaning of this term to include other things that 'appear' to us through the air:[10] in the second half of the work, he presents also meteorological facts, such as storms and winds.

In the poem *Phaenomena*, the rustic world is the dwelling place, above all, of farmers. Aratus repeatedly tells his readers that he will describe natural phenomena that are important for people who are involved in farming and agriculture.[11] The poet's interest in this rustic world is usually considered a tribute to Hesiodic poetry.[12] Hesiod's poem *Works and Days* highly prizes work and focuses on farming activities and their seasonal timing in Archaic Greece. This provided a model for later poets who wished to deal with the countryside environment, such as Vergil's *Georgics*. But we find a peculiar and quite 'dramatic' representation of the countryside world in the second half of the *Phaenomena* (778–1141), when Aratus deals with weather phenomena. He is interested in explaining natural events that foretell weather changes: the so-called *Diosemiai*, or 'weather signs'. Most of these signs he provides in list-form, arranging them into groups that refer to the same weather conditions (such as rain or a clear day). We learn about various natural phenomena, and he shapes the narrative such that it brings our attention closer and closer to what happens on the ground. Aratus mentions signs from various wild and livestock animals (909–1043), and then he openly talks about the world of farmers.

A description of a running farm, however, is not found in the poem. But we are shown glimpses of the farmers' life and work in the countryside. Farmers are, for example, careful observers of trees (1044–6), as these are indicative of what season is coming and what farming activities should be carried out (1051–4). The farm-owner (*alōeus*, 1045) is characterized here as an expert in interpreting (key) signs from trees. It is significant that Aratus hints also at the emotional state of farmers. At line 1045 and following, the *alōeus* is described as busy and somehow agitated ('he is always busily watching everywhere' for the signs). Indeed, calculating the right time of the season was key for ancient agriculture and, in the absence of modern technology, one had to rely on information drawn from nature. Aratus describes this fact but adds a psychological detail which implies a dramatization of the farmers' life in the countryside.

There is a passage later in the poem where we find a more explicit dramatization. Aratus is explaining various signs in animal behaviour. Some foretell season change and certain critical climate conditions (1064–93), such as long or stormy winters. Other signs, the last ones of the poem, are about coming rain (1104–41). The poet places a moralistic digression between these two sequences, when he refers to the uncertainties that beset farmers, as follows:

The mainland farmer does not like (*oude . . . chairei*) flocks of birds, when from the islands in large numbers they invade the cornlands at the coming of summer: he is terribly alarmed (*perideidie d'ainōs*) for his harvest, in case it turns out empty ears and chaff, distressed by drought. But the goatherd (*aipolos anēr*) is rather pleased (*chairei de pou*) with the same birds, when they come in moderate numbers, because he expects (*elpomenos*) thereafter a year of plentiful milk. So it is that we suffering restless mortals (*mogeroi kai alēmones . . . anthrōpoi*) make a living in different ways; but all are only too ready to recognize signs (*semat' epignōnai*) that are right besides us (*par posi*), and to adopt them for the moment (*es autika poiēsasthai*) (1094–103).

The poet mentions here two types of people who work in the countryside, the mainland farmer and the goatherd. He portrays them both as routinely seeking signs of nature – the presence of birds in this case – which foretell how the season is going to be. It seems that the arrival of too many birds (during summer) is taken by both types of agricultural workers as a sign of an incoming drought season. Aratus juxtaposes two different reactions from them, with their names and the verb *chairein* ('to rejoice') in a chiastic position. Moreover, we see further emotional details: the fear of the mainland farmer for his crops when the signs are bad (1096, *perideidie*); and the goatherd's hope for a well-fed flock (1100, *elpomenos*), when the signs are favourable. The information on the island birds is not an invention of Aratus, but, like most of the weather signs reported in the poem, it was widespread knowledge in Greece.[13] For example, another Hellenistic source of meteorological knowledge whose authorship remains disputed, the Pseudo-Theophrastus, presents the same information in this way (17):[14]

And during summer, when many island-dwelling birds show up in dense flocks, they signal rain. But if there are not many of them it is good for goats and herds; but if there are too many there will be a severe drought.

Compared to this explanation, Aratus' peculiar account becomes evident. With regard to the same weather signs, the poet gives particular emphasis to human emotions. First, he introduces the farmers and their emotional reactions to these signs, as I showed before. But this is not all, the poet also compares these to the human condition. The worry about nature signs characterizes not only farmers but all humankind.

Here, the poet's view is to some extent pessimistic: granted, nature signs are very helpful, but we must also reckon with the fact that humans live in a restless condition. Aratus uses the words *alēmōn* at line 1101 ('wanderer') and *mogeros* ('distressed'). It does not seem that weather signs make humankind stop worrying. For, the poet uses the expressions *par posi*, 'just at the feet' (i.e. 'close at hand'), and *es autíka*, 'too readily'. These would suggest that humans scramble to find the quickest pointers for their plans. By the end of the quote, the opposite reactions of the farmers appear to become an example of humans' distress with weather signs, not just an example of specific situations that meteorology explains.

There are some implications for the poem's meaning from the fact that farmers and humans share the same way of living. The rustic world becomes paradigmatic of how humans live anywhere on earth. Throughout the poem, Aratus very skilfully shifts the perspective of his readers from one of distance from the topic to one of closer engagement with it. But it is significant that some possibility for closer engagement is given when Aratus prompts the readers to identify with the farmers, for example, in the passage at lines 1094–103 quoted above. It has been argued that, with these references to farming, the poet aims at playfulness.[15] I argue below that they also achieve another goal, namely, they arouse the readers' empathy with the subject matter.

We have seen that Aratus pieces together descriptive and psychological details. I suggest that this results in an 'affective ecology' of the rustic world. In accounting for a different topic that arouses emotional response in literary works, namely situations of environmental injustice, Alexa Weik von Mossner uses the terms 'insider perspective' and 'outsider perspective'. With the former, readers feel for the character himself (such as the victim of environmental injustice); with the latter, readers empathize with someone else who in turn cares for the situation.[16] If we apply these ideas to the passage of Aratus just discussed, farmers then offer readers an 'insider perspective' into the challenges of interpreting the environment. This would explain why readers are not only informed about many important details of the countryside environment, but they are also encouraged to empathize with farmers who are immersed in it.

If this is the case, then I suggest that empathy serves the important purpose of making the rustic world a paradigm for the interactions between humans and the environment, in Aratus. To this end, the poet brings the 'insider perspective' to the extreme and makes his readers characters of his poem. In a programmatic passage of the *Phaenomena*, the long transition in the middle of the poem (758–77) which takes readers from the topic of astronomy to meteorology, the poet addresses his reader directly and places him in the same situation of the countryside people:

> . . . And if ever you entrust yourself to a ship, be concerned to find out all the signs that are provided (*kechrēmena keitai/sēmata*) anywhere of stormy winds or a hurricane at sea. The effort is slight, but enormous is later the benefit of being observant to the man who is always on his guard (*epiphrosunēs aiei pephulagmenōi andri*): in the first place he is safer himself, and also he can help another with his advice when a storm is rising nearby (758–64).

The poet invites his reader (here addressed with the second person singular) to take on the sailor's perspective. Sailing is critically exposed to nature's events, as much as it is farming. These two activities are somewhat complementary in the poem, as they appear to symbolize humans' dependence on the environment.[17] The poet has his good reason for pointing out that attaining knowledge about the signs of weather is quite advantageous and 'easy'. Indeed, this encourages readers to stick with the poem, now that the topic is about to change. But Aratus also brings in the insider prospective, by making clear, at lines 763–4, that the advantage has to do with something not secondary. This type of knowledge brings 'measureless advantage' (761) in that it allows humans to foresee weather conditions and situations of risk that may pose their own lives in extreme danger. Of course, this is true in so far as humans are identified with countryside people.

One key word in this passage is *epiphrosunē*, 'observation'. This is the state of mind expected from humans who look for those weather signs that 'lie delivered' (*kechremena keitai*, 759) to the benefit of humans, in the environment. The ability of being observant implies fixing the eyes on something, as the prefix *epi-* in *epiphrosunē* suggests. This is linked with a complementary feeling, one of constant vigilance. This is brought up with the phrase *aiei pephulagmenōi andri* (762), 'the man who is always on guard'. Readers have taken on the sailor's perspective by now and are, therefore, encouraged to feel the same emotion. Humans must stay alert all the time about phenomena in the environment because they have learnt that these can become helpful signs; but constant vigilance can easily turn into anxiety. Humans are restless creatures, Aratus maintains. As we will see in section 3 of this essay, in Aratus' poem, some reason for this anxiety is seen to come from the fact that signs from the environment are not always clear – disorder coexists with order. But before discussing this aspect, I will turn to Nicander's representation of the countryside world.

The rustic world in Nicander's *Theriaca*

Not much is known about the life of the poet Nicander of Colophon. He lived in the second century BCE and was active in the Attalid kingdom of Pergamon (in Asia Minor). Some works are of disputed authorship, but among those that are safely attributed to him and that deal with the countryside topics, we have the poems *Theriaca* (on venomous animals), *Georgica* (on farming activities) and, if it is not part of the latter, *Melissourgica* (on bee-keeping). I will concentrate on the *Theriaca*, which is, of these, the only fully extant (958 lines).

The *Theriaca* presents information on venomous animals and the remedies that can hinder the poisoning. These topics are drawn from a peculiar specialization of ancient knowledge which intersects the fields of ancient medicine and biology, that is, toxicology. The ancients collected information on dangerous animals, their characteristics, the places that they inhabited, and what remedies could be used for healing. We are only sparsely informed about this knowledge branch in the Hellenistic period, but we do know that it became quite popular in this epoch, even among the Hellenistic courts who offered patronage to poets; for example, we know of royals who kept toxicologists close to their entourage or were themselves familiar with plants that have healing powers.[18] This means that the *Theriaca* does not thematize 'obscure' or 'marginal' topics.

Unlike Aratus, Nicander occasionally refers to certain places or regions in his poem;[19] but, like him, he typically represents the environment without specific geographical references, although with those features that are characteristic of the countryside world. Nicander is very self-conscious about carrying on ideas found in Aratus, also thanks to both poets' admiration of Hesiodic poetry.[20] I want to point out that, regardless of Hesiod,

Nicander's work achieves a significant result on its own with his poetic representation of the rustic world. He makes this environment central to the message of his poem and exploits the meaning of the complex interactions between humans and the natural world.

In the prologue of the *Theriaca*, Nicander makes the countryside central for the whole message of this work. To his (real or fictional) addressee Hermesianax,[21] the poet explains that he will learn about the 'forms and bites of venomous animals' and 'the freeing of the troubles' with the right cures (lines 1–3). But the poet will not just tell Hermesianax these things for their own sake. Farmers too should be beneficiaries of this knowledge:[22]

> And the toiling ploughman (*poluergos arotreus*), the herdsman and the woodcutter, whenever in forest or at the plough one of them [*scil.* poisonous animals] fastens its deadly fang upon him, shall respect you for your learning (*periphrasthentos*) in such means for averting sickness (4–7).

The poet sets a special relationship between his internal reader, Hermesianax, and an ideal and yet distanced audience, namely the farmers.[23] One can call the latter 'fictional' also, but this does not mean that farmers are only part of a playful strategy of the author. We have seen with Aratus that countryside people function also as 'focalizers' and may arouse readers' empathy, by means of the insider prospective. Nicander retrieves Aratus' idea that the poem provides useful information to people who work in the countryside. This is suggested by the keyword *poluergos*, 'hard-working', referred to the ploughman at line 4. But unlike Aratus who speaks more generally of humans at work in the opening of his poem, Nicander here relies on Hermesianax as a sort of intermediary between the poet and countryside workers. Hermesianax is expected to pass down this knowledge to farmers and gain their trust.

Before turning to some highlights of the poem's pharmacological explanations, let us consider one last programmatic passage, namely the closure. Nicander presents himself here as a man of the country:

> So now you will treasure ever the memory of the Homeric Nicander, whom the snow-white town of Clarus (*Klarou niphoessa polichnē*) nurtured (957–8).

The poet mentions the city of Clarus, near Colophon, which raised him. Autobiography and poetological discourse are intertwined in this passage.[24] But there is also a third aspect, namely that this detail adds also to the construction of Nicander as a character in the poem. In what sense did Clarus 'nurture' the poet Nicander? Nicander was involved in the prestigious court of Pergamon, and we might expect him to be connected with other important cultural places of his time.[25] The 'character' with which Nicander presents himself here, however, is as someone who comes from a *small* village. For, he uses the term *polichnē* (line 958), a diminutive of *polis*, to mention his birthplace; that is, we are encouraged to think about Clarus as a rural place which is likely surrounded by many farms. This landscape fits the idea of the narrative of the poem as a collection of messages beneficial to farmers. In the poem's opening, Nicander sees Hermesianax as the most appropriate messenger with some special ties with countryside people (see lines 4–7 quoted above). But in the poem's closure, the poet himself emphasizes his own personal connection with this rustic world.

Once we start reading the poem's explanation after the prologue, we find that Nicander conjures the rustic world with many details, unlike Aratus who defers this to the second half of his poem. Nicander begins with an account of various techniques to ward off dangerous animals (21–156). He describes several situations of danger for humans in it. One key situation that appears to have caught the poet's attention (and imagination) is when humans rest outdoors, either within the space of the farm or out in nature. In lines 21–34, which kick off the poem's lessons, Nicander lists several situations of the day (or night) that may expose people to the terrible threat of *herpeta*, creeping animals (line 21). In surveying the various possibilities, the poet gives us a tour of the rustic world, in a key, initial position of the poem. Let us focus on some of the most interesting features of this passage.

First, we find many traces of human presence. Nicander mentions details of farms surrounded by fields (at line 21 'farmstead', *stathmos*, 'cottage', *aulion*; at line 29 'threshing floor', *halōs*); but there are also wilder places, such as thick forests, mountain gullies, dry hills. Yet these are also visited often by humans, especially those involved in rustic activities (see also the adjective 'pastoral' at line 28, *amorbaios*,[26] which describes these places). As Aratus does with his farmer, Nicander also makes his farmers 'focalizers', who allow us to experience the dangers of nature through them. Readers *feel* their struggles, as they find refuge outdoor in the fields after a steamy workday in the summer and making sure not to be bitten by lurking snakes (lines 21–34). This makes us empathize and pay closer attention to the countryside environment and the information Nicander shares about it.[27]

The rustic world described here has a twofold quality. On the one hand, it is a type of environment that humans inhabit and trust. This is well exemplified here by the image of humans finding for themselves a place to sleep anywhere outdoors in the countryside, during the hot days of summer (21–5). But, on the other, the rustic world is not a fully domesticized space. Danger is everywhere for humans. People are indeed most vulnerable when they let down their guard while sleeping; even when one rests at the farm (29). Nicander contrasts the beauty of serene springy meadows near farms with the equally fascinating metamorphosis of snakes that leave behind their old skin in spring and wander around blind so that – one must infer – they endanger humans who may step on them (30–4). Danger in the rustic world is conveyed with the language of battling (see, e.g. 21–2 *phugdēn ... diōxeai* 'chase [animals] and drive them out'). Floris Overduin has clearly pointed out that there is quite a significant amount of military language throughout the *Theriaca*, with which the poet characterizes the struggle of humans with these animals in the countryside. If Theocritus, a century earlier, had represented this environment as a serene and inviting space where rustic people converse amiably, Nicander no doubt turns the world of pastoral upside down.[28]

One key figure of the poem is the man named Alcibius. His story encapsulates these characteristics of the rustic world. Nicander refers twice to Alcibius in the poem, in connection to certain special herbs that this man apparently first discovered (541–9, 666–75). Alcibius is not explicitly described as a farmer, nor do we know anything about the period in which he lived. But we are told that he sleeps on a farm's threshing-floor (546–7); he also goes out to hunt and wanders in wilder places of the Troad region, near forests and cliffs (668–70, 672). Note that what Alcibius does is very similar to the activities that Nicander mentions with regard to farmers, in the quote above (21–34). Due to this aura of mystery, Alcibius appears to play the role of 'mythic farmer' and, thus, seems to be an important reference in the poem. At the same time, nothing is known about him from other authors. Alcibius may well then be Nicander's invention;[29] that is, he is a sort of fictional myth that, as I will now explain, speaks to the poem's whole message.

Both the two stories that Nicander recounts about Alcibius have the same message: the rustic environs are perilous, for there are threats that make them unpredictable and dangerous. In both stories, the hunter Alcibius or his dog are attacked by vipers. Nicander also shows that there are useful resources for survival in the countryside. Alcibius is responsible for finding new remedies against the viper's bite,[30] which in turn must bear his name (e.g. 541, 'Alcibius' bugloss', a plant from the Boraginaceae). With Alcibius' misadventures, Nicander emphasizes that nature helps humans with ready resources (i.e. medicinal herbs). In the first story, Alcibius is woken up by the pain of the viper's bite and immediately finds a plant whose root has healing power.[31] In the second story, his dog, while following a goat, is bitten by a viper. But the dog 'readily ate (*reia ... katebruxen*) the leaves of this herb and escaped deadly destruction' (674–5). The adverb *reia*, 'readily', 'easily', draws attention to Nicander's belief in the generosity of nature. The countryside is not only a place of danger but also of remedies that are easy to find. We see here another key parallel with Aratus. Both poets share the optimistic idea that there are plenty of helpful resources for humans who know their environment.

Countryside perils, and chaos aetiologies

Aratus and Nicander represent the countryside as an intermediate type of environment, which does not overlap with 'wild nature' nor is as anthropic as an ancient walled city. The rustic world is a type of space where humans leave their many marks (farms, domesticated animals, shepherd's trails) and exploit resources (agriculture, farming, etc.). The poets encourage us to empathize with farmers who are the protagonists of this world. But this space is also home to wild animal life, which is potentially dangerous. Humans are described as being very concerned with weather conditions and risks. We are, hence, quite far from a type of space that one could call a *locus amoenus* ('pleasant place').[32] Aratus and Nicander, I will now argue, provide cues to readers for explaining why the rustic world can be dangerously chaotic. Indeed, chaos is, in their view, a key feature of the countryside environment, as I will show.

In this essay, 'chaos' primarily means a condition of life in the universe, which is at odds with order.[33] I do not draw this meaning directly from the ancient Greek word *chaos*, whose etymology does not point to the idea of disorder, but means, instead, 'gap' and 'abyss'. I use the word 'chaos' in a more general sense. The ancient Greeks posited certain ideas about disorder which resemble what we call chaos (that is, lack of order). We find either the idea of disorderly phenomena in the universe, or the idea that there existed struggles in the contest for the ruling power over the cosmos (the Titans or Typhoeus, in Hesiod).[34] Both these ideas are relevant for explaining how Aratus and Nicander dealt with disorder in the countryside environment.

Aratus does *not* thematize chaos explicitly in the *Phaenomena*. The poet is indeed very vocal about order in the sky. We are told at the very opening of the poem that Zeus 'separated the stars and fixed the signs in the sky' (10–11 ... *ta ge sēmat'en ouranōi estērixen/astra diakrinas*). The verb *diakrinein* ('to distinguish', to 'separate one from another') brings forth the idea of order and organization. The constellations are presented as *agalmata nuktos iousēs* 'figurines of the passing night' (453); thus, they are like beautiful, well-crafted ornaments for the sky.[35] The celestial sphere is described as perfect as an object glued together by an expert craftsman (525–36).[36] These features indicate that the sky shares the characteristics of the *kosmos*. In ancient cosmological thinking, the universe is called *kosmos*, because it is thought to possess order and beauty; the Greek word *kosmos*, 'orderly design', 'arrangement' or 'decoration', fits well with this idea and becomes the right word for universe.[37] Aratus' sky is a reminder of the universe qua *kosmos*.

The poet, however, also conjures the idea of chaos. In the first instance (367–85), the poet is commenting on one of the few areas of the sky where stars are not shaped into constellations.[38] These nameless stars lie in a small space and are not very bright (367). They do not resemble the 'parts of a well-made figure' (370–1, *tetugmenou eidōloio ... meleessin*). We are faced, therefore, with a clear example of lack of order in the sky; Aratus contrasts this with the opposite situation, the many stars that, 'marching in ranks in order', 'along the same paths' (372), pass every year. To explain the situation, the poet embarks on an explanation of what is the cause of this, that is the aetiology of these phenomena.[39] We are told that 'some man from the past' (373) 'distinguished' the stars in the sky and 'gave shape' to them (i.e. the constellations).[40]

The identity of this first creator of the constellations is not given, which suggests that we are dealing with the 'first inventor' idea, that is, with the ancients' fascination with the remote past.[41] We are told, however, that he is responsible for making order in the sky (379–83). While Aratus starkly emphasizes this,[42] he also reminds us that there is a concomitant lack of order. He concedes that the first inventor could not 'name' or 'know' all stars (375–6) because 'there are so many all over the sky, and many alike in magnitude and colour, while all have a circling movement'. Seeing countless and identical stars suggests the idea of randomness and lack of *kosmos*;[43] note the alliteration and polyptoton[44] in the verses which stress this idea (πολλοὶ γὰρ πάντη, πολέων δ'ἐπὶ ἶσα πέλονται / μέτρα τε καὶ χροίη, πάντες γε μὲν ἀμφιέλικτοι 'there are so many all over the sky, and many alike in magnitude and colour, while all have a circling movement'). Thus, it is the case that Aratus enshrines the idea of cosmic order in this aetiological passage (367–85). But the poet opens and closes this aetiology with the reference to a shapeless and blurry area of the sky (367–70, 384–5), so as to remind the reader that the other possibility exists too.

Aratus appears to believe that there is chaos especially in human knowledge about the universe. Already, in the passage discussed above, we learn of the first inventor's shortcoming in knowing all stars (376, *oude daēnai*), even though these appear themselves chaotic, as we have just seen. The poet returns, later in the poem, to the idea that disorder is the result of human 'cognitive' failure. In the introduction to the new topic of meteorology (*Phaenomena* 758–77, mentioned above),[45] we have seen that Aratus observes the human condition of anxiety and *epiphrosunē* ('constant vigilance') when one is out in nature; and he adds that there is great advantage in understanding meteorological knowledge to cope with this anxiety (761–2). But, in the following lines, Aratus changes view quite radically (765–72), with the same oscillation that we found above. Now, suddenly, the environment is described as unpredictable (265–8); and 'an evil arrives unforetold' (768, *aprophaton kakon hiketo*).

In explaining why this situation of uncertainty may happen, Aratus makes it the fault of humans: 'we humans do not yet have knowledge of everything from Zeus, but much is still hidden, whereof Zeus, if he wishes, will give us signs anon' (768–71). The poet reiterates that Zeus is benevolent to humans (771–2), thus neutralizing the potentially disruptive comment made before, with regard to the *kosmos*. Scholars have sometimes read Aratus' comment about hidden knowledge as an allusion to disguised messages in the poem, such as his famous acrostics.[46] I want to stress, instead, that this passage also points to the idea of chaos in nature. Aratus combines the idea of unpredictable weather phenomena with Zeus' reluctance in making everything clear to us. At the very least, this suggests that humans have reasons for experiencing disorder, in nature. Thus, the countryside can become a place of anxiety for humans who suddenly experience the chaotic.

Nicander takes one step further than Aratus, by making a direct reference to chaos and by subtly rehearsing certain relevant myth stories of the Greeks. The poet provides an aetiology for why poisonous animals exist in the first place (8–20) with an explanation that combines two myths: the battle of the Titans with Zeus, and Artemis' punishment of Orion. Nicander first recounts that animals have venom in their body because they were created by the blood of the Titans: 'men say that noxious spiders, together with the grievous reptiles and vipers and the earth's countless burdens, are of the Titans' blood' (8–10). Based on the myth known in Greece, one infers that the blood mentioned here fell on the ground during the cosmic fight that these gods engaged in with Zeus. Nicander also makes a direct reference to Hesiod as source of this story (10–12). Despite the difficulties of this passage,[47] the poet does activate here the myth of the Titans combined with an allusion to Hesiodic poetry.

The importance of the Titans for Nicander is emphasized by the poet's return to them later in this passage when he recalls the story of Artemis and Orion. For, at line 13, when he brings in Artemis, she is referred to as *korē Titēnis* (she is, indeed, granddaughter of the Titans Phoebe and Coeus). Nicander emphasizes her link with the Titans rather than with her father Zeus. This allows him to connect the two myth stories. Besides, the alliance between Artemis and the poisonous scorpion with which she punishes Orion perfectly fits the main topic of the *Theriaca*. Whether or not Hesiod is Nicander's direct source on this aetiology for dangerous animals, the background of Hesiod's *Theogony* appears quite relevant. The *Theogony* presents a narrative about the formation of the universe in which Zeus succeeds in defeating his rivals, and then imposes a new and permanent regime of power and order.[48] The battle with the Titans,[49] the so-called Titanomachy (617–19), is central in this scheme. The result of this cosmic struggle is that Zeus becomes 'king of the gods' (881–5); the Titans lie neutralized in the depths of the earth, next to primordial Chaos, the yawning space that was generated first in the universe.[50] Mythic Chaos is closely associated with the Titans in Hesiod, because both are marginalized by Zeus.[51]

Thus, Nicander suggests that the 'battles' that humans face every day in the countryside against dangerous animals ultimately are due to a mythic battle for order, the Titanomachy. The blood of the Titans, caused by a cosmic battle in a dramatic moment of lack of order for the universe, would explain the situation of danger that farmers experience in the perilous countryside. Nicander, perhaps playfully, presents a strong message about chaos in relation to the topic of his poem. The dangers of nature in this rustic world can be seen as an image of chaos. As in Aratus' work, this representation of the chaotic universe coexists with a view that the environment is a helpful and vital space for human activities.

Both poets suggest that the rustic world, which is not a 'wild' space but a familiar one, just outside the walls of ancient *poleis*, is a complex environment. Humans inhabit it and venture into it with complex emotions, with hope and optimism, but also with anxiety and fear. In this perilous world, we discover that there are both resources and risks. Needless to say, and a perhaps surprisingly modern idea for us, it remains paramount for both poets that humans acquire knowledge and the ability to 'read' this complex rustic world.

Notes

1. Only some selective suggestions: on Theocritus and Callimachus, see Cusset 1999, Payne 2007, 2014b and 2019. Indeed, 'pastoral' imagery, which Theocritus helped to develop, has been debated in ecocriticism, see, e.g. Buell 1995: 31–52.

2. Schiller suggests this in his influential work *On Naïve and Sentimental Poetry* (see Golz 2005: 451), arguing that with Euripides nature becomes an object of contemplation rather than a 'whole' with human life; cf. Payne 2014b.

3. See, e.g. Payne 2007, 2014a, 2014b, 2016, and 2019; on Nicander as attentive observer and an 'alchemist' of nature, see also Sistakou 2012: 210–33.

4. Payne 2016: 97.

5. For a recent survey of Hellenistic didactic poetry, see Zimmermann and Rengakos 2014: 115–40. Harder (2011: 177), in assessing the evidence on fragmentary attestations of didactic poems, posits three categories of didactic poetry, two of which give prominence to practical use of knowledge. The poets' interest in useful aspects of the natural world, however, coexists with an interest in scientific or literary knowledge *tout court* and in gathering bits of (possibly obscure) knowledge.

6. Volk 2005 paves the way for this; more recently, Clausing-Lage 2019, for example, reads Aratus' poem with Gernot Böhme's 2013 concept of atmosphere and its ecological implications.

7. Cicero, in a famous passage of the work *De oratore* (69), couples the two poets for their common interest in writing poetry about knowledge topics, thus making them canonical for the genre. On the limits of the term 'didactic' genre, due to modern implications, see Vesperini 2015.

8. Text and translation here and below are from Kidd 1997 (any divergences are noted).

9. Cf. ibid.: 3–5. Biographical details are found in ancient *Lives* of the poet, but it is difficult sometimes to distinguish historical reality and legendary anecdotes.

10. Gee (2013: 7–12) discusses the implications for Aratus of the Greek verb *phainein* ('to be manifest' but also 'to seem').

11. Another category that benefits explicitly from this knowledge is the one of sailors. On both categories, see the survey of Fakas 2001: 100–48.

12. See, e.g. ibid., and Hunter 2014: 21–3, 100–11.

13. See Kidd 1997: 558, where the reference to Aristotle is especially noteworthy because it certainly antedates Aratus.

14. Trans. Sider and Brunschön 2007.

15. See Fakas 2001: 100–48. Fakas, in discussing Aratus' references to agriculture, speaks mostly of playful aesthetic effects that the poet wishes to achieve. For the lines 1094–103, Fakas (142–5) speaks of 'picturesque detail', 'intellectual distance' and 'masquerade'. I find Fakas' arguments on the style's distancing effect in these lines not fully convincing. The absence of directives to the farmer-addressee does not necessarily make these lines playful; and neither does the description of the two opposite emotions of farmers.

16. See von Mossner 2017: 83. Weik von Mossner's ideas about topophilia and embodied simulation are equally interesting (2017: 19–39) but cannot be addressed here due to space reasons.

17. Fakas (2001: 100–48) also treats the references to farming and to sailing as complementary, considering this to be a fictive aspect of the poem's didactic program.

18. Jacques 2002 collects and surveys the evidence on Hellenistic toxicology (xx–lxv, 269–309); on the popularity of this field at royal courts, see xv–xvii.

19. See ibid.: lxxxi–lxxxii.

20. See insightful arguments in Clauss 2006 on the link between Nicander and Aratus, and on Nicander's debt to Hesiod; Hunter (2014: 25–6) also shows that Nicander refers to them in a programmatic passage of the *Theriaca* (8–20), which I will consider in section 3 on a different matter.

21. On the still debated identity of Nicander's addressee, see Overduin 2015: 37–43.

22. Translations if unspecified are from Gow-Schofield 1953; the Greek text is from Jacques 2002.

23. Indeed, there is also a third audience implied here, Nicander's readers, which Overduin calls the 'external addressee' (2015: 42–4).

24. On this passage see Overduin 2019 and, for narratological considerations, Overduin 2015: 31–6. Clarus is one of the places that claimed the birth of Homer, and so this reference is functional to Nicander's own self-fashioning as a follower of Homer. But it is also significant that Nicander did hold a priestly office at the temple of Apollo in Clarus; thus, this reference has also some autobiographical meaning, see ibid.: 5–6.

25. A close relationship between Nicander and the Attalids is attested by the fragment of the *Hymn to Attalus* in which Nicander praises Attalus king of Pergamon (fr. 104 Gow-Schofield). The identity of the king in question is uncertain, but this fragment suggests at least a context of patronage for the poet at the Attalid court. Attalus the third (138–133 BCE) is a good

candidate for the *Hymn*, since he would share with Nicander also an interest in botany and poisons, see Jacques 2002: xviii–xix.

26. On this word, see ibid.: 4. It may also mean 'dark'. At any rate, the meaning of the whole quote depends on the idea that humans and animals meet in the places that the poet mentions.

27. So do phrases directed at the poem's addressee (e.g. l. 21) whose role in the text overlaps with ours; both the addressee and we, the readers of Nicander, 'listen to' the poet's exposition.

28. See Overduin 2014; for more references to military language, esp. 637–9.

29. Overduin also points out that 'it is almost as if Nicander eagerly wants to introduce this figure into mythology by pretending he is already part of it' (2015: 424).

30. On Alcibius as example of the Greek wide-spread idea of first inventor, see Overduin 2015: 109–12.

31. Lines 547–9: 'But he pulled a root from the ground (*autar ho gaiēs/rizan erussamenos*) and first broke it small with his close-set teeth as he sucked it, and then spread the skin upon his wound' (trans. adapted).

32. See Overduin 2014, who argues that Nicander subverts this topos and other characteristics of pastoral poetry.

33. Compare Martorana in this volume.

34. See Wohl 2019: 300–3, on Greek ideas about 'chaotic *kosmos*' (such as Heraclitus' famous fragment DK 22 B 124, ('the most beautiful cosmos is like the sweeping of scattered things'), and on ideas about *akosmia* ('disorder', 'lack of cosmos') in the natural world or in the *polis*. On disorder in Hesiod's narrative about Zeus' coming to power, see Strauss Clay 2009: 25–9.

35. See Volk 2012: 217.

36. See ibid.: 210–11.

37. See Horky 2019 (esp. 2–11, for a summary view on the ancient word *kosmos*).

38. Other passages about stars without detectable shape are lines 137–46, and 389–91. Cf. Gee 2013: 111–15, who surveys a few passages on disorder in Aratus, including the verses on the planets (lines 454–61); her viewpoint is that Aratus marginalizes disorder. I am more interested in pointing out that, as the lines 367–85 show, chaos/disorder is part of the universe.

39. On the importance of aetiology in the ancient world, see Reitz and Walter 2014.

40. *Ephrasat' ēd' enoēsen hapant' onomasti kalessai/ēlitha morphōsas*, '[he] devised and contrived to call all by names, grouping them in compact shapes' (374–5).

41. Cf. Kidd 1997: 320, and, on the entire passage, see 318–19.

42. See the emphasis on form and shape: *homēgereas . . . poiēsasthai asteras* 'to make the stars into groups', *epitax* 'in a row', *eidea sēmainoien* 'they could represent figures', *katharois enarērotes eidōloisi* 'fixed in clear-cut figures'.

43. Gee (2013: 111–12) also argues that we find the idea of cosmic disorder in this passage, and it is not just about failure in human understanding of the universe.

44. This is the repetition of the adjectives *polus* and *pas* with different endings.

45. See section 1.

46. See, e.g. Volk 2012: 226–7.

47. Scholars debate whether Nicander dismisses Hesiod here, and whether this story was in fact found in Hesiodic poetry (indeed, in the extant corpus, we find no matching reference to the blood of Titans), cf. discussion in Jacques 2002: 77–8, Overduin 2015: 183–4, and Barbara 2015.

48. On the key concept of order in Hesiod (and Homer) see Du Sablon 2014; on Hesiod's narrative on the formation of cosmos and the role of Zeus, see Strauss Clay 2009: 21–9.

49. On Titans in ancient myth, see Bremmer 2008: 73–93.

50. Hes. *Theog.* 116–25; cf. West 1966: 192–3.

51. On Titans and chaos, see Lincoln 2009.

CHAPTER 2

SHARED SUFFERING AND CYCLICAL DESTRUCTION: FAILURES OF ENVIRONMENTAL CONTROL IN THE *AENEID*

Aaron M. Seider

In its depictions of Aeneas' wanderings in *Aeneid* 3 and efforts to secure land in *Aeneid* 12, Vergil's epic foregrounds how the desire for environmental mastery may produce ruinous consequences. Throughout the epic, passages such as the sea snakes' attack on Laocoon and the transformation of the Trojans' ships into nymphs characterize the natural world not merely as a backdrop to humans' struggles, but as a participant in the action itself.[1] In *Aeneid* 3 and 12, several episodes foreground these issues at structurally significant moments in Aeneas' journey: in *Aeneid* 3, the Trojans' two initial attempts to found a city are linked with horrific environmental transformations, while in *Aeneid* 12 Aeneas' and Turnus' martial conflict spotlights the cyclical destruction of the environment which humans inhabit. Concentrating on these passages that bookend the Trojans' quest, I argue in this chapter that the efforts of both the Trojans and their foes to assert mastery over the environment damage themselves and their surroundings.

Even as the Trojans and their enemies yearn to understand their environment and claim a place within it, environmental forces come to the fore and destabilize human control. In the first section of my chapter, I focus on two episodes from *Aeneid* 3 where the Trojans attempt to establish a new home. In each of these episodes, the Trojans assert their control by choosing a location for their foundation, but the assumption that they can exercise mastery over their landscape and shape it to meet their needs is complicated when the natural world responds in ways that undermine assumptions of human understanding and blur the human/non-human divide. The chapter's second section considers passages from *Aeneid* 12, a book that highlights the Trojans' and Latins' attempts to control the built environment. In *Aeneid* 12, the characters' interaction with that built environment is cast as part of a cycle of failed attempts at control and ruinous consequences. The Trojans' effort to sack Latinus' city is characterized as part of a pattern of human dominion and destruction, while the role of a boundary stone in the final fight between Aeneas and Turnus raises questions about the impact of humans' desire to order the world around them.

In my analysis, I draw on work in ecocriticism that conceptualizes the relationship between human beings and the environment as one characterized by reciprocal influence and shifting constructions. The term 'landscape' evokes these ideas from a broad perspective, as this word describes a setting which is seen and interpreted by humans and which, in this process, shapes and is shaped by its viewer.[2] In this chapter, as I assess the Trojans' actions in different environmental settings, I use 'landscape' to denote their mental construction of the world surrounding them, from their own perspective and for their own uses. Such an approach enables this chapter's focus on how the Trojans imagine and interact with the natural world surrounding them and how the epic's construction of these interactions engages with Rome's ongoing expansion.

I will also bring to bear concepts relating to networks and inhabitation to support my analysis of the Trojans' attempts to found a city, first in Thrace and Crete, as described in *Aeneid* 3, and then in Latium, in *Aeneid* 12. In regard to networks, Serenella Iovino and Serpil Oppermann write how 'human and nonhuman players are interlocked in networks', where humans and their environments exercise varying degrees of control and success.[3] This approach facilitates my exploration of the Trojans' attempts to settle in Thrace and Crete in *Aeneid* 3. In each of these locations, as we will see, the environment responds to their ktistic efforts in dreadful ways, and the emotional impact of these interactions shifts the Trojans' understanding of the landscape and their place within it.[4]

Later, when Aeneas is on the cusp of founding his fated city in Italy in *Aeneid* 12, it is productive to apply a concept that focuses on how humans change the environment around them. The notion of 'niche construction', which explores how humans modify their surroundings in ways that respond to their own ideas and desires,[5] offers a useful approach to my consideration of how the Trojans and Latin engage with the built environment. Inherent in this concept is the idea that an organism 'changes the environment in a way that makes more sense to it and corresponds to the semiotic resources (sign systems) used by the organism.'[6] *Aeneid* 12 presents a vision of the environment as one that has been changed to meet the needs of its human inhabitants, and the efforts of the Trojans and their enemies to control this built environment for their political needs raises questions about the Trojans' imperialistic ambitions and the *Aeneid*'s political context. Following these analyses, in conclusion I consider the repercussions of the poem's exploration of questions about environmental knowledge, agency and suffering in relation to Aeneas' killing of Turnus and to the poem's historical context.

Aeneid 3: Environmental suffering

The Trojans' first two attempts to found a city produce environmental responses that bring emotional and physical pain. Unsure of their destination,[7] the Trojans attempt to start anew first in Thrace and then in Crete. These episodes concentrate on how the Trojans desire to understand their new surroundings. As Christopher Schliephake notes, the word landscape 'connotes how cultures attribute meaning and value to their physical surroundings';[8] and in both Thrace and Crete the Trojans approach the environment as a landscape they may use for their new settlement and fresh political beginning. In each location, though, the environment responds to the Trojans' attempts at foundation in a way that causes them pain and compels them to interrogate their assumption that they can harness the landscape in the way they wish. Twice, the Trojans change the meanings they attribute to these landscapes and choose to journey onward. In Thrace, when

Aeneas attempts to pull up branches for an altar, blood issues from the wood and the bush reveals that it is in fact Polydorus, an erstwhile companion transformed into a plant by the spears that killed him. This depiction of the environment as a cause of suffering continues in Crete. As soon as the Trojans build new homes there, a plague repels Aeneas and his men. In each location, the reaction of the natural world underscores the Trojans' lack of environmental understanding and their consequent inability to exert their will on their surroundings.

The Trojans' initial attempt to create a new homeland blurs the boundary between human and non-human and shows how the natural world reorients their beliefs and actions. Not long after Troy's destruction, the surviving Trojans sail to Thrace. Here, Aeneas chooses to put down his 'first walls' (*moenia prima, Aen.* 3.17) and rename his followers 'Sons of Aeneas' (*Aeneadae,* 3.18), political and cultural initiatives that assume that the physical surroundings will be a landscape that supports these new beginnings. But these attempts to fashion a new home and identity are met with a terrifying portent: the branches that the Trojan leader attempts to tear up for a religious ritual bleed and the bush itself speaks. Aeneas' introduction of the incident foreshadows the associations between humans' use of their surroundings and pain caused and even experienced by the environment (*Aen.* 3.22-26):

> *forte fuit iuxta tumulus, quo cornea summo*
> *virgulta et densis hastilibus horrida myrtus.*
> *accessi, viridemque ab humo convellere silvam*
> *conatus, ramis tegerem ut frondentibus aras,*   25
> *horrendum et dictu video mirabile monstrum.*

By chance there was a mound close by, on top of which there were cornel bushes and myrtle bristling with close-packed stems. I came up to it and tried to tear up the green wood[9] from the soil so that I might cover the altars with leafy branches, when I see a portent that is horrifying and extraordinary to tell.

Aeneas' framing of this scene does more than announce a horrifying portent: the terms *tumulus* (*Aen.* 3.22) and *hastilibus* (*Aen.* 3.23) call attention to how humans use the environment to create and mark pain. *Tumulus* can designate either a hill (a feature of the natural environment)[10] or a sepulchral mound (a feature of the built environment).[11] Later, when it is revealed that this location is where Polydorus was killed by spears, the mound's identification as a *tumulus* underlines the cruel irony that Polydorus did not receive a proper burial. *Hastilibus* likewise links aspects of the landscape and objects associated with death. The noun may designate either a natural object (a spear-like stem)[12] or a human-made weapon (a spear),[13] and, along with *tumulus*, it highlights the ways humans transform the environment as a means to produce and commemorate suffering. Lastly, line 26, which focuses on the emotional impact Aeneas endures in retelling this episode, invites his own audience (Dido and the Carthaginians) and by extension that of the poem, to contemplate their reaction(s) to these events, as well.

Aeneas' attempt to use these branches for a sacrifice reveals Polydorus' past and present pain and inspires fresh horror in the Trojans. As the Trojans' political and religious leader, Aeneas tries to pull up branches from the ground (*Aen.* 3.27-33, 3.37-40):

> *nam quae prima solo ruptis radicibus arbos*
> *vellitur, huic atro liquuntur sanguine guttae*
> *et terram tabo maculant. mihi frigidus horror*
> *membra quatit, gelidusque coit formidine sanguis.*   30
> *rursus et alterius lentum convellere vimen*
> *insequor et causas penitus temptare latentis;*
> *ater et alterius sequitur de cortice sanguis.*
>
> . . .
>
> *tertia sed postquam maiore hastilia nisu*
> *adgredior genibusque adversae obluctor harenae*
> *(eloquar, an sileam?), gemitus lacrimabilis imo*
> *auditur tumulo, et vox reddita fertur ad auris:*   40

For from the first branch torn from the ground, its roots broken, drops of black blood trickle and stain the earth with gore. A chill shudder shakes my limbs, and my blood thickens, cold with fear. Again I proceed to tear up the pliant stem of another bush and to search out the deeply hidden causes; and black blood follows from that one's bark ... But after I attack the shafts of a third with a greater effort and strain with my knees against the sand (should I speak or be silent?), a tearful groan is heard from the mound's depth, and a voice is brought to my ears in answer.

Trying to secure a propitious foundation, Aeneas yearns to use the landscape in productive ways. Instead, there is a 'a jarring combination of religious propriety and sacrilege.'[14] The Trojan's actions transform these bushes into an entity that produces confusion and terror for Aeneas, emotions which his rendition of this experience invites his Carthaginian audience and the *Aeneid*'s audience to feel as well. The boundaries between human and non-human are blurred and suffering arises for Aeneas and the environment around him.

The repetition of 'blood' at *Aen.* 3.28 (*sanguine*), 3.30 (*sanguis*), and 3.33 (*sanguis*) erases the boundary between human and non-human, both in terms of any separation between Aeneas and the bushes and between the bushes and Polydorus, the Trojan transformed in death. As Christine Perkell notes, 'Aeneas' intention [in pulling out a second branch] was to verify that this was the occurrence of a true omen, not a random occurrence.'[15] 'Uncomprehending of the nature of his action,'[16] Aeneas realizes that his interaction with this bush brings pain to him and Polydorus.

The next lines focus on his voice and that of the bush. Immediately after his own rhetorical question about whether he should speak or fall silent (*Aen.* 3.39), Aeneas describes the bush's 'groan' (*gemitus, Aen.* 3.39) and 'voice' (*vox, Aen.* 3.40). Polydorus' transformation into a tree is not complete, and he still possess certain human characteristics.[17] These similarities between human and non-human do not portend a shared benefit, though. Instead, there is only pain that extends outward: the bush drips blood and cries lamentably, Aeneas experiences confusion and horror, and, through his narrative, these emotions potentially spread to his present audience and the poem's larger audience.

After Aeneas tries and fails to pull a branch for a third time, the bush addresses him. As the bush becomes further anthropomorphized, its words make explicit the Trojans' misunderstanding of their environment (*Aen.* 3.41-48):

> 'quid miserum, Aenea, laceras? iam parce sepulto,
> parce pias scelerare manus. non me tibi Troia
> externum tulit, aut cruor hic de stipite manat.
> heu! fuge crudelis terras, fuge litus avarum.
> nam Polydorus ego. hic confixum ferrea texit   45
> telorum seges et iaculis increvit acutis.'
> tum vero ancipiti mentem formidine pressus
> obstipui steteruntque comae et vox faucibus haesit.

'Why, Aeneas, do you torture wretched me? Now spare me in my burial, do not pollute your pious hands. For Troy did not bear me as a stranger to you, nor does this blood ooze from a trunk. Alas! Flee these cruel lands, flee this greedy shore. For I am Polydorus. Here, an iron harvest of spears covered my pierced body and grew up in sharp javelins.' Then, overwhelmed in my mind with a two-edged fear I fell silent and my hairs stood up and my voice caught in my throat.

When Polydorus speaks, the blending of human and non-human is complete.[18] Killed by human-made weapons that he paradoxically characterizes as 'an iron harvest of spears' (*ferrea . . . / telorum seges, Aen.* 3.45-46), Polydorus is a bush that bleeds and talks, both of which actions terrify Aeneas.[19] As Lyndsay Coo notes, the inversion of a typical trope further intensifies the dreadful aspects of this experience: given that 'the making of natural material into weapons is a trope for the degeneration of man's relationship with nature', it might be reasonable to 'expect the opposite to have positive connotations'.[20] Initially, Aeneas tried to interpret the landscape in ways that were understandable and useful for himself and the Trojans. He saw Thrace as a land fit for his new city, and this bush as material fit for a sacrifice. Now he discovers his misunderstanding.[21] Compelled by the reaction of the natural environment, he buries Polydorus[22] and leaves Thrace.

The Trojans' experience in Crete further undermines the idea that they can treat their environment as a landscape that fits their needs without that environment reacting in turn. Having received an oracular instruction to seek out their 'ancient mother' (*antiquam . . . matrem, Aen.* 3.96), the Trojans interpret this enjoinment as directing them to Crete, the home of one of their ancestors. Here, their eagerness to settle is matched by the terrible consequences they and the landscape experience (*Aen.* 3.132-42):

ergo avidus muros optatae molior urbis
Pergameamque voco, et laetam cognomine gentem
hortor amare focos arcemque attollere tectis.
iamque fere sicco subductae litore puppes,   135
conubiis arvisque novis operata iuventus,
iura domosque dabam, subito cum tabida membris,
corrupto caeli tractu, miserandaque venit
arboribusque satisque lues et letifer annus.
linquebant dulcis animas aut aegra trahebant   140
corpora; tum sterilis exurere Sirius agros;
arebant herbae et victum seges aegra negabat.

Therefore, I eagerly work on the walls of our chosen city and call it Pergamum, and I encourage my people, happy in the name, to love their hearths and to raise up the citadel with homes. And now the ships were just drawn up on the dry shore, the youth were busy with marriages and new fields, and I was giving out laws and homes, when suddenly a decaying and wretched plague, from a spoiled part of the sky, came to our limbs and trees and crops, and the sickly season arrived.[23] Trojans were leaving behind their sweet lives or dragging around their sick bodies; then Sirius scorched our barren fields; the grasses were burning and the sick crop was denying sustenance.

This passage contrasts the Trojans' eagerness to shape this environment into their new home with the repercussions caused by their actions. The middle verse of this section (3.137) highlights this contrast and suggests that the Trojans' actions effect this change: in the verse's first half the alliteration of *domosque dabam* ('I was giving out homes') emphasizes the certainty behind Aeneas' action, while *subito* ('suddenly') hints at a new and unexpected turn.

A disastrous natural response attends the Trojans' attempt to take control of the landscape. Aeneas and his followers effect environmental change through farming and building, while they bring cultural innovation by naming the city and creating new marriages and laws. Just as in Thrace, the landscape reacts in remarkable ways. In contrast with the alacrity implied by Aeneas' narrative of the Trojans' work, his description of the ensuing plague offers 'the slow unfolding of a sinister climax.'[24] At first, he introduces the change as confusing and terrifying in its suddenness (*subito*, *Aen.* 3.137) and deleterious effects (*tabida*, *Aen.* 3.137).[25] The situation only gains clarity with the appearance of *lues* ('plague') in *Aen.* 3.139. The horror of this new reality is emphasized by the hyperbaton between the adjective *tabida* ('decaying') and the noun *lues* ('plague') it modifies. Moreover, this construction calls attention to how the plague links the Trojans' bodies and their environment through their shared suffering: *membris* ('limbs') is directly next to *tabida* ('decaying') at the end of *Aen.* 3.137, while *arboribusque satisque* ('both trees and crops') abuts *lues* ('plague') at the start of *Aen.* 3.139. As Hunter Gardner writes, the plague 'leaves the Cretan settlers poised on a threshold between the dissolution of one age and the inception of another that has yet to be realized'.[26] The Trojans fail in their efforts to transform their surrounding environment into a landscape that serves their needs, and they can realize neither a new age nor a new city.[27]

The Trojans' failures to manage the environment to their purposes, first in Aeneas' work to harvest branches for an altar in Thrace and then in the Trojans' efforts to settle in Crete, raise questions about control and knowledge. In a piece on humans' perception of the world and the challenges of their relationship with place, Edward Casey writes that 'The problem of landscape is thus that landscape represents to us, not only our relationship with place, but also the problematic nature of that relationship—a relationship that contains within it involvement and separation, agency and spectacle, self and other.'[28] In Thrace and Crete, the Trojans look out at the natural world and construct it as a landscape that they may control and use for their goals.[29] Their subsequent experiences highlight how they misread the environment surrounding them. From the Trojans' perspective, these failures may be attributed to their lack of knowledge. Neither Thrace nor Crete are the locations promised to them by fate, and this raises the implication that, once they do come to that destined location, they may be able to impose their understanding on the environment and use it as a landscape fit for their new foundation.

Aeneid 12: Building up cycles of destruction

The Trojans suffer in Aeneid 3 when they attempt to transform the natural environment into a landscape that supports their new home, and they are compelled to shift their understanding of Thrace and Crete before departing each location. Once they reach Italy, the location decreed by fate for their city, they confront a new challenge: unlike in Aeneid 3, where the Trojans are the sole human protagonists in the environments they wish to conceive of as landscapes fit for their inhabitation, here, they strive for territory in a land other people already live.

Within this context, as well as within a consideration of the Aeneid's place in Augustan Rome, the concept of 'niche construction' proves useful for showing how the Trojans try to found their city within an environment that has already been shaped by and has shaped the humans who inhabit it. Such ideas of environmental determinism and change resonate within the Aeneid's larger historical milieu, as the Romans continued to expand their political territory and, in doing so, continued to wage war in new environments and to exert their control over these environments. Writing about niche construction, Timo Maran notes: 'By manipulating the environment for its aims, an organism transfers its modeling activities back to the environment; it changes the environment in a way that makes more sense to it and corresponds to the semiotic resources (sign systems) used by the organism.'[30] This is especially relevant to the Aeneid's second half, where the built environment that the Trojans find in Italy is a product of ways that other humans have changed that environment and added sign systems to it in a way that makes sense for them.[31]

Two episodes in *Aeneid* 12 spotlight how the Trojans' and Latins' attempts to manage the built environment produce chaos and destruction. First, Aeneas, frustrated by his inability to fight Turnus, plans to raze Latinus' city, a tactic that evokes the cyclical environmental destruction brought on by hopes of political mastery within the poem, wherein one group of humans constructs a built environment, only for another group of humans to destroy it before building anew. Then, near the epic's end, an ancient boundary stone plays a pivotal part in Aeneas and Turnus' duel, and the role of this marker suggests that futility attends human efforts to order and control the landscape.

In the first of these two episodes Aeneas plans to destroy Latinus' city, an idea that arises out of his anger over his lack of control. The notion of niche construction emphasizes how humans modify their surroundings in a way that make sense to them. A sequence of events in battle (his wounding by a spear, his inability to track down Turnus) have already baffled Aeneas when he is further frustrated by the unscathed state of Latinus' city (*Aen.* 12.554-60):

> hic mentem Aeneae genetrix pulcherrima misit
> iret ut ad muros urbique adverteret agmen   555
> ocius et subita turbaret clade Latinos.
> ille ut vestigans diversa per agmina Turnum
> huc atque huc acies circumtulit, aspicit urbem
> immunem tanti belli atque impune quietam.
> continuo pugnae accendit maioris imago.   560

At this point his most beautiful mother sent a plan[32] to Aeneas to go the walls and turn his troops to the city immediately[33] and disturb the Latins with a sudden disaster. While tracking Turnus through hostile troops, he brought his gaze here and there, he saw the city, untouched by so great a war and safely at peace. Straightway the image of a greater fight inflames him.

Venus fixes Aeneas' vision on Latinus' city and the safety it has enjoyed, and, while gazing at this built environment, he remembers the 'greater fight' (*pugnae maioris*, *Aen.* 12.560) that culminated in Troy's destruction.[34] The emotions sparked by his recollection incite him to attack Latinus' city, and the associations of *accendit* ('inflames') with fire[35] both recall the fires that accompanied Troy's destruction and foreshadow Aeneas' use of fire against this Italic city.[36] This causal link between past and future attacks on cities draws attention to how efforts at political dominion cause cyclical destructions of the built environment in the poem.

The location and content of Aeneas' subsequent speech reinforce this notion (*Aen.* 12.561-69):

> Mnesthea Sergestumque vocat fortemque Serestum
> ductores, tumulumque capit quo cetera Teucrum
> concurrit legio, nec scuta aut spicula densi

deponunt. celso medius stans aggere fatur:
'ne qua meis esto dictis mora, Iuppiter hac stat,   565
neu quis ob inceptum subitum mihi segnior ito.
urbem hodie, causam belli, regna ipsa Latini,
ni frenum accipere et victi parere fatentur,
eruam et aequa solo fumantia culmina ponam.'

He calls the leaders Mnestheus and Sergestus and strong Serestus, and he seizes a mound to which the rest of the Trojans army runs at once, and, close-packed, they put down neither their shields nor spears. Standing in their midst on the high mound, Aeneas says: 'Let there be no delay to my orders, Jupiter is on our side, and let no one go more slowly on account of the sudden nature of my undertaking.[37] Today the city, the cause of war, the kingdom itself of Latinus, if it does not agree to accept the bridle and, having been conquered, to obey, I will destroy from the foundation and I will make its smoking peaks equal with the ground.'

As Aeneas speaks, he occupies a mound from which he can address the mass of soldiers. This location is designated as a *tumulus*, a word that, as noted earlier, may describe either a natural hill or a human-made sepulchral mound. This detail expands the temporal scope of the destructive interplay between different groups of humans in the poem, who seek to impose their own signs and meanings on the landscape and, in doing so, bring devastation to the built environment. Not only might this *tumulus*, now used for its hortatory advantages in urging on destruction, later become transformed into a burial mound that memorializes the deaths incurred by such an attack, but it may already fulfil that function now, memorializing burials that occurred after other battles over the control of the environment.

Turnus' perspective on this destruction highlights how one set of humans (the Trojans) is now undoing the very ways that another set of humans (the Latins) manipulated the environment for their own utilization and understanding. When Aeneas addresses his men, he promises to burn the city's wooden peaks and bring its structures to the ground; when Turnus views the besieged city, his perspective reveals how Aeneas' attack undoes his efforts to create this built environment (*Aen.* 12.672-75):

ecce autem flammis inter tabulata volutus
ad caelum undabat vertex turrimque tenebat,
turrim compactis trabibus quam eduxerat ipse
subdideratque rotas pontisque instraverat altos.   675

There, indeed, a whirling column of flame was rolling to the heavens and was starting to engulf[38] a tower, a tower which Turnus himself had raised with its jointed beams and had set on wheels and had covered with high gangways.

The text 'follows Turnus' gaze,'[39] which simultaneously moves upwards through the city and backwards through time. Turnus views the current destruction of this tower through the lens of his past efforts to build it. The repetition of *turrim* in *Aen.* 12.673 and 12.674[40] intensifies this conflation of two temporal perspectives, as Turnus' construction of the tower and Aeneas' destruction of it become simultaneous. As this passage underlines, human modifications of the environment are linked with destruction in a cycle spurred by the desire for political mastery. Shaken by this urban attack, Turnus decides to engage Aeneas in single combat, and, in the second episode under consideration here, the role of a boundary stone in their battle further highlights the futility of human attempts to order the landscape. Standing alone against his foe, Turnus spies an ancient boundary stone and hurls it at the Trojan (*Aen.* 12.896-902):

> *nec plura effatus saxum circumspicit ingens,*
> *saxum antiquum ingens, campo quod forte iacebat,*
> *limes agro positus litem ut discerneret arvis.*
> *vix illud lecti bis sex cervice subirent,*
> *qualia nunc hominum producit corpora tellus;*   900
> *ille manu raptum trepida torquebat in hostem*
> *altior insurgens et cursu concitus heros.*

And having said no more Turnus looks around and sees a giant rock, an ancient giant rock, which by chance was lying on the plain, having been placed on the land as a boundary to decide disputes about the fields. Scarcely could twelve chosen men lift that rock on their necks, men with bodies such as now the earth produces; that one was seizing it and heaving it with a trembling hand toward his enemy, the hero rising higher and sped up in his running.

Having cast his spear and shattered a sword on Aeneas' shield,[41] Turnus seeks a new weapon. He seizes an enormous stone, one whose designation as 'ancient' (*antiquum*) signals the length of time it has been set in this location.[42] Pausing the narrative at this dramatic moment, Vergil spends an entire verse (*Aen.* 12.898) describing the stone's function to settle boundary disputes, 'a non-idealizing detail . . . that hints at a resolution of a conflict very different from the present situation.'[43] Previously the stone gave meaning to the land for farmers: it was a means of ordering and arranging the environment. Now Turnus hurls it in the hope of killing another person. This connection with violent conflict highlights the human desire to order the world by destructive force as well as the impossibility of achieving that order. First, Turnus' removal of the stone from the field ends its previous function, as wherever it falls, it has left its previous location and can no longer divide the fields.[44] Secondly, its removal foreshadows the changes in land control effected by Aeneas' victory, and hints that even seemingly everlasting markers of human control of the environment are but temporary.

Turnus' attempt to weaponize this boundary stone fails, and Vergil's treatment of this universalizes the evanescent nature of environmental control. While the earlier verses emphasized Turnus' heroic strength, the poem now links his failure with the experience of the *Aeneid*'s audience (*Aen.* 12.903-14):

sed neque currentem se nec cognoscit euntem
tollentemve manu saxumve immane moventem;
genua labant, gelidus concrevit frigore sanguis.   905
tum lapis ipse viri vacuum per inane volutus
nec spatium evasit totum neque pertulit ictum.
ac velut in somnis, oculos ubi languida pressit
nocte quies, nequiquam avidos extendere cursus
velle videmur et in mediis conatibus aegri   910
succidimus; non lingua valet, non corpore notae
sufficiunt vires nec vox aut verba sequuntur:
sic Turno, quacumque viam virtute petivit,
successum dea dira negat.

But he recognizes himself neither running nor going nor lifting the immense rock nor throwing it with his hand; his knees waver, his blood grows cold with a chill. Then the rock itself, having rolled through the empty air, neither made its way through[45] the entire space nor delivered a blow. And just as in dreams, when sluggish quiet presses the eyes at night, we seem to want to continue our eager running to no avail and in the midst of our attempts we fall sick; our tongue is not strong, our known strength does not meet our body's need and neither voice nor words follow; thus to Turnus, whatever way he sought with virtue, the dread goddess Allecto denies success.

Turnus faces defeat in his effort to control the environment in two ways: both in his use of the boundary stone to strike Aeneas and in his goal of using it to keep the Trojans from settling on his land. Turnus' experience is linked to the first-person experience of Vergil's readers through the verb 'we seem' (*videmur*, *Aen.* 12.910), which 'strongly aligns the readers' sympathy with Turnus.'[46] Turnus' inability to throw this stone successfully is emphasized by this passage's vivid description and allusion to Homeric verses.[47] It is also associated with the epic's audience, as the first-person plural verb 'we seem' (*videmur*, *Aen.* 12.910) invokes the experiences of the poem's readers. Already in *Aeneid* 3, Aeneas' comments about his narrative invite both his Carthaginian audience and the poem's audience to experience his terror in Thrace and Crete; now this simile in *Aeneid* 12 brings together Aeneas' ancient foe and the epic's contemporaneous readers, a link that universalizes the repercussions of Turnus' experience. The concept of niche construction considers how an environment's human inhabitants attempt to order it to their needs. In this passage in *Aeneid* 12, Turnus tries to use a boundary marker, a reification of this urge to bring order to the environment, to kill Aeneas and thereby prevent the Trojans from settling in Latium and ordering it to their own needs. The association of Turnus' failure with the experience of Vergil's audience raises the question of whether they, or, more broadly speaking, any, humans can control the environment they inhabit.

These passages focusing on Aeneas' attack on Latinus' city and Turnus' ill-fated attempt to strike Aeneas with a boundary stone point toward humans' inability to control the environments which they attempt to shape as their homes. Indeed, this perspective is reinforced by a brief episode earlier in *Aeneid* 12. Here, after Aeneas' errant throw lodges his spear in the trunk of a tree sacred to Faunus, the hero cannot remove his weapon. Eventually, it is Venus who must accomplish this task,[48] a moment that highlights the stark difference between humans' and gods' abilities to control the environment.[49] This detail, which showcases even Aeneas' need for divine intervention in his engagement with the natural world, reveals how both Aeneas and Turnus experience failure in their aspirations to control the environment, a shared experience that, along with the comparison of Turnus with the epic's audience, universalizes such failures of environmental control and the destruction they occasion.

Conclusion: Urban and imperial foundations

In this chapter, I have argued that *Aeneid* 3 and 12, rich with examples of humans' engagement with the environment, offer an opportunity to gauge how the Trojans are depicted as interacting with the world surrounding them at the beginning and end of their quest. This has larger implications for the narrativization of the history of Rome, and perhaps more broadly for the understanding of human/non-human interaction. In two episodes from *Aeneid* 3, the Trojans attempt to transform the environment surrounding them into a landscape they can use for a new home, and they suffer as a result. In Thrace, the bush that is Polydorus speaks and bleeds when Aeneas attempts to pull out its branches, while in Crete the Trojans are driven off by a plague. At the end of the epic, meanwhile, when the Trojans do know where they are supposed to settle, Aeneas' and Turnus' actions highlight the inability of humans to exercise long-term control over the environments they modify and inhabit. Aeneas' impulse to sack Latinus' city reveals the cyclical nature of the destruction of the built environment, while Turnus' attempt to strike Aeneas with a boundary stone fails, and its link with the experiences of the poem's audience suggests that this sort of failure to establish long-term control over the landscape is a universal one.

In conclusion, I would like to glance at the repercussions of these ideas as they relate to the evocation of Rome's foundation in the poem's final lines and to the larger context of Vergil's epic. The narrator's choice of *condere* to describe Aeneas' deadly sword thrust into Turnus (*Aen.* 12.950) recalls the epic's first use of that verb in the exclamation 'How great a labour it was to found the Roman race!' (*tantae molis erat Romanam condere gentem! Aen.* 1.33). As Sharon James elucidates, Vergil is the first to use *condere* to mean 'bury the sword', a meaning which at *Aen.* 12.950 links Rome's foundation with a 'form of civil conflict'.[50] In addition to this evocation of civil conflict and its association with Rome's foundation, *condit* associates Rome's foundation with the other similarly imperialistic attempts at environmental control in *Aeneid* 12. Earlier in this book Turnus watches the tower he built be consumed by flames (*Aen.* 12.672-75), while the stone that for many years had adjudicated boundary disputes was taken up without success in another fight about land control (*Aen.* 12.896-907). Against this background, the act of foundation, with all the control and permanence that it promises, may only have a short-lived result.

These episodes also raise questions about Roman aspirations for geographic expansion and control.[51] In the *Aeneid*, passages such as the transformation of the Trojans' ships, constructed from lumber harvested from Mount Ida, into nymphs, evoke the cost of colonializing politics and imperial goals.[52] Meanwhile, writings such as Caesar's *Bellum Gallicum* and Augustus' *Res Gestae* speak of territorial growth and domination.[53] In these texts, both mental and physical control are exerted over the environment. Intellectually, Caesar and Augustus imagine the environment as a landscape fit for their and Rome's needs. They describe how, physically, the Romans impose their meaning and order on the natural world. Such descriptions of forays into new lands raise the question of an 'empire without end' (*imperium sine fine*, *Aen.* 1.279), much like what Jupiter promises the Romans in the *Aeneid*.

In the world imagined by this phrase, as well as for the territory imagined by Caesar or Augustus, boundary stones would be unnecessary. Within Roman territory, the environment could be imagined as a landscape ordered to Rome's needs and absent any internal differentiation. Meanwhile, the incessant outward movement of the empire's borders would obviate the need for any markers there as well. Vergil's epic, though, in its treatment of the beginning and ending of Aeneas' journey to found a new city, undermines these aspirations for human control. Through their depiction of failed foundations and the inability of humans to regulate space, *Aeneid* 3 and 12 imagine a world where efforts to transform the environment into an 'empire without end' result only in transience and destruction.

Notes

1. Armstrong 2019: 15–18 considers the meaning and ramifications of an ecocritical approach to the Vergil's corpus. Phillips 1978–9 offers general thoughts on the landscape of the *Aeneid*, while Vuković 2020 considers the landscape of a specific episode from *Aeneid* 7 and Seider 2021 focuses on *Aeneid* 8 and environmental control. For recent analyses of space in Roman literature, see Fitzgerald and Spentzou 2018 and various chapters from McInerney and Sluiter 2016.

2. For considerations of recent developments in the theorization of landscape, see Felton and Gilhuly 2018 and Häussler and Chiai 2020.

3. Iovino and Oppermann 2014: 5. See also Cohen 2014.

4. Felton 2018 explores the relationship between landscape and the emotion of dread in Greek and Roman literature.

5. See Maran 2014: 150.

6. Ibid.: 150.

7. Horsfall 2006: *ad* 5 considers how much information at this point Aeneas has received from the gods about his fated destination.

8. Schliephake 2020: 41.

9. For the translation of *silvam*, see Perkell 2007: *ad loc.*

10. Glare 1996: *tumulus* 1. Armstrong 2019: 154 also notes this and the next meaning of *tumulus*

11. Ibid.: *tumulus* 2. See also Horsfall 2006: *ad loc.* on the Trojans' transformation of this into a funeral mound at 3.62.

12. Glare 1996: *hastile* 3.

13. Ibid.: *hastile* 1 and 2. Coo 2008: 196 notes the 'sinister meaning' and 'true significance of the situation' that are hinted at by the various meanings of *tumulus* and *hastilia*.

14. Armstrong 2019: 153.

15. Perkell 2007: *ad* 3.31–3. Armstrong 2019: 154 remarks on Aeneas' 'reluctance to take the hint.'

16. Thomas 1988: 266.

17. Armstrong 2019: 154–5.

18. Coo 2008: 195 analyses how Aeneas' narrative portrays the branches which Aeneas tears out as coming 'directly from the still sentient body of Polydorus.'

19. See Horsfall 2006: *ad* 47.

20. Coo 2008: 194.

21. Hardie 2007 notes how this episode may be cast as 'a perverted foundation story' through its potential allusion to how Romulus' spear began to grow where it fell.

22. Tueller 2010: 357 comments on this episode's epigrammatic elements, such as its immediacy and the presence of a voice from the tomb, and its context, which is conducive to two different types of epigram: 'an epigram or dedication of vow-fulfillment' for founding a city and 'a sepulchral epigram.'

23. See Horsfall 2006: *ad loc.* for this understanding of *letifer annus*.

24. Ibid.: *ad* 137.

25. As Perkell 2007: *ad loc.* notes, the 'jagged word order here . . . suggests Aeneas' distress in making sense of the experience.'

26. Gardner 2019: 145.

27. Armstrong 2019: 211 n. 178 notes the plague's extensive effects.

28. Casey 2011: 21.

29. Armstrong 2019: 87 and 152–5 discusses this episode as a failed foundation.

30. Maran 2014: 150.

31. See Hughes 2015: 15 and Schliephake 2020: 14–17 for further exploration of this idea.

32. See Tarrant 2012: *ad loc.* for this translation of *mentem*.

33. Ibid.: *ad loc.* on the translation of *ocius*.

34. Ibid.: *ad* 554–60 notes the 'double motivation' in these verses. On the memory of Troy, see Berlin 1998, and see also Tarrant 2012: 232 and Seider 2013: 178 n. 63.

35. Glare 1996: *incendo* 1 and 2.

36. Tarrant 2012: *ad loc.*

37. For the translation of *Aen.* 12.565-66, see Tarrant 2012: *ad loc.*

38. See ibid.: *ad loc.* on the translation of *tenebat*.

39. Ibid.: *ad* 672–3.

40. See Wills 1996: 145 n. 48 and Tarrant 2012: *ad* 673–4.

41. On the shattering of the sword, see ibid.: *ad* 731.

42. For other, literary implications of *antiquum*, see ibid.: *ad loc*. Huskey 1999: 78 notes how the rock's size and age are emphasized by the length of its description as well as the verses' repeated words and heavily spondaic meter.

43. Tarrant 2012: *ad* 897–8. Fratantuono 2007: 395 argues that the removal of the stone shows the end of separation between the Trojans and Italians as Aeneas' fated victory approaches.

44. Thaniel 1971 and Huskey 1999 remark on the religious nature of boundary stones and how Turnus' action here may be interpreted as an act of religious sacrilege. Mader 2015: 593 views Turnus' attack with the stone as 'the anarchic gesture of a man who has no stake in maintaining the civilized order it stands for.'

45. On the translation of *evasit*, see Tarrant 2012: *ad loc*.

46. See ibid.: *ad loc*.

47. See Mader 2015: 590–1, who notes that Turnus' action of throwing the rock is characterized as 'an archetypical heroic gesture' (590).

48. See *Aen.* 12.765-87.

49. Barchiesi 1995 notes the differences in the experience of suffering by the gods and humans in the *Aeneid*, and these differences in divine and mortal interactions with the environment help elucidate mortals' struggles in establishing long-term control over the natural and built landscape.

50. James 1995: 636.

51. For an analysis of how the depiction of landscape may reflect political anxiety in a work close in time to the *Aeneid*, see Gramps 2018 on dread in Horace's *Odes*.

52. See Hardie 1994: 88 for commentary and bibliography on this passage (*Aen.* 9.77-122).

53. In particular see Cooley 2009: 218–56 for analysis and bibliography of *Res Gestae* 26–33.

CHAPTER 3
CHAOS AND *KOSMOS*: AN ECOCRITICAL READING OF SENECA'S *THYESTES*
Simona Martorana

Introduction

The narrative of the *Thyestes* features some of the most gruesome and appalling scenes of Seneca's dramatic writing. After welcoming his brother Thyestes and Thyestes' sons, Atreus takes his nephews with him to the innermost and concealed area of his palace (ll.650–6), where he kills them, cuts their corpses into pieces, and cooks their limbs in a pot (ll.691–788). Thereafter, Atreus serves the flesh of the two boys as dinner to Thyestes, who eats them, unaware of Atreus' misdeeds (ll.983–7). Thyestes' discovery of the horrible truth happens gradually, during a tense dialogue between Atreus and Thyestes (ll.995–1051), which reaches its peak when Atreus ambiguously replies to his brother that he holds 'whatever survives' of his sons 'alongside what does not survive' of them: *quidquid e natis tuis/superest habes, quodcumque non superest habes* (ll.1030–1).[1] Atreus' revenge against his brother for having slept with his wife has been accomplished, thus producing an escalation of *scelera* ('heinous crimes'), which is a *Leitmotiv* within the drama.[2]

This chapter focuses on the fourth choral ode of the *Thyestes* (ll.789–884), which famously features apocalyptic natural phenomena, and the following section of the drama, namely the final act. By rereading these passages through ecocritical and post-human lenses, I demonstrate that natural collapse is not directly related to Thyestes' and Atreus' crimes (as per traditional interpretations) but articulates a more complex view of *natura* ('nature') as an independent and self-governing system. After outlining my theoretical framework in the next section, I will proceed with a close reading of the fourth choral ode vis-à-vis the final act of the drama, in order to show that the apparent contradictions between the two passages concerning the representation of natural forces can be explained through the adoption of a 'post-human' perspective.

Natural (re)action: Theoretical framework

Disruption of cosmic cycles, exceptional natural phenomena and apocalyptic events prominently feature in the fourth choral ode of Seneca's *Thyestes* (ll.789–884), where they are framed as a reaction of *nature* to the terrible crimes that are perpetrated in the tragedy.[3] According to a Stoic interpretation of the *Thyestes*,[4] this cosmic disruption may be said to articulate the concept of 'sympathy'. Building upon Stoic materialistic views, the notion of 'sympathy' (from the Greek *sumpatheia*) postulates the interaction (the 'co-affection') between elements of the universe, and therefore the interrelation between physical and psychic spheres.[5] In the *Thyestes*, the breaking of human and moral laws, namely, the unbalance determined by Thyestes' impiety, is articulated at a physical level by the disruption of natural laws.[6] Moreover, the apocalyptic events that the chorus describe can be read as a literary translation of the Stoic conflagration (or *ekpurōsis*), which asserts cyclical destruction and reformation of the world.[7] This cosmic destruction reflects, at the physical level, the disruption of each social and familial law, as well as moral principles, within the human community.

The fourth choral ode of the *Thyestes* is not the first instance where we can find a connection between human actions and non-human elements or natural phenomena in Seneca's dramas.[8] An example close to the *Thyestes* is the storm at *Agamemnon*, ll.406-578, which can be read as a consequence of the impious actions of the Achaeans in Troy and at the same time anticipates the disgraceful events (most importantly, the murder of Agamemnon) that are about to happen in the drama. Another instance can be observed at the beginning of the *Oedipus* (ll.1–81), where Oedipus' patricide and incestuous relationship with his mother cause a pestilence that affects the whole population of Thebes. The natural disasters in the fourth choral ode of the *Thyestes* are very similar to the examples mentioned; yet, there is no direct reference to the fact that these apocalyptic phenomena were propelled by a deity – or by fate – as a punishment for Atreus' and Thyestes' impious deeds.[9]

Exceptional natural phenomena are among the topics of another work by Seneca, the *Natural Questions*, where the treatment of natural disasters is both similar to and different from that of the tragedies. While the tragedies and the scientific treaty share a corprealistic conception of the cosmos (and therefore of the natural world), the *Natural Questions* tend to rationalize and 'normalize' natural disasters as a part of the whole cosmic mechanisms.[10] But is a Stoic interpretation possible for the natural collapses featuring in the *Thyestes*? Does the text of the drama imply that *nature* is reacting to human moral evil, as it seems? Can the disruption of natural laws and catastrophic natural events be attributed *tout court* to the Stoic doctrine of conflagration?

These questions represent a point of departure for my re-examination of the fourth choral ode vis-à-vis a section of the subsequent dialogue between Atreus and Thyestes. In the dialogue, Thyestes wonders why gods and natural forces are not reacting to his crime (ll.1035–51, 1068–96), thus pointing out a fundamental ambivalence in the portrayal of *natura* within the drama. On the one hand, the depiction of nature shows an overlap between human experience and the natural world, as well as presenting humans as parts, co-actors, in an organic whole; on the other hand, precisely this incorporation of human experience in the natural cosmos reveals how the complexity of natural phenomena cannot be grasped by human observers, whose view of nature remains partial and extremely limited. By drawing on various strands of ecocritical and post-human theory (particularly, the works of theorists such as Rosi Braidotti, Jeffrey Jerome Cohen, Donna Haraway and Bruno Latour, as well as American literature scholar and eco-theorist Hubert Zapf), I show how this seemingly contradictory attitude of nature problematizes a straightforward interpretation of natural collapses as *sympathetic* (in the Stoic sense) and consequential to human evil. In doing so, my reading of the *Thyestes* engages with scholarship that has shown how Seneca's dramas complicate the (Stoic) principles endorsed in his philosophical prose.[11] While, to some extent, human experiences and the natural, non-human world seem to overlap, at the same time natural elements, such as earth (ll.1006–7, 1020), are shown to be apathetic and distant from humans' desires and expectations.[12] The intermingling of human and non-human components of the cosmos undermines humans' epistemological and ontological prominence over other non-human entities.

This ecocritical interpretation builds upon recent scholarly works that have demonstrated the importance of Environmental Humanities for the study of the ancient world, particularly those challenging anthropocentric views of nature and natural phenomena in Classical authors. Among these studies, the works of Christopher Schliephake and the volume edited by Hunt and Marlow have been crucial in providing a theoretical background, as well as a methodological strategy to navigate ancient literature, history and material culture through an ecocritical lens.[13] Hunt and Marlow, for instance, acknowledge in the introduction to their volume the challenge that the application of contemporary issues and modern theory to ancient texts poses. While environmental changes are sometimes addressed by Classical writers, such as Theophrastus,[14] ancient societies did not experience the global, critical scale of environmental damage that modern technologies and globalization have created. The ancient world cannot give us answers on how to tackle water pollution, reduce the ozone hole, or further develop renewable energies; yet, it can give us an idea about how to change our attitudes towards the global environment, and engage with the natural world more harmoniously.

By walking the line between keeping a distance from the past and imposing it wholesale on the present, this chapter endorses the contemporary challenge to a reified notion of nature by resituating it within a distant context, that is, the Classical past. Ecocritical theories encourage us to dismantle traditional dichotomies in the light of the close advent of a 'post-human' world, where the borders and differences between man and woman, nature and culture, subject and object (and human and machine) are blurred and indistinguishable.[15] This quasi-organicist view not only leads us to perceive natural elements and phenomena in terms of an embodied experience, but also proves that humans are a part of a universal, cosmic whole, and *our* human point of view is unavoidably too limited to understand and judge natural forces. The portrayal of the 'environment' (namely the natural world, as well as natural phenomena and collapses)[16] featured in the fourth choral ode of Seneca's *Thyestes* encourages us to question the idea of nature as being coherent and explainable because connected to human action, or even as being intelligible from a human perspective.

Apocalypse now: The fourth chorus of Seneca's *Thyestes*

The fourth choral ode of the *Thyestes* (ll.789–884) blurs the differences between human experience and nature, between anthropomorphic divine agents and natural events, and between the crimes of two men (Atreus and Thyestes) and the disruption of natural and divine laws. By starting with an invocation to the sun as *parens*, 'parent' (l. 789), the chorus set the ground for shortening the distance, and breaking the boundaries, between a natural element, the sun, the divine personification of the sun as 'Phoebus' (l. 793) and the humanization of that natural element, that is, the human perception of the sun as something familiar and benevolent, as a parent, 'father' at 789.[17] The mention of the sun as *parens* enhances the connection between the sun as a natural-divine entity and the plot of the drama, where a father, Thyestes, has just eaten his sons. At the same time, the invocation to the sun (anticipated by the Messenger at ll.776 and 785) establishes a thematic connection with Atreus' self-presentation as the sun, which happens slightly later in the drama (Sen. *Thy.* 896–901):

> *etiam die nolente discutiam tibi*
> *tenebras, miseriae sub quibus latitant tuae.*
> *nimis diu conviva securo iaces*
> *hilarique vultu; iam satis mensis datum est*
> *satisque Baccho: sobrio tanta ad mala*   900
> *opus est Thyeste.*

Even though the daylight is unwilling, I shall dispel for you the darkness that conceals your sorrows. Too long you have lain there feasting with a carefree and cheerful expression. Enough devotion has been given to the banquet, enough to wine: for suffering so great, we need Thyestes sober.

In this passage, Atreus does not simply compare his actions to the tasks of the sun, he also implicitly claims to replace the sun by metaphorically dispelling Thyestes' ignorance, thus shedding light on the truth, namely his murder of Thyestes' sons and, later, Thyestes' *teknophagia* (the consumption of these children). Therefore, the chorus's mention of the sun as the 'father of earth and heaven' at l. 789 sinisterly recalls the other father of the drama, Thyestes, as well as establishing a link to Atreus' self-depiction as the sun, thereby stressing the connection between moral evil (the crimes of the two brothers) and physical elements and/or phenomena.

This attribution of quasi-human features to an astronomical object blurs the boundaries between human, divine (cf. the sun as 'Phoebus' at l. 793) and the astronomic sphere, as well as providing a non-human element with agentic force: the sun actively turns (*vertis iter*, l. 791) and dissipates (*perdis*, l. 792) the light of the day (*diem*, l. 792). In the same choral ode, a few lines later, other celestial bodies are also personified through their identification with semi-divine entities, and hence provided with agency: it is said that Vesper, the evening star, is not yet summoning the stars ('the lights of the night'; *nocturna ... lumina*, l. 795); the sunset is mentioned through an elaborated periphrasis and a reference to the 'turning of the Western wheel' (*Hesperiae flexura rotae*, l. 796).[18] While this process can be seen as a form of 'humanization' of non-human natural elements, the agency bestowed upon an astronomic body also articulates the progressive de-centralization of humans as self-conscious actors within the narrative, thereby undermining 'their fantasies of sovereign' and control over their non-human surroundings – to borrow a phrase from Jeffrey Jerome Cohen's work on the agency of stones.[19]

This description of the sudden departure of the sunlight at an unusual time of the day represents a sort of eclipse (or 'retrogression', as Rosenmeyer puts it);[20] an unexpected natural phenomenon that emphasizes human lack of control over and understanding of natural forces. Furthermore, the chorus remark on how the *arator*, 'the ploughman', is amazed at the abrupt appearance of the evening (literally, 'wonders at the sudden arrival of suppertime'; *stupet ad subitae tempora cenae*, l. 800), when 'his oxen is not yet exhausted' (l. 801).[21] The reference to the ploughman, along with the 'sun' and 'Vesper', contributes to the incorporation of natural elements and phenomena into human experience. This incorporation, however, does not lead to a better comprehension of natural events by human characters. Indeed, the chorus openly profess their astonishment for the unconventional natural phenomena they are witnessing: 'What has driven you out of your heavenly course? What cause has forced your horses down from their fixed path?' (*quid te aetherio pepulit cursu?/quae causa tuos limite certo/deiecit equos?* ll.802-4).[22] The overlap between the natural and human world, and the attribution of agentic power to the former, challenges the active role of human beings both at the ontological and gnoseological level, claiming the centrality of non-human forces.[23]

The interaction and reversal of power dynamics between humans and non-humans become even more explicit when the chorus express their fear for the coming disruption of natural laws, and the return of primordial chaos that they see as the result.[24] Having described the loss of the 'regular cycles of the heaven' (l. 813, *solitae mundi periere vices*), with personified sun, dawn, moon and stars switching their tasks and positions (ll.815–27), the chorus state that their hearts are trembling due to the great fear ('our hearts are trembling, trembling because they are shaken with enormous fear'; *trepidant, trepidant/pectora magno percussa metu*, ll.828–9). Everything is shaken by a fatal ruin, the chaos will overcome both humans and gods ('lest formless chaos overcome again gods and humans'; *iterumque deos hominesque premat/deforme chaos*, ll.832–3), and nature (l. 834) will cover again lands, sea and stars: 'and once more earth and girdling sea and the wandering stars of the jewelled sky be hidden by nature' (*iterum terras et mare cingens/et vaga picti sidera mundi/natura tegat*; ll.833–4).[25] From these lines, it appears clearly how humans, along with gods, are being taken over by non-human agentic forces, *chaos* and *natura*.

According to some scholars, this account draws a picture of *natura* as reacting predictably to human actions, particularly to human evil.[26] By contrast, I argue, the focus on the agency of nature at lines 833–4, and its connection to the fear of the chorus, not only stresses the overlap between human subjective feelings (fear; anxiety; trouble) and the external landscape, but it also articulates the inability of humans to find coherent explanations for natural events.

This sense of chaos and incoherence does not concern only the characters within the narration, but also affects the formal features of the passage, which seems unsettled from a stylistic point of view. Similar to natural phenomena, the text remains fundamentally ambiguous and extraneous to its human 'observers', namely its readers:[27] at the formal level, because of its unusual meter, alliterative sounds and rhetorical choices (e.g. the *geminatio* of *trepidant* at 828);[28] at the syntactic level, because of the subject position of non-human entities; in terms of content, because it describes unexplainable and uncommon natural events.

To these apocalyptic natural phenomena, one can add the confusion between constellations, which is described in detail later in the choral ode (e.g. ll.835–74).[29] While these phenomena seem to actually take place in the drama, the other fears of the chorus (the return of primeval chaos and nature's overtaking of sea, lands and stars, with the consequent restoration of primordial indistinctness) will not be fulfilled.[30] This discrepancy between the words of the chorus and what happens in the drama confirms that the human perspective on natural events is only partial. Human involvement in natural phenomena and catastrophes does not make human beings more knowledgeable about nature or natural processes.

The questioning of human epistemological capabilities is accompanied by an ambivalent attitude of the chorus in the final lines of the ode. First, the chorus sarcastically wonder whether 'out of so many people', it is judged that they 'deserve to be crushed by the overthrow of the axis of heaven' (*nos e tanto visi populo/digni, premeret/quos everso cardine mundus?*; ll.875–7), and that they are therefore witnessing the 'final age' of the world ('has the final age come upon us?'; *in nos aetas ultima venit?*; l. 878). This somewhat individual and subjective interpretation of cosmic events is disavowed in the following section of the drama, as (contrary to what the chorus state) natural phenomena will not lead, in fact, to the end of the world. While pointing out their individuality, the chorus also find parallels between their human condition and that of the rest of the world, including animate and inanimate beings, and therefore downplay the central role of humans as judges, and drivers, of natural processes. The participants of the chorus urge themselves to abandon the complaint, as 'one that does not want to die when the whole world perishes with them is greedy for life' (*vitae est avidus quisquis non vult/mundo secum pereunte mori*, ll.883–4). This last sentence of the ode confirms the ambivalent way in which the chorus, along with other characters within the drama, engage with the natural world.

Re-placing humans: The apathy of the natural world

After the choral ode, the fifth act opens with Atreus' joyful reaction at the sight of Thyestes' cannibalistic feast (ll.885–919).[31] The tragic irony created by Thyestes' unawareness of his impious meal is reinforced by his excessive delight and celebrations, as well as his false belief in reconciliation between himself and Atreus (ll.920–69). In an intense dialogue with his brother, Thyestes first discovers that his sons have been killed by Atreus and then realizes that he has just eaten them. After finding out that his sons have died, he wonders why *tellus* ('earth') does not react to such a *nefas* ('impiety'): *sustines tantum nefas/gestare, Tellus?* ('earth, can you bear to carry such an unspeakable crime?' ll.1006–7). The verb *gestare* is frequently used in Latin texts to indicate the carrying of a baby, thereby evoking the representation of earth as (the great) mother, a quasi-anthropomorphic deity.[32] Thyestes asks why the earth does not swallow Atreus and himself or does not drag them to the *chaos inane* ('empty void/chaos', l. 1009). While Boyle correctly understands *chaos inane* as an indication of the underworld, the expression also recalls the *deforme chaos* ('formless chaos') produced by the disruption of natural laws at l. 833.[33] Thyestes' exclusion from this chaos, along with the earth's putative refusal to drag down him and his brother Atreus, seems to contradict the cosmic conflagration described in the previous choral ode.

This contradiction, which is implied by Thyestes' astonishment at the lack of any reactions to his crimes, shows how the exceptional natural phenomena outlined in the choral ode only superficially reflect a sympathetic, coherent, response of nature to human crimes. In Seneca's Stoic theorization, the notion of a sympathetic relationship between human and cosmic forces coexists with, and is complementary to, the Stoic idea of providence as independent from human action, as well as unintelligible from a human perspective.[34] From Thyestes' point of view, the passivity of natural elements is articulated by the immobility of the earth, which 'lies motionless, as a stolid mass' (*immota, Tellus, pondus ignavum iaces?* l. 1020), as well as the absence of gods, who seem to have gone away (*fugere superi*, l. 1021). Thyestes' allocutions depict the earth as a living organism, with independent will and agency.

This personification of the earth is a literary topos that goes back to accounts of an ancestral and pre-Olympian divine order, where Earth, or Gaia, featured as a goddess. For example, as a character in Hesiod's *Theogony*, Gaia holds a terrifying power and at the same time is a wise advisor.[35] In his rereading of the idea behind the mythological figure of Gaia, the philosopher Bruno Latour shows the potential of rethinking Gaia as a living entity.[36] In his view, Gaia, made up of a myriad of different organisms, is neither active nor passive; Gaia engenders the constituents of the world and, concurrently, is engendered by each organism living in it.[37] Latour's vibrant Gaia, which comprises and nurtures other organisms, as well as merges with them, accentuates the blurring of boundaries between various components of the world. Gaia is both immanent and transcendent; she generates and is generated; she is distant and at the same time close to human beings. In other words, this notion of Gaia exemplifies the fluidity in the representation of natural elements in the *Thyestes*. Nature first appears close to human feelings and interrelated to human action; subsequently, it is represented as detached and independent from humans. While human epistemological prominence is denied, the ontological incorporation of humans as components of the cosmos stresses their interconnectivity with natural elements, which makes them 'objects among objects',[38] unmarked entities in an independent and self-regulating system.

This coexistence of distance and closeness emerges from the words of Thyestes, who expects from the earth a sympathetic reaction to his crimes, but all he gets is complete detachment and apathy. Thyestes' remarks on the passivity of the earth and natural elements (and gods as representatives of non-human forces) are antithetical to the description of chaos and disruption of natural laws that were witnessed by the chorus.

After the previous exceptional natural events, Thyestes would expect additional, more individualized punishments by nature for his brother's and his own abject crimes. These punishments, however, do not take place; nature does not comply with Thyestes' views or expectations. Nature, along with its components, remains inexplicable and ambiguous to Thyestes' understanding. Although his wishes are unheard by nature, Thyestes still tries to make sense of, and apply, his human-centred perspective to the natural phenomena that were previously described by the chorus, after he has found out that the flesh of his most recent meal is, in fact, the dismembered bodies of his sons (Sen. *Thy.* 1035–7):

> *hoc est deos quod puduit, hoc egit diem*
> *aversum in ortus. quas miser voces dabo*
> *questusque quos? quae verba sufficient mihi?*

> This was what shamed the gods, this drove the day back to where it rises. What words, what laments shall I utter in such misery? What speech will suffice me?

By linking the subversion of natural laws to his cannibalistic feast, Thyestes rationalizes natural phenomena as consequence, and response, to his crimes. Similarly to the chorus, Thyestes seems to be inclined to interpret the disruption of natural laws in Stoic terms, namely as a sympathetic reaction of nature to Atreus' and his own abject actions. The account of natural disasters, however, as well as subversion of natural laws, are the result of the incorporation of natural phenomena into personal experience and, vice versa, the projection of emotions and feelings into the natural surroundings. This sort of subjectivization of the external landscape is not new to Senecan drama, and can be found in other passages of his tragedies, such as Oedipus' description of the plague of Thebes at *Oedipus,* ll.1–70. As noted by Walde, the plague devastating the urban and rural landscape is not simply an articulation of Oedipus' moral evil but is also a projection of Oedipus' feelings and perceptions.[39]

The subjectivization of natural surroundings and Stoic interpretation of natural phenomena are not necessarily mutually exclusive, as subjectification may be another way to convey the idea of a sympathetic connection between human and non-human world. Yet, the ambivalence of what is understood as natural responses to human actions – namely, the coexistence of active reaction and passivity of the natural world – articulates the limitedness of an anthropocentric and reified view of nature. The dislocation of the central place of humans within the cosmos goes beyond a Stoic interpretation of Senecan dramas, or Seneca's own philosophical views, transcending the distinctions among philosophical doctrines. If humans are *post-humanly* intermingled with natural phenomena, their position as privileged observers of both human and non-human events is undermined. Accordingly, their epistemological potential is annihilated by their ontological belonging to the cosmos as an independent and autonomous system.

The engagement with the natural world in the *Thyestes* thus posits a broader question about the capability of human characters to control and understand the meaning of the natural world, and accordingly displays human limits. This difficulty at meaningfully engaging with the natural world further emerges from Thyestes' invocation of natural and divine entities after the discovery of his cannibalistic meal. While invoking a punishment for his impiety, Thyestes expects a reaction from gods and natural forces (1068–96), which are once again personified and humanized.

Alongside the sea (*maria*, 1069), the gods (*di*, l. 1070), hell (*inferi*, l. 1070) and earth (*terrae*, l. 1071), Thyestes invokes the darkness of a personified 'night' (*nox*, l. 1071), with a request of making space for his laments ('attend to my words'; *vocibus nostris vaca*, l. 1072).[40] The night is further humanized, as Thyestes seems to take her as the only advisor and confident left to him: 'I am abandoned to you, you alone see my misery' (*tibi sum relictus, sola tu miserum vides*, l. 1073). After the night, Thyestes invokes Jupiter through a periphrastic epithet ('you exalted ruler of the skies'; *summe caeli rector*, l. 1077), asking him to provoke storms, thunder and lightning, as well as to 'avenge the stolen daylight' (*vindica amissum diem*, l. 1085) and strike at him: 'strike at me, hurl the fiery brand of your three-forked weapon through this chest' (*me pete, trisulco flammeam telo facem/per pectus hoc transmitte*; ll.1089–90). While addressing natural elements and gods, Thyestes at the same time acknowledges that gods seem not to be touched by his impiety, 'nothing moves the gods' (*nihil superos movet*, l. 1092).[41] Given that gods are not punishing him for his actions, Thyestes wishes that at least an eternal night will remain to cover his crimes with darkness (*aeterna nox permaneat*, l. 1094). Like Jupiter, however, the night also ignores Thyestes' requests.

Thyestes' invocations represent a widespread topos in the ancient dramatic genre, where the characters, usually unsuccessfully, appeal to gods or other natural entities for help.[42] At the same time, the apathy of gods and natural forces is supported by the Stoic idea of providence as autonomous, ineffable and independent from human action. Literary tradition and Stoic doctrine may well have played a role in Seneca's portrayal of divine and natural forces in the fourth choral ode and the final act of the *Thyestes*. However, the patent contradictions in the representation of non-human entities, which appear, simultaneously, close to and distant from the human characters, as well as actively involved in the narrative and passively detached from the events, articulate the limits of an anthropocentric view of nature. The combination between literary motifs and Stoic doctrine stresses once more the partiality and inadequacy of the human (character) for the understanding of natural phenomena. Accordingly, in this text, the role of humans as the central focus of the narrative and privileged observers of both human and non-human events is challenged and reconsidered in light of the increased acquisition of agentic and narrative force by natural, astronomic, semi-divine or divine entities.

Conclusion

Apocalyptic responses to human evil actions certainly are not new to Latin imperial poetry, from the eclipse following Caesar's death in Ovid's *Metamorphoses* 15 (ll.729–842), to the plague of Thebes as a result of Oedipus' crimes in Seneca's *Oedipus* (ll.1–81), to the exceptional natural phenomena anticipating the civil war between Caesar and Pompey in Lucan's *Pharsalia* 1 (522–83). What is different here in the *Thyestes* is the profound contradiction between a supposedly *sympathetic* and consequential reaction of nature to human evil and what can be defined as an *apathetic* attitude of natural and environmental features. This indifference, which coexists with the supposedly sympathetic reaction, indicates that Thyestes' hopes, wishes and invocations will not be fulfilled. Gods as representatives and masters of natural phenomena, and as personifications of natural elements, stay silent, seemingly passive; nature does not respond to the expectations of the human characters but remains profoundly ambivalent. By building on ecocritical theory, I hope to have shown that, in Seneca's *Thyestes*, nature is not ambivalent or incoherent per se, but it may appear ambivalent to humans' partial and limited point of observation, that is, the chorus's and particularly Thyestes' point of observation. As an independent organism, a system, the natural world takes directions that are not clear to human expectations.

Notes

1. 'At one level his words mean that Thyestes has all that is left of his sons . . . But, of course, Atreus intends his words to operate also literally, with a different sense for *habes*: "you have (outside you) all that remains", "you have (inside you) all that does not remain". Atreus' pleasure (and power) in seeing Thyestes fail to comprehend the full meaning of his words is evident'; cf. Boyle 2017: 432–3; see also Littlewood 2004: 185. The Latin text of Seneca's tragedies is from the Loeb's edition, Fitch 2004, unless otherwise stated; the English translation is also from Fitch 2004, with changes.

2. Schiesaro 2003: 27–8, 77–8, and 130, Littlewood 2004: 198 and 228–36, Martorana 2022: 270.

3. Throughout this essay, 'nature' will be written with lowercase 'n'. Although this survey endorses the idea of nature as a coherent system of relations, embedded with an independent agency, and does not reject the Stoic concept of nature as an organism, but rather builds on it, the upper-case 'Nature' conveys a post-modern anthropomorphic, highly human-centred notion of nature that is contrary to the main argument of this essay, which maintains that nature's agency is unintelligible to humans. For some general readings of *natura* in Seneca's drama, see Boyle 1985: 1284–347, Vottero 1998: 291–303, Fedeli 2000: 25–45, Rosenmeyer 2000: 99–119.

4. For a 'Stoic interpretation' of Senecan dramas, and its connected issues, see Hine 2004: 173–220.

5. Volk 2006: 183–200, Tarrant 1985: 204–16, Boyle 2017: 363–7. On how Stoic sympathy leads to a cosmobiologic, organic, view of nature, see Holmes 2019: 239–70.

6. For a detailed analysis of *natura* in Seneca's *Troades* and *Thyestes*, see Matias 2009. More specifically, in his *Natural Questions* Seneca refers to cosmic interconnectedness in highly materialistic terms, addressing it as 'the unity of a body' (*unitatem corporis*; QNat. 2.6.2, with Rosenmeyer 1989: 108–10), as well as pointing out the Stoic idea of a community of feelings and aspirations between cosmic objects and human morality.

7. Volk 2006: 190–2, Boyle 2017: 365–6.

8. For the flight of the sun as a possible consequence to horrible crimes within Senecan drama, cf. *HF* 939–42, *Med.* 28–31, *Pha.* 676–9, *Ag.* 295–7, and 908–9.

9. The chorus listen to and sometimes comment on the Messenger's account of the murder and cooking of Thyestes' sons, which forecasts the flight of the sun (776–87). However, there is no direct reference to the connection between Atreus' (and Thyestes') crimes and the following cosmic disruption; see Davis 1989: 424.

10. See e.g. the earthquakes in *QNat.* 6, with Williams 2006: 124–46. The conception of the soul (and passions of the soul) as a corporeal substance derives from the Stoic notion of 'sympathy', whereby every human, non-human, animate or inanimate entity is a part of the cosmic whole. For Stoic materiality, as well as the overlap between divine and physical spheres, see e.g. Long and Sedley 1987: 272–304, 359–68, passim; Rosenmeyer 1989: 37–112; Inwood 2005: 157–200, 224–48.

11. See Rosenmeyer 1989, on the relationship between the tragedies and Stoic physics; see Schiesaro 1997: 89–111 and 2003, as well as Gunderson 2015: 105–47, on tragic characters vis-à-vis Stoic ethics.

12. Certain contradictory aspects of the ode vis-à-vis other sections of the drama have been noticed by Picone 1984: 106–15, Davis 1989: 431–4, Schmitz 1993: 201–5, Volk 2006: 193–4, Mazzoli 2014: 571–3.

13. Schliephake 2016, 2020; Hunt and Marlow 2019.

14. E.g. Theophr. *Caus. pl.* 5.14.2-3; Lane 2011 on Plato's *Republic*. For other examples, see Harper 2017, Cordovana and Chiai 2017.

15. See Braidotti 2002, 2013.

16. The notion of 'environment' has developed only recently, starting with the industrial revolution and evolving throughout the twentieth century. 'Environment' can be broadly defined as the circumstances, objects or conditions by which one is surrounded, since the word derives from the French *environs*, literally 'surroundings'. However, 'environment' is understood by some people simply as nature, or non-human world, or a system of relationships between humans and non-human beings and objects (see Garrard 2012: 1–17). That the word 'environment' is relatively recent does not imply that pre-modern populations were indifferent to their relationship with the natural world or did not develop a conception of nature as a complex system of relations (see Schliephake 2016: 1–15, Hunt and Marlow 2019: 2–12, Schliephake 2020: 1–31).

17. The reading *parens* (instead of *potens*) has been accepted following Nenci's remarks on the occurrence of this epithet in Greek literature, where it qualifies the sun at, for instance, Aeschylus' *Choephoroe* 984. The reference to the sun as *parens* is here coherent with the plot of the drama, which has a father (Thyestes) eat his sons; cf. also Sophocles' frag. 752 (Lloyd-Jones), see Davis 1989: 432 n.41, Nenci 2002: 180–2, Boyle 2017: 368; see also Tarrant 1985: 205 (*pace* Zwierlein 1986).

18. According to Boyle 2017 (369), Vesper is mentioned as a marker of time in these lines. For the image of the sun's daily journey, cf. *Pha.* 286 (*Hesperias . . . metas*), Ov. *Met.* 3.145 (*meta . . . utraque*).

19. Cohen 2015: 9.

20. Rosenmeyer 1989: 156–7. For a review of the discussions concerning this natural phenomenon, see Torre 2018: 440–1; for an interpretation of this motif against other Roman as well as Greek sources, see also Bonandini 2022: 50–77.

21. This is the only occurrence of *arator*, 'ploughman', within Senecan drama and may have been drawn from Ov. *Met.* 8.218-19, see Boyle 2017: 370.

22. Davis 1989: 431–3.

23. See Zapf 2016: 85.

24. For the links between Ovid's description of the primordial chaos and the underworld in the *Thyestes*, and for some remarks on Seneca's reception of the Ovidian episode of Tereus and Procne, see Tarrant 2002: 349–60, see also Schiesaro 2003: 178–90, Littlewood 2008: 253–9.

25. In this passage, Boyle 2017 (377–8) also notices the role of *natura* (and Fate) as the primary agent of the world's return to chaos, which adheres to Stoic views of conflagration. This Stoic principle is contradicted by the fearful reaction of the chorus, which appears to be non-Stoic. At line 834, I chose to de-capitalize the word *natura* (following Viansino 1993 and Nenci 2002; *pace* Fitch 2004 and Boyle 2017), in agreement with the conception of the natural world that is adopted in this essay (see discussion in n.3).

26. For the connection between human feelings, physical suffering and natural landscape within Senecan drama, see Segal 1983: 172–87.

27. While analysing the presence of the natural world in a poem by Emily Dickinson, Hubert Zapf (2016: 31) comments that the poem unfolds the 'rich semantic potential' of the natural world, using 'the interfusion of metaphor and narrative' to create an 'uncanny dialectic of familiarity and strangeness, of the visible and the invisible, of presence and absence, of communication and isolation, of life and death as basic forms of being in the world'. Similarly, in the fourth choral ode, familiar natural elements have transformed into something distant, impalpable and impossible to grasp.

28. Boyle 2017: 375.

29. Ibid.: 377–85; for a detailed analysis of this passage vis-à-vis contemporary astronomical knowledge in the Roman world, see Torre 2018: 440–88.

30. Boyle (2017: 388) sees in this denial of the chorus' fears (or prediction) a 'gap between Stoicism and the world'.

31. For Thyestes' feast as a sinister spectacle that is displayed in front of Atreus' eyes, see ibid.: 397–8; for Thyestes' cannibalistic banquet, see e.g. Aygon 2003: 271–84, Pociña 2003: 251–70; on *teknophagia*, see Haley 2018: 152–73.

32. Cf. *TLL* VI 2.1963.2-1969.17, *s.v.* 'gesto'.

33. Boyle 2017: 427. For chaos in Senecan drama, see Mazzoli 2016.

34. Cf. *SVF* 2.944, 2.950, 2.954, 2.956; also Sen. *Prov.* 1, 5.6-7, Long and Sedley 1987: 333–43.

35. Hes. *Theog.* 104–206.

36. Latour 2017: 81–94; and cf. the discussion in Usher, this volume.

37. Latour 2017: 98.

38. 'A thing among things', as Merleau-Ponty (1964: 163) would put it.

39. Walde 2012: 71–94.

40. For *vacare* as 'being empty for', cf. *OLD*, *s.v.* 'vaco'; Boyle 2017: 442.

41. Cf. ibid.: 'As elsewhere in Seneca tragedy (*Hippolytus, Phaedra, Oedipus, Medea*), a prayer for self-destruction receives no response' (446); cf. e.g. Theseus at *Pha.* 1242–3.

42. Cf. e.g. Aesch. *PV* 88–92, Soph. *Phil.* 936–8, Sen. *HF* 1054–60 with Tarrant 1985: 238.

PART II
CONNECTION

CHAPTER 4

THE INTERSPECIES AND TRANS-CORPOREAL MESH IN EURIPIDES' *BACCHAE*

Maria Combatti

In his study, *The Bacchae: The Theatrical Body*, Rush Rehm states that 'as the (anthropomorphic) god associated with physical transformation, Dionysus works in and through the bodies of all the characters in the play, radically transforming the spaces they occupy'.[1] These words emphasize the importance of the body in the *Bacchae*, where the god adopts a human disguise and the bacchic frenzy of the chorus' women leads to the dismemberment of Pentheus, who embodies the sole resistance to Dionysus. Rehm's reading stresses the relationship between bodies and spaces according to various categories like physical contact, fusion and fragmentation. The spaces of the play's world show the coming together, the merging, and the breaking down of disparate bodies (of humans, animals, vegetables and material objects) until they come to rest in the fragmented body of Pentheus, which symbolizes the ruined house and the fragmented city, and through which the audience experiences 'its own kind break down'.[2]

Rehm's interpretation helps us to think beyond structuralist oppositions and reimagine physical and spatial relations based on juxtaposition, union and transformation. In these terms, Victoria Wohl has observed that a dynamic of 'becoming-other' characterizes much of the action of the play.[3] Dionysus becomes human, Theban women become maenads, Pentheus becomes animal, and the play closes with predictions of future transformations into snake, hero and divinity. As she points out, the Dionysiac 'contagion spreads and mutates', letting individual integrity explode, such that the tragic hero becomes a 'polymorphous nomad, unfixed in place and shape'.[4] Building on such insights, in this chapter, I examine Dionysus' pluralistic and transformative action as spreading over the *Bacchae*'s environments (both urban and natural) and invading the bodies inhabiting those environments.[5] However, while Rehm and Wohl offer a human-centred approach by mainly focusing on human bodies, I look at the mutual interdependencies between human and nonhuman entities by emphasizing all the relations between different but connecting natural and material realms of which humans are only a part.

My reading of the *Bacchae* puts studies of the play into dialogue with contemporary theoretical paradigms such as ecocriticism, posthumanism and environmental humanities, highlighting the complex dynamics of human relations with the 'more-than-human'[6] world.[7] For example, Downing Cless has read the *Bacchae* through an ecocritical lens, emphasizing how nature (natural phenomena, mountains, fields, and animals of many kinds) is a continuously active part of the plot and imagery of the play.[8] In Cless's opinion, the centrality of the natural world in the play is 'a thing of the past, just a mythical throwback', motivated by 'Euripides' skeptical view of human misappropriation of nature's agency'.[9] In these terms, Pentheus' tragic reversal would be related to his 'eco-hubris' and thus to his arrogant confidence that he can control nature by restraining the actions of the wild revels. However, while appreciating Cless's approach, I propose a different interpretation of the human–nature interactions in the *Bacchae*.

I read the play through an ecological conception that looks closely at the interaction of all things and shows how the bodies of humans, animals, plants and material entities are entangled in a nonessentialist relationship within the play's physical environments. In so doing, I engage with the concept of 'mesh' developed by Timothy Morton.[10] It suggests that all things in the world, from the smallest particle to the largest organism, are interconnected and interdependent. One of the key ideas behind the mesh is that traditional ways of thinking about the world often rely on hierarchies and distinctions between different things, which are inadequate for understanding the complex and dynamic nature of reality.[11] According to Morton, all things are 'strange strangers' in the sense that they are utterly independent but also composites of the other, as they share, for example, their cell structures.[12] Drawing on these concepts, I examine how things inhabiting the *Bacchae*'s environments are enmeshed and swap the same fragmented form. More specifically, I investigate how the royal palace, animals, dresses, plants and human bodies within the play are interlinked under the Dionysiac destructive force, which deconstructs them and shatters them all into pieces: the royal palace is destroyed by the earthquake, the cattle are torn into pieces, Pentheus' bacchic dress is fragmented into different parts, the tree is torn apart, and Pentheus' body is dismembered.

Deconstruction, fragmentation and transformation are the elements that characterize Dionysus' and the maenads' actions in the play, which scatter, multiply and transform bodies. In these terms, we can read the Dionysiac action through the lens of the 'rhizome', a concept developed by Gilles Deleuze and Félix Guattari, which apprehends connections, multiplicities, and expansions in opposition to differences, hierarchies and boundaries.[13] According to Deleuze and Guattari, the rhizome is heterogeneous and multiple and works with trans-species connections, functioning as an assemblage for new concepts, bodies and thoughts. The rhizome is a model of thought and organization fundamentally different from the traditional model of the 'tree', which operates according to hierarchy and sharply opposed differences between things existing in nature.[14] Unlike the tree, which has a rigid structure with vertical and linear connections, the rhizome grows horizontally and is open-ended. In this chapter, I use this concept to analyse the main events of the play, which are, as I have already mentioned, the destruction of the royal palace, the *sparagmos* ('ripping apart') of the cattle, the deconstruction of Pentheus' dress, the maenads' assault on the tree, and the dismemberment of Pentheus. These events, I argue, are an integral part of a rhizomatic patterning that illustrates the Dionysiac action that is also found in the deconstruction and fragmentation of the authoritarian power embodied by Pentheus.[15]

Finally, I build my discussion on ecofeminist studies that productively engage with human bodies' materiality in their relationship with the nonhuman world.[16] I look closely at Stacy Alaimo's theory of 'trans-corporeality', which conceives of the human body as an entity 'immersed in the flows of the world and in which social, cultural, and material/geographic agencies intra-act.'[17] I draw on this theory to trace the effects of the Dionysiac force upon the bodies of Pentheus, animals, plants and material entities, from which a new bodily assemblage emerges, namely, the thyrsus topped with Pentheus' head at the end of the play. As a result of an interspecies and trans-corporeal mesh, the thyrsus points to complex interactions of 'natural-cultural' dynamics, from which other enmeshments stem, like, for example, the transmutation of Cadmus and his wife Harmonia into snakes at the end of the play.[18]

The propagation of the Dionysiac force

As soon as he arrives in Thebes, Dionysus 'changes his form from the divine into human' (*morphēn d'ameipsas ek theou brotēsian*, 4), taking the role of the Lydian stranger, leader of the bacchants.[19] On the stage, the god sees the ruins of his mother's house and tomb, which he covers with 'clustering green of grapevine' (*ampelou/botruōdei chloē*, 11–12).[20] In this way, he transforms the stage set from a space of devastation into a luxuriant place, with an action that highlights his transformative power, which permeates all things and alters the environment.[21]

Dionysus' action extends to the offstage setting, including the people, city and land of Thebes. In particular, he clothes the Theban women in 'fawnskin' (*nebrida chroos*, 24) and puts the 'thyrsus, the ivy javelin' (*thurson kissinon belos*, 25) in their hands. He then drives them from their houses to the mountains, where 'they sit on the rocks, in the open air, beneath the green fir trees' (*chlōrais hup' elatais anorophous hēntai petras*, 38), and sends the bacchants to beat their 'drums' (*typana*, 59) 'about the royal palace' (*basileia t'amphi dōmata*, 60). Finally, as the chorus' leader says in the *parodos*, the bacchants initiate the entire Theban community to the Dionysiac cults (65–71): the whole city of Thebes joins the god's worshipping by crowning its head with ivy and abounding in 'evergreen leaves and lovely berries' (*chloērei/milaki kallikarpōi*, 107–8), dancing like a bacchant 'with sprays of oak and fir' (*druos/elatas kladoisi*, 109–10), and draping over its dappled fawn skins 'tufts of white twisted wool' (*leukotrichōn plokamōn/mallois*, 112–13). As a result, 'the whole land comes to dance' (*ga pasa choreusei*, 114) as Bromius leads his followers to the mountains. The effect of Dionysus' impact upon the earthly world is potent: 'the ground flows with milk, flows with wine, flows with the nectar of bees' (*rei de galakti pedon, rei d'oinō/rei de melissan nektari*, 143–4), while Bacchus runs, dances and shouts, 'whipping his long fine curls in the wind (*trupheron plokamon eis aithera riptōn*, 148–50).

The *parodos* shows a proliferating environment of material encounters between humans, animals, plants and objects. Many movements go on, and many things happen: there is a sense of sprouting, bursting, expanding and meshing. The Dionysiac action blurs the boundaries between humans and nonhumans, as all entities experience the ecstasy of the bacchic rites. This intricate network of interconnections invites us to see the Dionysiac force as a rhizomatic *milieu* ('environment') in Deleuze's and Guattari's words. According to the two philosophers, the *milieu* is not just a static background against which individuals and groups interact but a dynamic and ever-changing field of forces and influences. It is composed of multiple layers, from the global to the local, and it is constantly in flux as new connections and relationships are formed and old ones are dissolved. In these terms, Dionysus' and the maenads' actions can be seen as a flux of multiple connected forces that spread over the entire environment, from Asia to Thebes, and grow into multiplicity, variety and change.[22]

The only person who resists the Dionysiac invasion is King Pentheus, who tries to restrain the diffusion of the bacchic rites by imprisoning the Lydian stranger in his palace. While Dionysus is trapped in the palace, the chorus of bacchants sings the second *stasimon* (519–75), reaffirming their faith in the Dionysiac mysteries and blaming the king for his blasphemy. In this ode, the chorus-women depict distant places in heaven (Olympus) and on the earth (lands, woods, rivers), letting the audience visualize a vast cosmic space permeated by the god's proliferating force against Pentheus' restrictive scheme. First, Dionysus' voice is heard on the stage from within the palace. Then, by singing in a lyric exchange with the chorus, the god calls on the 'goddess Earthquake' (*Ennosi potnia*, 585) to shake the earth. Thus, the chorus leader predicts and describes the collapse of 'Pentheus' palace' (*ta Pentheōs melathra*, 587), while 'above the pillars the great stones break apart' (*laina kiosin embola/diadroma*, 591–2). At this point, Dionysus invokes the lightning to burn down the whole palace (594–5). Consequently, the chorus-women throw their 'trembling bodies' (*tromera sōmata*, 600) to the ground as Dionysus attacks the palace and turns it 'upside down' (*anō katō*, 602).[23] Finally, the god enters the scene and describes how he liberated himself from the chains and escaped after razing the palace to the ground; 'the whole thing', now, 'lying shattered in ruin' (*suntethranōtai d'apan*, 633).

The explosive combination of earthquake, thunder and fire highlights Dionysus' destructive action's full force as it is entangled with natural phenomena. The disastrous event represents a potent warning to both Pentheus and the audience not to underestimate the consequences of Dionysus' anger.[24] The last image of the palace, in ruins, points back to the demolition of Semele's precinct and looks forward to the other deconstructions and destructions of the play, including the *sparagmos* of the cattle, Pentheus' dressing in bacchant clothes, the maenads' assault on the tree, and the *sparagmos* of Pentheus. All of these represent single and interconnected phenomena of the Dionysiac, rhizomatic flux of destruction and transformation.

The *sparagmos* of the cattle and the dressing of Pentheus

The earthquake scene has shown a complex conception of human and more-than-human interrelations, which extend to both on- and offstage settings. Like the palace, the women tremble and fall to the ground as the effects of the earthquake pass from the palace to their bodies. The entanglement between women's bodies and the material environment is further emphasized in the first messenger speech, which concerns the maenads' activities on Cithaeron (660–774). The messenger describes a mountain landscape where the whole environment partakes in Dionysiac ecstasy. The initial scene is that of a peaceful place where the sun sheds its light on the earth (679–80), the grazing cattle climb the uplands (677–8), and the bacchants lie in a deep sleep on tree branches on the ground (684–5).

Then, agitation starts taking hold of the place: Agave, Pentheus' mother, hearing the lowing of the cattle, stands up and wakes her companions from sleep. Thus, the women give themselves to the Dionysiac frenzy: they tie their fawnskins with writhing snakes that lick their cheeks (697–8), breastfeed gazelles and young wolves (699–700), and crown their hair with ivy, oak, and flowering bryony (702–3). Finally, miraculous flows pour forth: 'a fountain of cool water' (*drosōdēs hudatos notis*, 705), 'a spring of wine' (*krēnēn oinou*, 707), 'a well of white milk' (*leukou pōmatos galaktos*, 708–10) and 'sweet streams of honey' (*glukeiai melitos roai*, 711) dripping from the *thyrsoi*.

Victoria Wohl reads the 'strange and exciting syntheses' between the women's bodies, animals, and plants and the miraculous flows that erupt from the earth as manifestations of the maenads' erotic pleasure and an answer to their desire.[25] In contrast, I consider these bodily and environmental encounters as vibrant expressions of the effects of the Dionysiac action, which transits across human bodies and the wider environment, drawing them into a mutual and symbiotic relationship. The entanglement between the maenads' bodies and the mountain environment becomes a collision between the two entities, as the *sparagmos* of the cattle shows, 733–47:

> We (Pentheus' men) ran away and thereby escaped
> being torn to pieces by the bacchants. But they, with no iron weapons
> in their hands, attacked the grazing cattle.
> You could have seen a woman tearing
> a bellowing fatted calf asunder with her hands
> while others tore heifers to pieces.
> You could have seen their ribs and cloven hooves
> scattered this way and that (*anō te kai katō*): pieces drenched with blood,
> hung dripping from the fir trees.
> Bulls that till then were violent, with anger in their horns,
> were thrown to the ground, dragged by countless female hands:
> stripped of flesh was torn into pieces
> faster than you could blink your royal eyes.[26]

In this passage, rather than focusing on the women's frantic behaviour and the ritual or sacrificial aspect of their hunting, as most scholars have done, I want to concentrate on the bodies of the animals in relation to the broader environment.[27] The messenger's depiction of the *sparagmos* invites the audience to visualize a landscape of fragmentation characterized by the presence of pieces of animals' bodies scattered all around the environment. Ribs and hooves are dispersed in the mountain, pieces of meat drip their blood from trees, and bodies of bulls stripped of their flesh are dragged and thrown everywhere. The stunning maenadic force is integral to this fragmentation, as the women's bodily parts, notably their bare, countless hands, are mixed with the animals' pieces all over the environment. Finally, this depiction resonates with the description of the destruction of the royal palace (633): indeed, as the palace has been turned 'upside down' (*anō katō*, 602), so the cattle are scattered 'this way and that' (*anō te kai katō*, 741).

Once the messenger has exited the stage, Dionysus proposes that Pentheus should wear the bacchant costume to go to the mountain and spy on the maenads undisturbed (912–16). The dressing scene has fostered a great interest in scholars.[28] But, while they have focused on Pentheus' gender permutation and sexuality, I examine the scene as an integral part of the patterning of the human and nonhuman interactions of the play through the way in which it advances the material enmeshment between Pentheus' body and clothing. In this respect, it is worth noting that each item of the bacchant attire is called *schēma* ('shape', 832), a word that is often used in ancient texts for the form and figure of the body.[29]

This comparison between body parts and clothing items has been anticipated in the scene of the *sparagmos* of the cattle, where Euripides uses the expression 'garments of flesh' (*sarkos enduta*, 746) to refer to the stripped flesh of the bull's bodies. At 830, Pentheus asks Dionysus 'what clothes he must wear' (*stolēn de tina phēs amphi chrōt' emon balein*). Thus, the god lists the attire items, probably touching Pentheus' body parts.[30] First, he will make Pentheus' 'hair grow long on his head' (*komēn men epi sō krati tanaon*, 831). Next, he will give him 'robes falling over his feet' (*peploi podēreis*, 833) and 'a headband for his head' (*epi kara mitra*, 833). Finally, he will add a '*thyrsus* for his hand and a spotted fawn skin' (*thurson ge cheiri kai nebrou stikton deros*, 835). As a result, Pentheus will go through the town as 'a man-turned-woman' (*gunaikomorphon*, 855).

As these lines suggest, the bacchant costume, coextensive with Pentheus' body, deconstructs his identity, mutates his gender,[31] and alters his perceptive faculties. Indeed, when he enters from the palace dressed as a bacchant, he sees double, 'two suns' (*duo men hēlious*, 918) and 'two Thebes' (*dissas de Thēbas*, 919).[32] The description of Pentheus' dressing shows an interactive enmeshment between the single clothing items (wig, headband, robe, fawnskin, *thyrsus*) and Pentheus' bodily parts (head, feet, hand), which is, in the end, also reflected upon the surrounding environment. Therefore, the dressing scene, we may say, aids in creating a trans-corporeal landscape in which the human, the self, the material and the wider environment are all entwined in a complex dynamic of interchanges.

The assault on the tree and the *sparagmos* of Pentheus

While Dionysus escorts Pentheus to the mountains, the chorus sings the fourth *stasimon*, in which the bacchants encourage the god to reveal himself and let Pentheus fall to the maenad throng (977–1032). Then, an attendant of Pentheus, who had also accompanied him to Cithaeron, enters the stage as a second messenger. He announces Pentheus' death, first describing the assault on the fir tree on which the hero has been perched to observe the maenads and then reporting the *sparagmos* of Pentheus.

Scholars have proposed different interpretations of the tree scene, emphasizing allusions to sacrificial or hunting rituals.[33] Downing Cless has argued that the depiction of the maenads' attack on the tree may relate to Euripides' critique of deforestation, partly due to the Peloponnesian War.[34] I read the scene differently, foregrounding a natural-cultural entanglement between the tree and Pentheus' authoritarian power.[35] As the messenger informs the audience, once on Cithaeron, Pentheus and Dionysus stop in a 'grassy valley' (*poiēron napos*, 1048), in 'a meadow surrounded by cliffs' (*agkos amphikrēmnon*, 1051) and 'shaded by pines' (*peukaisi suskiazon*, 1052). Here, Pentheus asks Dionysus to climb the 'tall-necked fir tree' (*elatēn hupsauchena*, 1061) so that he can better see the women's activities. At this point, the god reached the 'highest branch of the fir tree as tall as the sky' (*elatēs ouranion akron kladon*, 1064) and 'bent it down, pulled it, pulled it to the dark earth' (*katēgen, ēgen, ēgen es melan pedon*, 1065), until 'it was curved like a bow' (*kuklouto d'hōste toxon*, 1066) or 'a wheel-curve' (*kurtos trochos*, 1066). Then, he seated Pentheus 'atop the fir branches' (*elatinōn ozōn epi*, 1070) and set the trunk straight again (*orthou methiei*, 1071). The tree finally was fixed, straight, towering to heaven' (*orthē d'es orthon aither'estērizeto*, 1073) with Pentheus on its back.[36]

In the lines above, the reference to the tall structure of the tree emphasizes how the plant emerges beyond the other trees in the surrounding environment. This depiction triggers a strong resonance in the spectators' imagination, letting them vividly perceive Pentheus' high position. From this viewpoint, we may say that the tree embodies Pentheus' authoritarian power and his will to impose order and control upon the wild revels. The easy way the tree's branch submits to Dionysus, however, signifies the natural participation in the impending defeat of Pentheus.

In the mountain space that isolates the tree and its tall figure, Dionysus shouts to the women to capture Pentheus. Then, silence falls, and, the messenger tells us, 'the forest valley was still, the leaves were still' (*siga d'hulimos napē/phull'eiche*, 1084–5), while the maenads started running towards the tree and leaping over the rocks (1091–94). When they saw Pentheus perching on the tree, they climbed a great towering rock opposite the tree (1097) and started pelting the man with stones, fir branches and *thyrsoi* (1096–9).[37] Finally, seeing that they could not reach Pentheus, they 'shattered the tree with branches of oak' (*druinous sugkeraunousai kladous*, 1103) and 'tore up its roots with crowbars' (*rizas anesparasson asidērois mochlois*, 1104). Then, they gripped it, put their 'countless hands' (*murian chera* 1109) to the tree and 'pulled it out of the ground' (*kaxanespasan chthonos*, 1110) so that Pentheus 'falls to the ground' (*piptei pros oudas*, 1111–12).

In these lines, the maenads' hands, branches and crowbars become agents of mutual intra-action, the branches and crowbars becoming prosthetic extensions of the women's hands. The women's countless hands, which pull the tree out of the ground, may be compared to rhizomatic formations that invade and rupture the arborescent structure coinciding with Pentheus' power. As Deleuze and Guattari state, 'to be rhizomorphous is to produce stems and filaments that seem to be roots, or better yet connect with them by penetrating the trunk'.[38] In these terms, the maenads' assault on the tree incarnates the rhizomatic infiltration of the Dionysiac force into Pentheus' hierarchical, tree-like power. Finally, the tree, like the palace, the cattle and the bacchant costume, lies in ruins.

Pentheus' body is now on the ground amid the broken branches and the extirpated trunk. The women get Pentheus in their hands and start his *sparagmos*.[39] As I have suggested at various points in this chapter, I read the hero's dismemberment as part of the entanglements between human and nonhuman entities, encompassing the array of Dionysus' destructions of the material symbols of the authoritarian power incarnated by Pentheus. In what follows, I focus on bodily matter, highlighting the enmeshment of Pentheus' body with plants, animals and objects as the final testimony to the Dionysiac destructive flux of action, which transits across human bodies and the wider environment.

Pentheus' mother begins the killing of her son until her companions join her in the *sparagmos*, 1129–43:

> Ino was destroying his (Pentheus) other side,
> tearing his flesh, and Autonoe and the whole horde
> of bacchants attacked him. Shouts were everywhere at the same time–
> he groaning with all the breath he had in him,
> and they raising the sacrificial cry. One woman was carrying an arm,
> another a foot still in its boot, his flanks
> were stripped bare of flesh, and every woman with bloodied
> hands hurled Pentheus' flesh about like a ball (*diesphairize*).
> His body lies scattered (*keitai de chōris sōma*), some of it among the sharp
> rocks, other parts in thick-growing woods,
> no easy thing to look for. As his luckless head,
> which his mother happened to take in her hands,
> she fixed on the point of her wand and carries it,
> as if it were the head of a mountain lion, through the midst of Cithaeron,
> leaving her sisters with the maenad companies.

By depicting a scenario like that of the *sparagmos* of the cattle, in this passage, bodily parts (flesh, arm, foot, flank, hands), voice sounds (shouts, groaning that reminds of the cattle's lowing), clothing items (boot), biological matter (blood), natural elements (woods, rocks), animal bodies (lion) and objects (wand) are inextricably entangled. I place the depiction of Pentheus' *sparagmos* in dialogue with Maurice Merleau-Ponty's ontology of 'flesh', which describes the 'crisscrossing' or 'intertwining' between the human body and things existing in the world.[40]

This notion is further illustrated by the image of Pentheus' flesh, which, the messenger reports, the maenads 'threw about like a ball' (*diesphairize*) and dispersed in the surrounding space. In this way, Pentheus' flesh enters into composition with the environment, while his 'body lies scattered' (*keitai de chōris sōma*) among the rocks in the thick woods. In association with the palace's ruins, the bodily pieces of the cattle, the clothing items, and the tree's parts, Pentheus' fragmented body viscerally materializes the ultimate disintegration of his identity and power. But Pentheus' dismemberment is not annihilation since his head becomes part of the *thyrsus*, Dionysus' emblem, which is usually crowned with ivy or vine leaves. In rhizomatic terms, Pentheus' *sparagmos* becomes what Deleuze and Guattari call an 'a-signifying rupture', which indicates the ability of the rhizome to start anew on one of its old lines or new lines.[41]

The *thyrsus*

Carrying the *thyrsus* topped with his son's head, Agave enters the scene (1165–8). In a lyric dialogue with the chorus, the woman, still beset by the Dionysiac frenzy, manifests her pride over the animal she has caught in honour of the gods. She describes Pentheus' head with a variety of expressions. In Agave's eyes, her son's head is a 'new-cut tendril' (*helika neotomon*, 1170), 'a young whelp <of a mountain lion>' (<*leontos agroterou*> *neon inin*, 1174), a 'beast' (*thēros*, 1183), and 'a young calf, whose cheek is just growing downy under his delicate crest of hair' (*neos ho moschos arti/genun hupo koruth' apalotricha/katakomon thallei*, 1185–7). By encouraging Agave, the women of the chorus finally ask her to show the citizens her 'great prize' (*sēn nikēphoron*, 1200). These lines make it clear that Pentheus' head becomes a metaphorical aggregate that encapsulates different realms, including the human, animal, vegetal and material.

The exchange between Agave and the chorus is interrupted by the entrance of Cadmus, who, seeing Agave in her frantic state (1238), encourages her to return to sanity. As the stichomythia between the two starts, the old man asks Agave to look correctly at the *thyrsus* and asks her 'whose head' (*tinos prosōpon*, 1277) she has in her hands. At this point, the woman realizes that she is holding her son's 'head' (*kara*, 1284). Cadmus uses the term *prosōpon* for the head, which most scholars have interpreted as the actual 'mask' of the actor who played the part of Pentheus, emphasizing the close relation of the religious and the tragic in this play.[42]

Catherine Kalke has noted that the *thyrsus* maps back onto the phallic image of Pentheus atop the fir tree and the masked Dionysus on the pole raised in the Dionysiac processions.[43] By emphasizing the cross of boundaries between object, person and divinity, Melissa Mueller also reads the *thyrsus* as the material transformation of Pentheus into the cult statue of Dionysus that was initially processed at the start of the festival.[44] I consider the *thyrsus* as the embodied product of the material encounter between the various entities (both human and nonhuman) that have been affected by Dionysus' destructive force throughout the play. No longer human, Pentheus becomes a new assemblage. In this light, the *thyrsus* represents the symbol *par excellence* of the interspecies and trans-corporeal mesh between the human (Pentheus' head), animal (Pentheus' head seen as that of a lion), natural (stalk of the *thyrsus*, trunk of the tee and even pillar of the palace), and material/theatrical (Pentheus' mask) entities.

This enmeshment of the human and more-than-human world becomes a universal state of being in the play. Indeed, Cadmus and his wife Harmonia will be transformed into nonhuman creatures, as Dionysus tells the king: 'changing your form you will become serpent' (*drakōn genēsēi metabalōn*, 1330). The final part of the *Bacchae* is fragmentary. Here, Agave regrets her action and wishes she would never be reminded of the *thyrsus* (*thursou mnēma*, 1386). But the memory of the *thyrsus* haunts the future by prospecting an open-ended, rhizomatic landscape of culture, nature and imagination crisscrossed by 'multiples forms' (*pollai morphai*, 1388), as the last conventional statement of the chorus shows.

Notes

1. Rehm 2002: 200.
2. Ibid.: 213.
3. See Wohl 2005. She reads the *Bacchae* by using Deleuze's and Guattari's notion of 'becoming', which is a process of change within an assemblage (e.g. body). In 'becoming-other' the assemblage is drawn into the territory of another assemblage, changing its properties and bringing about a new unity. More specifically, Wohl uses the notion to address the play's 'bizarre gender permutations' and its 'multiple, productive and transformative sexuality.'
4. Ibid.: 150.
5. Drawing on the paradigm of the 'environmental humanities', I use the term environment instead of space as it covers up social, cultural as well as material aspects as grounding principles of human-nature interaction. For a discussion of human-nature interactions in the environmental humanities and their application to the ancient world, see Schliephake 2020: 1–12.
6. For a discussion of the term 'more-than-human' see the introduction to this volume, particularly note 36.
7. I mainly engage with studies of the play which focus on embodiment and space; see Foley 1980 and 1985, Zeitlin 1985, Rehm 2002: 200–14, Konstantinou 2018: 113–44, Worman 2021: 93–130. On ecocritical studies of Greek tragedy, see Cless 2010: 17–29 and Bakola 2019. On posthuman studies and the ancient world, see Bianchi, Brill and Holmes 2019, Chesi and Spiegel 2020. For recent works in the environmental humanities and the ancient world, see Hughes 2014, Schliephake 2017 and 2020.
8. Cless 2010.
9. Ibid.: 27–9. Also, as Cless observes, it seems reasonable to assume that the wartime situation in Athens near the end of the Peloponnesian War affected Euripides' critics.
10. See Morton 2011: 19–30. The concept of the mesh has gained popularity in a range of disciplines, especially in ecology. In his writings, Morton suggests that, by recognizing the interconnectedness of all things, we can better understand the complex systems and processes at work in the world and develop more effective ways of addressing the challenges facing humanity and the planet.
11. This conception ties in well with the ancient notion of *zōē*, which refers to the kind of life that for the Greek philosophers encompassed animals, plants, the cosmos, the divine and the human. The notion of *zōē* is linked to the Presocratic (and Hippocratic) definition of life, in which different, interrelated forms, including human beings, are conjoined with the wider environment. For a discussion of the interconnectedness of all living forms in the Presocratic philosophy, see Zatta 2018. For a discussion of the ways in which early Greek philosophy applies to tragedy, see Allan 2005 and Holmes 2010.
12. On the concept of 'strange strangers', see Morton 2010: 275–9.
13. See Deleuze and Guattari 1987.

14. The classic example of this kind of thought would be the *Arbor Porphyriana*, Porphyry's tree of species. Deleuze refers to the Porphyry's *Isagoge*, see Porphyry 1975: 37, which provides a formalization of Aristotle's account of species and genera in medieval logic. The difficulty with such an approach is that it creates a sharp division between things in nature, which, on the contrary, have more gradated distinctions.

15. I argue that Pentheus with his authoritarian behaviour incarnates the model of the tree as a hierarchical structure organized only around a central point, without considering that root systems are also capable of developing from other parts of the plant, such as the stem or leaf.

16. See Alaimo and Hekman 2008. For an overview of ecofeminist theories, see Gaard, Estok and Oppermann 2013.

17. See Alaimo 2010: 7–11 and 2020: 177–91. She borrows the term 'intra-action' from Barad 2007 to explain the mutual constitution of entangled agencies between humans and nonhumans. This term contrasts with the usual 'interaction', which instead assumes that there are separate individual agencies. Alaimo 2010: 48 also talks about a 'trans-corporeal landscape,' as she refers to the presence of toxic substances in the bodies of humans, animals, plants and rocks in a given disrupted environment.

18. I borrow the notion of 'natureculture' from Haraway 2003. Natureculture is a synthesis of nature and culture that recognizes their inseparability in ecological relationships that are both biophysically and socially formed. For a discussion of the ways in which this notion applies to the ancient world in connection with socioeconomic, religious, and environmental dynamics, see Schliephake 2020.

19. On Dionysus' mask and dramatic role in the *Bacchae*, see Foley 1980, Vernant 1988, Chaston 2010: 179–238, Billings 2017. There is a distinction in nomenclature between the two groups of women forming the chorus and following Dionysus: the Lydian maenads are usually called 'bacchants' (βάκχαι) whereas the women of Thebes are 'maenads' (μαινάδες). However, as Konstantinou 2018: 117 has pointed out, there is no uniformity on terminology in Antiquity, nor is there one among scholars today. On the chorus of the *Bacchae* and their different roles, see Murnaghan 2006: 99–100, Arthur 1972 and Bierl 2013.

20. As Dodds 1960: 61 has noted, on the stage may have been a tomb and the ruins of Semele's house, where the woman raped by Zeus gave birth to Dionysus. Over the fence surrounding the tomb vine-shoots may have trailed. The façade consisted of the royal palace, which formed the back-scene.

21. Otto 1965: 151 has observed that the vine mirrors the two Dionysus' features of enlightenment and destruction which appear in Dionysiac ecstasy with staggering force. Chaston 2010: 201 associates the garlanding of the tomb/hearth to the garlanding of the thyrsus, which needs to be 're-garlanded' to renew the maenads' force.

22. See Deleuze and Guattari 1987: 1–25.

23. This scene has been variously discussed by scholars, who have mainly focused on the realization of the actual 'special effects' on stage, including lightning and earthquake. For a bibliography, see Dodds 1960 147–9, Castellani 1976, Segal 1982, Foley 1985, Fisher 1992, Thumiger 2006: 60 n. 3, Seaford 2018.

24. Segal 1982: 92 has observed that the palace's collapse signifies the initial dissolution of Pentheus' authoritarian personality. See also Thumiger 2006: 193, who has argued that the destruction of the palace implies a kind of 'destructive *sparagmos* of the human world.'

25. Wohl 2005: 149.

26. The translation is adapted from Kovacs 2003 and Grene and Lattimore 2013.

27. For a bibliography on the *sparagmos* of the cattle, see Thumiger 2006 and 2008, Henrichs 2012.

28. For discussion of the dressing scene, see Dodds 1960: 172, Foley 1980: 113–14, Segal 1987: 169, Seaford 1981: 258–61, Zeitlin 1985: 6–64, Wohl 2005: 147, Worman 2021: 101–5.

29. See Eur. *Ion*. 239, *Med*. 1072. Also, Holmes 2018: 73, who notes that *schēmata* indicate the bodily organs after Aristotle.

30. See Foley 1985: 209 who notes that Dionysus adjusts Pentheus' costume, touching his head, hands and feet, thereby consecrating him as his victim. For a detailed examination of the iconographic depiction of Pentheus' attire, see Mimidou 2013.

31. For a bibliography on Pentheus's gender permutation through dressing, see note 22 and Segal 1978 and Buxton 2009.

32. Foley 1985: 250 relates the image of the two suns to Pentheus' and Dionysus' saffron costumes. As she puts it, 'if both Dionysus' and Pentheus' costumes were saffron, the audience as well as Pentheus would see two suns, two brilliant yellow costumes moving side by side.'

33. See Burkert 1966: 107–8, Seidensticker 1979: 181–90, Csapo 1997, and Bednarek 2019.

34. Cless 2010: 28.

35. Kalke 1985: 417, Csapo 1997: 284 and Chaston 2010: 226 see the tree as an image mapping with the *phalloi* carried in Dionysiac processions.

36. For a discussion of Dionysus' action upon the tree, see Bongers 2002 and Stieber 2006.

37. For a discussion on the pelting of Pentheus as evoking the pelting of an animal victim or evoking the image of a hunt, see Bednarek 2019.

38. Deleuze and Guattari 1987: 15.

39. The scholarly debate about Pentheus' *sparagmos* has produced copious and variegated interpretations concerning ritual, psychological, familial, sexual and metatheatrical aspects. For a general bibliography and recent trends in scholarship, see Reitzammer 2017: 298–311.

40. See Merleau-Ponty 1968: 130–55. The generality of flesh embraces an 'inter-corporeality' or "inter-animality," an anonymous sensibility shared out among distinct bodies' (172).

41. See Deleuze and Guattari 1987: 6–22.

42. For a discussion about Pentheus' mask and the *thyrsus*, see Segal 1985: 166–7, Foley 1980: 130–1, Rehm 2002: 209–10, Chaston 2010: 225–38, Mueller 2016a: 68.

43. Kalke 1985: 417.

44. Mueller 2016b: 70.

CHAPTER 5
THE RELATIONALITY OF DARKNESS IN THUCYDIDES
Esther Eidinow

Introduction: The darkness of night

Night battles

In the fifth century BCE, battle regularly ended at nightfall. During the Peloponnesian War there was, as Thucydides tells us, only one battle between great armies that took place at night (7.44.1): the battle at Epipolai. Indeed, as Dowden notes, 'the verb νυκτομαχεῖν does not appear before Appian and must be a Hellenistic classifying conceptualisation';[1] nevertheless, this does not mean that actually fighting at night is unknown.[2] And, while that specific term may not be used until later writers, nevertheless, Thucydides' account features a number of types of conflict that occur during hours of darkness.[3] This chapter sets out to explore how Thucydides uses language to communicate what his characters encounter when they fight at night, focusing specifically on the perceived nature, and experiences, of darkness, and the ways in which those were and are conveyed to the reader.

In general, across the *History*, that is not achieved by conveying the quality of the night itself: Thucydides offers little description of darkness itself, but rather focuses on its affects, as I will explore in the first part of this chapter. In that context, the use of two terms stands out as exceptional: *skoteinos*, an adjective for dark, which Thucydides uses twice in the description of the siege of Plataea;[4] and *skotos*, the related noun, which Thucydides uses twice in his *History* – once in the description of the Plataean siege, and, again, of a failed attack by sea. While these terms seem to be equivalent words for describing or evoking darkness, I will argue that they communicate different experiences. Building on this, in the second and third parts of this chapter I investigate uses of the term *skoteinos* and *skotos* as descriptors of 'darkness', which provide insight into a semantic network that reaches beyond the experience of the colour of darkness at night, to encompass other, related, physical and emotional experiences.[5]

My approach to the investigation of these colour terms focuses on human actors (as embodied and meaning-making entities) but also aims to draw into the foreground the non-human network of which humans are a part, through the concept of affordances.[6] As with previous work on ancient nympholepts, where I have considered a relational approach to emotions involved in experiences deemed religious in Antiquity,[7] I am intending to elucidate something of the lived experience of our historical subjects. In that previous work, I drew on Martin Buber's notion of I and Thou to draw out the sense of entanglement between mortal and space, place and nymph.[8] Here, I am focusing on the affordances of language to explore how the meaning of something as apparently obvious as the colour of the night sky becomes intricately entangled with the 'untidy and dispersive entanglement' of 'biological, inorganic, natural and technological actors' – which, at any point, humans might describe as comprising their 'environment'. To that list of categories of actors, I wish to add two more. The first are what a secular society may describe as supernatural actors; this is, in part, because of the nature of the ancient society that is the focus of this essay, but I am also inspired here by modern work on a non-secular Anthropocene.[9] As my argument will demonstrate, the ancient environment included human, non-human and more-than-human actors. The second set of actors that I want to add here are words themselves, with a particular focus in this essay on colour terms; I explain this further below.

Embodied colour

I start with the idea that a colour term is not simply a description of a single external quality, but may convey a bundle of embodied experiences, building particularly on previous work by Michael Clarke on colour categorization in the ancient world.[10] Clarke argues against taking a universalist understanding of colour categorization, which, he states, depends on the basis of widespread experience of what he calls 'a Kodachrome world', that is, 'a world where the prevalence of high-quality printing, fabric dyes, coloured plastics and the screen media mean that our perceptual world is crammed full of visual stimuli crossing the entire range of colours in the spectrum, presented overwhelmingly at bright saturated values on flat static surfaces'.[11] Instead, examining the ways in which colour terms are used in ancient Greek texts, he argues that their semantic logic reveals that a colour term is 'more like a verb than a noun': a culture's prototypical concept, which underpins the meaning of a colour is 'a kinetic phenomenon at a fundamental level of the language's ordering of experience'.[12] By this, he means that a culture's colour term may encompass a range of meanings that are more or less closely associated with the prototypical concept of that colour, but are associated with other related sensory experiences. These experiences may not necessarily be the chromatic aspect of the prototypical concept, but rather some other aspect or set of aspects, from several domains of experience: indeed, that concept, 'is at the meeting point of several cognitive domains which English keeps apart – colour, light, movement and even mental states – and, as if to balance the punctual precision of that definition, the range of hue values permissible in a member of the category is much wider than one would expect of a semantic structure restricted to the domain of colour'.[13]

Thus, while the cultural prototype may provide a 'cognitive reference point', other things may be described with the same colour term, because they participate, more or less, in other related aspects, and this provides a semantic range of meaning for that colour term. Clarke illustrates this idea by examining the constellation of members of the category *chlōros* – a term that, he argues, does not merely designate colour, but also signals a number of other experiential aspects, including vibrant life and fertilizing wetness. He depicts a series of concentric circles, moving from 'A', near the prototypical concept, out to D and then E, further out from the concept, with each new circle indicating an experience of the colour term that is more distantly related to the initial, prototypical concept, and conveys different sensory experiences. Thus, the term *chlōros* may be used to describe a plant full of fresh green life (at position 'A') – a sense of the colour that is very close to the prototypical idea – but it may also be used to describe, for example, river-water (at position 'D'), which is only 'vaguely associated with greenness' and while moist is not so associated with vitality. [14]

In what follows, I will use these arguments to propose how we may better understand the intended effects of the colour terms used by Thucydides in his descriptions of night battles and explore what this may indicate about the embodied experiences they may be intended to evoke. To support this approach, I want to introduce into the argument the concept of 'affordances': 'action possibilities' that an organism perceives in its immediate environment; what the environment 'offers the animal, what it *provides* or *furnishes*, either for good or ill'.[15] In this approach, as Gibson says, 'an affordance is neither an objective property nor a subjective property, or it is both if you like. An affordance cuts across the dichotomy of subject-objective';[16] in other words, the 'organism (animal or human) and environment' are 'mutually defined relational aspects of one another'.[17]

Clarke's observations about ancient Greek colour-terms, and his argument that a person's conceptualization of colours incorporate and are structured in terms of patterns of embodied experience, align with research into theories of grounded cognition. These argue that individual, social and cultural factors can have a physical effect on brain processes that, in turn, shape experience and knowledge. Drawing on research on the development of concepts, we can perhaps develop Clarke's argument to suggest that colour concepts are not held as abstract ideas in the brain, but rather that colour perception may also be grounded in modality-specific systems of the brain. Elsewhere, I have drawn on the theory of grounded cognition (as outlined by Lawrence Barsalou) to explore how mind, body, and physical and social environments were inextricably linked in the creation of ancient Greek conceptions of the divine, which could be triggered by linguistic stimuli.[18] Here, drawing on relevant research, I put forward the possibility that perception of colour may also be dependent on colour knowledge retrieval, and that this too is triggered by linguistic stimuli.[19]

This is not to argue that the brain functions as a computer,[20] in which 'knowing is having permanent concepts stored in memory' (as Gibson describes it – in order to reject it[21]). Rather, it is to suggest, as current theories of grounded cognition argue, that brain processes are online dynamic states, such that, for example, a concept can be described as 'a dynamical distributed system in the brain that represents a category in the environment or experience and that controls interactions with the category's instances'.[22] The brain processing described as 'predictive engagement', in which 'the brain, as part of and along with the larger organism, actively responds in ways that allow for the right kind of ongoing attunement with the environment – an environment that is physical but also social and cultural' seems to align with some theories of ecological enactivism,[23] or indeed with Gibson's own understanding of perception;[24] and perhaps from Gibson's own understanding of 'perception'.[25]

In that context, I want to use the notion of affordances to explore the experiences not only of those fighting in the night battles, as described by Thucydides, but also of the audiences of those descriptions, building on naturalistic accounts of language that argue that we should understand language as acquiring meaning in context, emerging as a property of human interactions, which have developed into social norms.[26] As Stephen Cowley argues, 'language can be conceived of as an action'.[27] He evokes this with the term 'wordings', which are defined as 'readily repeated aspects of vocalizations that, for speakers of a community, carry historically derived information'.[28] Thus, our interaction with language is highly contextual, with particular words corresponding to particular events, passed down from adult to child, but also dynamic and emergent. In these ways, we might think, as Matthew Harvey argues, of wordings in terms both of affordances themselves that offer meaning with regard to the relationship with the environment, and as themselves changing the environments (and the affordances) in which they occur.[29]

Thus, in what follows, I draw on the research above to explore terms used by Thucydides for describing darkness, investigating what they may communicate about the perceived affordances of the environment. By examining their use in contemporary and later literature, I also explore these 'wordings' as affordances themselves, with the potential for shaping different interactions with the environment. My aim here is to offer a richer understanding of the experiential environment that Thucydides evokes – and, in turn, participated in creating – through his descriptions of 'darkness'. I hope that this investigation may offer some insight into the power of Thucydides' writing: *skoteinos*, *skotos* and their cognates, I argue, not only convey perceptions of colour as experienced in the environment, but also the cognitive, emotional and embodied experiences that were a part of those perceptions.

Battles at night: Thucydides' words for darkness

In Book 7.42-46 of his *History*, Thucydides describes how the Athenians attack Epipolai by night[30] – and his emphasis is on confusion: at 7.44.1: 'The Athenians were now thrown into such helpless confusion' (*en pollei tarachei kai aporiai egignonto hoi Athenaioi*); 7.44.3: 'The rout of their forward troupes had now created complete confusion' (*ta prosthen tēs tropēs gegenēmenēs etetarakto*); 7.44.7: 'once the panic had started' (*epei hapax etarachthēsan*).[31] And the audience is told repeatedly of the lack of clear, reliable vision: e.g. 7.44.2: 'Although there was a bright moon they saw each other only as men do by moonlight, that is to say, they could distinguish the form of the body, but could not tell for certain whether it was a friend or an enemy.' As Thucydides says explicitly (7.44.1), 'in a night battle . . . how could anyone be certain of anything?'

Instead, the predominant sense that he describes is sound: the Syracusan soldiers cheering each other on; the Athenians constantly asking for the watchword – the only way to recognize one another (7.44.4); the paeans of each side. The soldiers start to fight each other as *phobos* ('fear') seizes them, only pulling back just in time (7.44.6–7):

Whenever the Argives, Corcyraeans, or other Dorian contingents on the Athenian side raised their paean, the effect was to frighten [*phobon pareiche*] the Athenians just as much as the enemy's paeans. So in the end, once the panic had started [*epei hapax etarachthēsan*], all over the army friends were colliding with friends and nationals with their fellows, not only terrifying one another [*ou monon es phobon katestēsan*], but actually proceeding to combat, which was stopped just in time.

This reference to *phobos* takes us to another night manoeuvre: the retreat after the Sea Battle at Syracuse (Thuc. 7.80.1–6). This is a comparatively succinct description, which forcefully conveys the emotional experience of the army (Thuc. 7.80.3):

As can happen in any army, especially a very large one, panic-fears [*phoboi kai deimata*] broke out – not least because they were marching at night, through enemy territory, and with the enemy not far away – and they fell into confusion [*tarachē*].

This is fear of a very particular kind: the phrase *phoboi kai deimata* at 7.80.3 recalls not only the fears of and confusion of the night battle at Epipolai, but also introduces another element – the supernatural. *Deimata* is a term used again by Thucydides only at 2.102.5, to describe the terrors that pursue a matricide:

The story goes that when Alcmeon the son of Amphiaraus was a fugitive after the murder of his mother he received an oracle from Apollo indicating that he should settle in this land: the riddle was that he would not have release from the terrors [*lusin tōn deimatōn*] until he found and set up home in a place which at the time when he killed his mother had not yet been seen by the sun nor yet existed as land, since all the rest of the earth was polluted by him.

The implication is of something other-worldly – a cosmic punishment for the crime committed. It brings to mind the pursuit of Orestes by the Erinyes as described in Aeschylus' *Libation Bearers* (283–9; here and below, trans. Sommerstein 2009):

He spoke too of other assaults of Furies, generated by the blood of a father: the dark weapon of the powers below, arising from those of one's kin who have fallen and beg for justice, together with madness and empty night-time terrors, derange him, harry him, and chase him from his city.

As Mercedes Aguirre has analysed in her exploration of the context of the Erinyes, these are monsters specifically related to night.[32] Thus, Thucydides, in using the term *deimata* seems to be offering information about the quality of the fear felt by his characters, and its relation to night, encompassing both a sense of confusion and the presence of the supernatural. But in terms of the qualities of the darkness of night, the passage seems to offer very little – at least, at first sight.[33] In fact, Thucydides uses a couple of specific terms to describe the night – *skoteinos* and *skotos*, usually simply translated as 'dark' or 'darkness' – which, I want to argue, are rich with associated experiential meaning. Let us turn first to the adjective *skoteinos*.

Skoteinos: The dangerous darkness of night

In the description of the siege of Plataea, *skoteinos* occurs twice in rapid succession (3.22.1 and 5):

> When the Plataeans had all prepared, they waited for a stormy night of rain and wind, and also no moon, to make their exit. They were led by the same men who had proposed the enterprise. First, they crossed the surrounding ditch, then they came up to the enemy wall, undetected by the guards who could not see the in the darkness [*ana to skoteinon*] and could not hear their approach through the bluster of the wind.
>
> There was an immediate hue and cry, and the whole besieging army rushed up onto the wall. In the darkness [*skoteinēs nuktos*] and stormy weather they had no idea what had caused the alarm . . .

There is no doubt that *skoteinos* is a rare term in prose of this period: it occurs nowhere else in Thucydides, and Herodotus does not use it. Rather, it seems to have had more poetic qualities for which we can turn first to passages in tragedy, where it is used in a variety of ways to evoke darkness and associated experiences. For example, Sophocles' Oedipus describes his own physical blindness (Soph. *OT* 1325–6; trans. Lloyd-Jones 1994):

> Your presence is not hid from me, but I recognise your voice, though I am in the dark (*skoteinos*).

And it is blindness that the chorus in Euripides' *Herakles* alludes to when they use this term (Eur. *Her.* 638–41, trans. Kovacs 1998):

> But age is a burden that always
> lies heavier than the crags of Aetna
> upon the head, and over my eye
> it casts a veil of darkness (*skoteinon*)

Both of those ideas of blindness carry, in turn, further associations: in the Sophoclean passage, it is an association with ignorance; while the references by the chorus in Euripides' *Herakles* to old age may lead the audience to think of death. The same association is made by Alcestis in Euripides' play of that name when she refers to the darkness that dims her eyes (Eur. *Alc.* 385, trans. Kovacs 1994): 'Already now my sight is dimmed with darkness (*skoteinon*)'.

The next two examples may also allude to similar associations. At first sight, they are about the darkness of a physical space. The first, a passage from Euripides' *Bacchae* (610–11, trans. Kovacs 2003), refers to a dungeon:

Dionysus: Were you disheartened when I was taken inside, thinking I would be thrown into Pentheus' dark (*skoteinas*) prison?

In the second, from Euripides' *Phoenissae*, the term is used to describe a scabbard (276–7, trans. Kovacs 2002):

Polyneices: come, let me put up my sword into the dark (*skoteinas*) of its encasement and ask these women standing near the house who they are.

To these initial understandings, additional associations may be brought. In the first, ignorance: the darkness of the dungeon in which Dionysus is imprisoned offers a metaphor for Pentheus' inability/refusal to see the stranger for who he really is. In the second, notions of death are a fitting association for a weapon.

Looking to other poetic forms, we find the term used again to evoke more than darkness: in *Nemean* 7, when Pindar refers to 'blame' talk as *skoteinos*, he is, as Carne-Ross observes, using the term 'because it consigns an action or person to oblivion'[34] (Pind. *Nem.* 7.61-63, trans. Race 1997):

I am a guest-friend. Keeping away dark (*skoteinon*) blame,
like streams of water I shall bring genuine fame
with my praises to the man who is my friend

This, perhaps, offers a useful point at which to consider the emotional affordances of these associations. Across all of the passages so far cited, we trace a sense of fear, each time with its own particular 'flavour', from fear of the threat of death (Alcestis and Polyneices) to fear of the unknown (Pentheus), to fear of being made wholly unknown (Pindar). This idea of *skoteinos* as bringing fear, as being dangerous is vividly conveyed in Aeschylus' *Libation Bearers* (658–62), when Orestes says:

Take a message to the masters of the house; I've come with news for them. And hurry, because night's dark (*skoteinon*) chariot is already advancing rapidly, and it's time for travellers to drop anchor in houses that make all visitors welcome.

With these associations made, when we return to Thucydides' description of the events at Plataea we may see this term in a new light. This is a description of the darkness experienced by those on watch, rather than those attacking. The affordances it offers are of a particular, negative, type. The description evokes their lack of sensory information: they are sightless without even a moon; their hearing is blocked by the roar of the wind. And, as the second use of the term underlines, they are ignorant of what is going on around them. The word *skoteinos*, I suggest, has been quite deliberately employed here to evoke not only meanings specific to the night-time context, but also to introduce very particular associations; and not only those that we have explored, but also, the very genre, the tragic, in which they appear. This is a dramatic moment, and Thucydides wants his audience to picture the scene as vividly as if it were on stage.

The legacy of this use of the term can be glimpsed in other writers. Plato uses it in descriptions of the experiences of those who, in terms of the ideal citizen that he is constructing, are, in various ways, incomplete. One example is the places that women prefer to dwell, rather than enter the citizen life of the city (Pl. *Leg.* 6.781c; trans. Bury 1926):

> The female sex would more readily endure anything rather than this: accustomed as they are to live a retired and private (*skoteinon*) life, women will use every means to resist being led out into the light, and they will prove much too strong for the lawgiver.

And, elsewhere, the term is used to describe a badly constructed argument (Pl. *Resp.* 8.558d, trans. Emlyn-Jones and Preddy 2013):

> 'Do you want us, then,' I said, 'to define first essential desires and those that aren't, so we won't be wandering about in the dark (*mē skoteinōs*) in our discussion?'

It also comes to describe a state of not-being, almost an absence of self (Pl. *Soph.* 254a, trans. Fowler 1921):

> Stranger: The sophist runs away into the darkness of not-being, feeling his way in it by practice, and is hard to discern on account of the darkness (*skoteinotēta*) of the place. Don't you think so?

When we look for its use in specific military contexts, we find it frequently in the work of Aeneas Tacticus,[35] where there are plenty of references to night, but only four uses of this term, *skoteinos*, all in situations with a marked similarity to the siege of Plataea. Thus, Aeneas Tacticus uses *skoteinos* in his description of the (almost) betrayal of the great city of Teos in Ionia by the gatekeeper to Temenos the Rhodian. We are told (18.13; in the category 'Other Kinds of Relief'): 'To that end they agreed on, amongst other things, a dark and moonless night [*nukta aselēnon kai skoteinēn*] during which the gatekeeper would open up and Temenos would come in with mercenaries.' In the section headed 'Patrols', the dangers faced by sentinels who do not – or cannot – keep a good enough watch is introduced by Aeneas Tacticus (22.12), with a reference to the dark winter nights [*tais cheimerinais kai skoteinais nuxin*]: during which 'they should throw <a succession of> stones on to the outside of the wall and cry "Who goes there?", in a pretence of seeing somebody'. Under the category of 'Additional Tokens of Recognition' (25.2), Aeneas Tacticus instructs his reader to arrange that 'On dark nights [*tais skoteinais nuxin*] the man demanding the password could add some other vocal sound, or, preferably, make a noise'; and a similar concern with the habits of the watchmen '... on dark nights [*en tais skoteinais nuxi*]' occurs in the section on 'Patrols' (26.6).[36]

It appears from these uses, that Aeneas Tacticus introduces this term *skoteinos* when he wants to suggest a particular experience of night, one that presents a more than usually greater threat. As we will see, it seems likely that Aeneas Tacticus was following Thucydides in his evocation of this experience. We can see this through their shared use of a second term, often translated as darkness: *skotos*; I turn to this term next.

Skotos: The deceptive dimension of darkness

The Thebans have entered the city of Plataea, and attacked by the Plataeans they are trying to flee (Thuc. 2.4.2):[37]

> ... as the onslaught continued with a huge din, joined by the woman and slaves shouting and screaming from the roofs and pelting them with stones and tiles, and with heavy rain falling throughout the night [*kai huetou hama dia nuktos pollou epigenomenou*], they panicked and turned to flee. They went running through the city, but the streets were dark and muddy [*en skotōi kai pēlōi*] (it was the end of the month and there was no moon) and most had no idea of the routes to safety, whereas their pursuers knew how to prevent their escape: so the majority met their death.

Again, the 'darkness' is not total, this time because of the moon, which causes problems for the fugitives. The visual confusion is here explicitly coupled with physical obstructions: Thucydides creates the delightful zeugma *en skotōi kai pēlōi* – (caught) 'in darkness and in mud'.

This notion of physical incapacity and visual and mental confusion occurs in Thucydides' other examples: *skotos* is used to describe the context in which the Plataeans stand on the edge of a ditch and fire their weapons against the approaching Thebans (3.23.4):

> The Plataeans, standing on the edge of the ditch, could see them the better out of the darkness (*ek tou skotous*), and aimed their arrows and javelins at the unprotected parts of the enemies' bodies: they themselves were out of range of the torches, and the less visible for their glare. So even the last of the Plataeans managed to cross the ditch in time, though it was a difficult struggle.

In this case, darkness is broken by the light of torches, and the presence of this light actually makes matters worse for the Thebans: the Plataeans can see, but cannot really be seen. *Skotos* here seems to be evoking the experience of the Thebans, even as it describes the physical setting of the Plataeans, and this is a darkness that is, while not quite dark, profoundly confusing. This visual bewilderment produces physical disorientation, and we see this also in the final episode, which, again, draws attention to the experience of *skotos*. Astyochos' fleet, sailing to Syme, and hoping to take the enemy by surprise (8.42.1) loses its coherence in the rain and fog (*huetos kai ta ek tou ouranou xunephela*) of the night, which 'disoriented his ships in the darkness (*en tōi skotei*) and created confusion'. There is a verbal link here to the earlier appearance of *skotos*: the word *huetos* (rain) is otherwise only used by Thucydides at 2.4.2 and 2.5.3.[38] At 2.4.2, as we have seen, the rain is part of what creates difficulties not only of vision, but also of movement. Something similar occurs at 2.5.3, where having to march in the rain (*en huetōi*), prevents the Thebans from marching fast enough towards Plataea (2.5.3) – so when they arrive (too late), they find 'their men in Plataea were either dead or captured and held alive'.

If we look backward, to possible influences on Thucydides' use of *skotos*, we find it used frequently by Homer in the *Iliad*, to indicate a warrior's moment of dying. It is used in two key expressions: for example, *Il.* 4.460-62: 'and into his forehead drove the spear, and the spear-point of bronze passed into the bone; and darkness enfolded his eyes (*skotos osse kalupsen*), and he crashed as does a wall, in the mighty combat.'[39] And, for example, *Il.* 5.45-47: 'Him Idomeneus, famed for his spear, pierced with a thrust of his long spear . . . and he fell from his chariot, and hateful darkness seized him (*min skotos heile*).' These two phrases reinforce the arguments made above about *skoteinos*, which noted not only the visual perception evoked by the term, but also the embodied experience of it, and suggested the presence of supernatural dangers. *Skotos* seems to be not just a colour, but also to have substance, insofar as it covers the eyes of the warriors. Indeed, that first phrase seems to indicate a sense of agency, which is, in turn, reinforced by the idea of darkness itself seizing the warrior as if in ambush, in the second phrase. These associations with a darkness that is also a death that is somehow personified offer some rationale for Thucydides' use of the term in the passages discussed above.

When we turn to examine the use of the term in Homer's *Odyssey*, we find it employed with a slightly different emphasis, which adds some further insight to Thucydides' use of it. *Skotos* occurs only once in the *Odyssey*, as part of Odysseus' attempts to hide his scar from his nurse, so that she will not recognize him and reveal who he is to the suitors (Hom. *Od.* 19.388-89): 'Odysseus sat him down away from the hearth and straightway turned himself toward the darkness (*skoton*).'[40] This episode does not have the more direct associations with death that are manifest in its uses in the *Iliad*; instead, it introduces a notion of darkness as an instrument of concealment and deception. These seem to be particularly relevant dimensions of its future use: for example, when we turn to Herodotus' *History*, we find the term *skotos* used twice – in neither case to describe the quality of night, but with a strong emphasis on concealment, deceit and ignorance.[41]

The first example occurs during a story about Rhampsinitus, King of Egypt (Hdt. 2.121E5) – a story that Herodotus himself professes not to believe. Rhampsinitus tried to identify the individual who has managed to steal from his treasure chamber, using his daughter to trap the thief. Setting her to work in a brothel, he tells her to ask all her clients (and he instructs her to accept everyone as a client) what the worst thing is that they have done. The thief reveals himself – but when she then grabs for him, 'in the darkness (*en tōi skotei*), the thief put a corpse's arm in her way'.[42] Use of the term *skotos* here introduces a poetic element, suitable for the scarcely believable story that Herodotus is self-consciously recounting. In the next chapter (121F), Rhampsinitus rewards the thief's ingenuity by giving him his daughter in marriage: a typical folktale. But *skotos* also offers the audience of this episode a number of useful dimensions of darkness, other than the visual. Not only does *skotos* evoke the physical darkness of the room, it also suggests a cognitive darkness, of unknowing and deceit, where a brothel-worker is actually a princess, an unknown client is a knowing thief, and the body part he offers belongs to a corpse. A similar dimension of *skotos* is apparent in the other passage in which it appears, a description of the Sevens' attack on the Magi (3.78.4): 'Darius stood there in a quandary, because it was dark' (*en skotei*; lit. 'in darkness') and he was worried about stabbing his ally, Gobryas. Again, the term primarily describes the lack of light in a room; but it also alludes to the darkness of ignorance, here experienced by Darius.

These emphases on cognitive confusion are found in other writers' use of this term, where it offers a similar rhetorical power. For example, we can turn again to Plato's *Laws*, where *skotos* is used to refer to the darkness of ignorance and deceit (Pl. *Leg.* 837a and 864c). Or the vividly recounted speeches of Demosthenes, where *skotos* is used to describe the ignorance of his fellow Greeks (19.226: 'while those whose lives are devoted to your service ... encounter in you such dullness of hearing, such darkness of vision [*tosouto skotos*]); and an ignorance that is possibly caused by the deceit of an enemy (18.159: 'only, as it seems, there is a cloud of darkness [*ti skotos*] between you and the truth').[43] With these associations, it appears in phrases that set the scene with a particular emotional nuance (Dem. 21.38: 'the man who hit the *thesmothetes* had three excuses: drink, love, and inability to recognize him because the incident happened at night and in the dark [*dia to skotous*]'); or to prime the reader to expect deceitful behaviour (Dem. 21.85: 'And when it was already evening and dark [*skotous*], this man Meidias came to the magistrates' office ...').[44]

Building on this understanding of the semantic network of *skotos*, when we return to Aeneas Tacticus (*Praef.* 2.6), we see that he seems to have followed Thucydides closely in his description of the night attack upon Plataea – and he uses the term *skotos* to evoke the context in which the Thebans are unable to escape. The allusion to 'darkness' here, is coupled with their ignorance of their surrounding; rather than the mud and rain, the obstructions are caused by the wagons that the Plataeans have used to block up the streets and allies. But I think Aeneas Tacticus is doing more than following Thucydides in this episode: the choice to use *skotos* is also prompted by the embodied experiences conveyed by the term, including lack of light, ignorance and confusion.

Similarly, other uses of the term in Aeneas Tacticus' writing draw attention to this range of experiential meaning. At 18.14, *skotos* is used to describe the moment in which the key action of betrayal occurs – and obviously is not seen. The darkness that it evokes is one that is not only literal – of sight – but also metaphorical, communicating a lack of insight. At 22.13 and 26.3, *skotos* describes nuanced states of darkness. At 26.3, it is a stormy darkness, where the storm makes the visual confusion worse; at 22.13, it conveys a sense of confusion relating to the experience of darkness by the patrol, since the sounds that they are making prevent them from hearing their attackers.

From all these examples, *skotos* appears to be a term that brings with it not (or not only) a meaning of 'darkness', but (also) a set of embodied experiences: it may introduce a sense of physical disablement, of being obstructed from being able to act. This can include confused vision and a related, potentially dangerous, ignorance or bewilderment; and, finally, it may also convey the capacity or intention to create this kind of confusion and ignorance – a powerful deceit.

Conclusion: 'Darkness' as affordance

This chapter has examined the terms that Thucydides used to describe darkness in night battles, *skoteinos* and *skotos*. Rather than viewing them as simple colour terms, it has raised the question of how meaning and experience interact – and investigated the specific embodied experiences that these terms may have conveyed. In doing so, this has, I hope, demonstrated how, in the contemporary understanding of these terms, human, non-human and more-than-human actors were 'ensnarled'.[45]

As descriptors of environments, this chapter has argued, these terms for 'darkness' were relational: they were used to communicate to readers the affordances of those environments; how and what they offered, for good or ill, as action possibilities, both for characters within the narratives and for those reading about them. In that process, in addition, this chapter has suggested, these words are to be regarded as non-human actors: they themselves also brought (and continue to bring) affordances – and thus participate in, and expand, the experiential networks that describe and create the environment.

Notes

1. Dowden 2010: 119 n. 4.

2. Ibid.: 110.

3. E.g. attack or attempted attack: 4.135, 7.4.2; escapes or manoeuvres that could have led to fighting: 1.115.4, 3.112.2, 4.67.3, 5.58.2, 6.7.2, 7.80.1-4; darkness is used for military strategy 7.73.3. Fighting is abandoned because it is getting dark: 1.51.2.

4. Thuc. 3.22.1 and 5.

5. Grand-Clément 2020: 241–8 discusses the emotional associations of *melas* and *kyaneos* (alongside terms for white and purple) in ancient Greek texts referring to religious ritual; she does not address these terms for the darkness of night.

6. As Gibson 1979 (see more below).

7. Eidinow 2023 (see more below).

8. Buber 2020 (see more below).

9. Which – as Cohen (2013: xxv) notes – has been evoked by different ecotheorists via words

such as 'mangle', 'network', mesh, meshwork, etc. On a non-secular Anthropocene, cf. Latour 2013, Latour 2014, Bubandt 2018.

10. Clarke 2004.

11. Ibid.: 132; Witzel 2019 (an example of recent research in this area) challenges the basis of traditional research on colour categorization (nature vs. nurture, which gives rise to a universalist-realist debate), arguing instead for the 'complex interaction of multiple constraints and determinants' in colour categorization.

12. Clarke 2004: 134. Bradley (2013) interprets Clarke as arguing that colour was 'an object-centred experience', such that 'ancient colour experience could tap into smell, touch, taste and even sound' (2013: 140). Here, I focus on (what I read as) Clarke's emphasis on the embodied experience of the world.

13. Clarke 2004: 136.

14. Ibid.: 135 for the overall description and the quotation.

15. Gibson 1979: 127 (italics in original); discussed in Eidinow 2023.

16. Gibson 1979: 129.

17. Szokolszky 2019: 18; see also Malafouris 2019: 3; cf. Eidinow 2023. In introducing this idea here, I am not indicating an ideological adherence to ecological psychology (EP) as opposed to enactivism I, as examined by Read and Szokolszky (2020): they emphasize how these differ from each other, insofar as ecological psychology argues that sensation does not equal perception, whereas enactiviI(E) emphasizes the contribution of the organism in making sense of their environment. Raab and Araújo (2019) distil this difference as the accepting or not of mental representations (where EP does not accept them and E does). I favour the idea that mental representations are involved, in the sense that the sensorimotor processes are activated by perceptions (and vice versa), in particular but not only because this also helps to explain the role of language and other dimensions of the social. On these aspects and their need for development in Gibson's writings, see Still and Costall 1991.

18. E.g. Barsalou 2016; Eidinow 2022.

19. Kyle Simmons et al. 2007, Amsel et al. 2014, Conca et al. 2021.

20. See Epstein 2016 for a wonderfully clear rejection of this idea.

21. Gibson1979: 258.

22. Barsalou 2016: 11.

23. Gallagher and Allen 2018: 2634.

24. E.g. as Kiverstein and Rietveld (2018: 1593) posit when they frame their combination of ecological and enactive approaches: 'Agents engage in activities that allow them to explore for possible structure, pattern and regularity in the environment before arriving at stable structures that allow them to maintain the coordination of their activities to affordances.'

25. Gibson 1979: 256: 'a perceptual system that has become sensitized to certain invariants (information) and can extract them from the stimulus flux can also operate without the constraint of the stimulus flux'. Also cited by Kiverstein and Rietveld 2018: 158.

26. As opposed to the impression given by the 'written language bias', which conveys the impression that words are inherently stable units of meaning. For this section, I am indebted to the lucid account of Harvey 2015.

27. Cowley 2011: 185.

28. Ibid.: 186.

29. Harvey 2015: 124: wordings are 'communal technologies, whose structure and effects on action and affordances are stabilized by inter-agent coordination.'

30. Throughout this section, as Hornblower (2008) observes, there are persistent allusions to another famous night conflict, the Doloneia, as described in Book 10 of the *Iliad*.

31. Trans. here and below, Hammond 2009. See Pelling 2022 on this passage.

32. The Erinyes are daughters of Earth in Hesiod, but in Aeschylus (and later iconography), they have become daughters of night (as Aguirre 2010: 138 argues).

33. At the siege of Epipolai, the moon is mentioned, but only as a way of confirming the Athenians' inability to see anything; the quality of light and dark is not described.

34. Carne-Ross 1985: 142.

35. Trans. here and below: Whitehead 2003. We might expect to find it in Xenophon's military writing: but he rather uses it to evoke the affordance of landscape in *On Hunting*, describing the experience of difficult terrain for a fleeing animal (5.21); and for a net-keeper tracking a hare (6.5). In the *Memorabilia*, it evokes the experience of the viewing of an image (3.10.1) and the experience of the darkness of night (4.3.4).

36. Cf. Hermocrates' use of darkness to confuse the Athenian soldiers: 7.73.3.

37. *Skotos* can be a masculine or a neuter noun; here it is the masculine form, but in 3.23.4 it is neuter. It is not clear to me why Thucydides selects one or the other form.

38. See Hornblower 2008 on these passages.

39. Trans. here and below, Murray 1924.

40. Murray 1919.

41. This is not because most events happen at other times (there are 102 uses of *nux*, according to Powell's *Lexicon*); *skoteinos* is not used.

42. Here and below, Waterfield 1998.

43. Trans. (both passages) Vince and Vince 1926.

44. Trans. MacDowell 1990.

45. Cohen 2013: xxv.

CHAPTER 6

THE ONLY CONSTANT IS CHANGE: THE ENVIRONMENTAL DIMENSION OF PLUTARCH'S *DE DEFECTU ORACULORUM*

Christopher Schliephake

Around the end of the first century and early second century CE, Plutarch of Chaeronea (*c.* 45–120 CE) wrote his most important extant literary works. As a young man, he studied philosophy at Athens and would come to be recognized by his contemporaries as a Platonist. Returning from prolonged journeys throughout the Mediterranean, Plutarch came back to his small, but historically significant hometown in Boeotia during the last decade of the first century CE. His family estate was only a day's ride away from the influential oracular sanctuary of Delphi, where Plutarch soon became one of the two permanent priests – a position he would hold until his death some thirty years later.[1] During that time, he embarked on his ambitious project of the *Parallel Lives*, a juxtaposition of biographies of great Roman and Greek statemen from the past. While he is probably best known for these moralistic character studies, he also finished his most accomplished philosophical texts during this period. Most of these were later assembled in a collection we now refer to as the *Moralia*, which brought together essays on a vast array of subjects, many of which reflect the encyclopaedic knowledge of their author.[2] The *Moralia* also contain Plutarch's philosophical inquiries into theological issues. Amongst this group are a series of philosophical dialogues set in Delphi and focused on the oracular activity as well as the medium of the site – the Pythia – a fact that led Plutarch to term them 'Pythian dialogues' (*Pythikoi logoi*, cf. Plut. *De E* 1.384E).[3]

That Plutarch wrote these texts when he was a priest at Delphi has not been seriously challenged by anyone. As a scholar has recently put it, they make up the core of his philosophy and particularly his Platonism.[4] As the dialogues engage with fundamental questions concerning the gods, humankind, and the communication (and intermediaries) between them, they also take their recipients on a tour through the site itself, anchoring the abstract philosophical discussions within a concrete geography and history. This gave Plutarch the chance of reflecting on the central role that the sanctuary had played (and continued to play) in human affairs and on how far divination was a topic relevant to philosophy.

In his text *De E apud Delphos* ('The E at Delphi'), Plutarch discussed the age-old wisdom that cultural memory connected to the earliest periods of the site. These found a material manifestation in a series of aphorisms attached to the Apollo temple, which were traced back to the oldest known philosophers of Greece. In *De Pythiae oraculis* ('The Oracles at Delphi No Longer Given in Verse'), he dealt with another matter of transhistorical importance, namely, the question of how the prophetic utterances of the Pythia had changed over the ages and why, at present, her prophecies were given in prose, whereas tradition held that, in the past, they had been delivered in verse. Finally, in *De defectu oraculorum* ('The Obsolescence of Oracles') he explored possible reasons for a decline in oracular activity on the Greek mainland in his own time, while also offering a complex account of divinatory mechanisms primarily connected to so-called *daimons*, semi-divine beings that played a role in the divinatory process.

Taken together, these dialogues make up the centrepieces of Plutarch's philosophy, which combined critical reflection on fundamental theological questions with intricate explorations of human knowledge and the material frameworks in which cultural practices of communication and meaning-making took place. That Plutarch chose the generic form of the philosophical dialogue to express these ideas is important, because it gave him the chance to bring together different perspectives, to confront opposing viewpoints and to turn his search for truth into a possibly open-ended and highly relational enterprise.[5] Much like the aphorisms attached to the sanctuary of Apollo, which resonated in cultural memory, the many voices that Plutarch combined in his Pythian dialogues turn these texts into complex philosophical reflections with multiple levels of signification. One level concerned how humans had, over the course of history, looked to Delphi as a place that provided them with invaluable guidance in the face of existential questions and threats. At another level, they looked at the transcendental mechanisms that determined the workings of oracular consultation, ranging all the way from discussions of the basic functions of human communication to the lunar dwellings of *daimons* and how they impacted the soul.

In this essay, I want to look at yet another dimension, one that concerns the environmental aspects of Plutarch's Pythian dialogues. Taking *De defectu oraculorum* as my main analytical example, I want to examine the role that material processes play in Plutarch's reflections. By 'environmental', I mean, first, the spatial configurations that are embedded in the narrative, which relate to Delphi's geography and how it is connected with other places around (and beyond) the Mediterranean world. Secondly, drawing on recent approaches in the environmental humanities and how they have rendered the interplay between cultural texts and the material dimensions of the world, my use of the term 'environmental' also involves the ways in which Plutarch reflects on materiality and the human body in his theory of divination. The levels of signification referred to above are thereby not to be seen as separate, but rather as co-constitutive parts of what we could refer to as Plutarch's holistic outlook. By juxtaposing various argumentative strands and by asking his recipients to think about how they connect, Plutarch invited a multi-perspective view of how the world worked and how humans were part of an environment teeming with non-human forces, the unstable nature of which both determined changes in the visible and intelligible realm, and demanded that both humans and their institutions adapt to ever-shifting conditions.

In what follows I will start with a brief discussion of previous scholarship on *De defectu oraculorum*. While the prevalent sense of change that Plutarch presents in this text has been highlighted by a number of readings, my interpretation focuses on the spatio-environmental aspects that frame his account. By analysing how Plutarch writes about Delphi and the material dimensions of the site, particularly those related to the soil, I will show how changes in oracular activity as presented in *De defectu oraculorum* were connected to physical processes in the natural world. As I want to suggest, Plutarch thereby presents his recipients with a take on divination that is both embodied and environmental.

The spatial framework of *De defectu oraculorum*

As already mentioned above, one central question lies at the heart of Plutarch's *De defectu oraculorum*: why did many oracles find themselves in a process of decline and why had some even vanished altogether? (*De def. or.* 5.411E) In scholarship there has been a lot of debate about how far Plutarch's question can be seen as the expression of a general perception of change in oracular activity in the late first and early second century CE. Although the archaeological evidence suggests that some oracular sites such as Delphi and Didyma saw comparatively less building and dedicatory activity around that time, we cannot speak of a substantial decline in either a cultic or a material way – and there were some places, such as Claros, where we can witness considerable growth (not least due to Roman investment).[6]

In consequence, Bendlin states that 'we cannot speak of a *general* decline of materially-impoverished oracles from late Hellenistic times'.[7] As he also observes, Plutarch nevertheless seems to assume that this was the case and to answer his question by referring to a 'political, miliary, and demographic decline of Greece since the Hellenistic period, which caused the depopulation of the land and the decay of many rural, extra-urban areas, which is where many traditional oracles obtained their clientele'.[8] While it is true that Ammonius, Plutarch's teacher and one of the interlocutors of the dialogue, uses this argument to offer an explanation of why some oracles fell silent (because in some areas there was simply no one to visit them anymore) and why the number of prophetesses at Delphi was reduced (cf. *De def. or.* 8.413E–414C), there is more to Plutarch's answer.

As Bendlin himself recognizes, the depopulation of Greece 'is itself actually a familiar literary topos in Plutarch's day'.[9] It can be traced back to at least Polybios' time (second century BCE; cf. Polyb. 36.17). While its factual basis has been the matter of some controversy, it can certainly be read as the expression of socio-political changes that had happened since the advent of Rome in the eastern Mediterranean.[10] Yet Plutarch does not dwell on this for long, and the argument is introduced at a very early point in the dialogue. In fact, most of his dialogues are structured in a way that allows him to express the viewpoints that he deems most important towards the end.[11] The argument that relates the apparent decline of oracular activity to depopulation is used by Ammonius to refute the Cynic stance that attributes its demise to a general moral decline (cf. *De def. or.* 7.413A–C). Plutarch's Middle-Platonist viewpoint is expressed by his brother, Lamprias, the main narrator and certainly most important voice of the dialogue, who holds that god is removed from earthly matters. This is not to say that Apollo has turned his back on humans, for he still cares for them and is open to what they have to say to him (*De def. or.* 7.413C).[12] But it also means that Ammonius' argument that the god actively guides oracular activity (and can actually react to processes of depopulation by abandoning more or less deserted sanctuaries), must be refuted as well. According to Lamprias, the gods exist in an unattainable realm, removed from all worldly affairs, and, if they have any bearing on what happens in oracles, then this influence must not be sought in any direct or causal relationship (an aspect we will come back to below).

Lamprias' argument is complex and it is not introduced right away. Rather, the text begins with a brief story that introduces one of its main motifs, namely the geography of oracular activity around the Mediterranean (cf. *De def. or.* 1.409E–F). According to a well-known myth, two eagles or swans had flown from opposite corners of the world and met at its very centre, just above the Apollo oracle at Delphi, a place that Greek tradition consequently referred to as the *omphalos*, 'navel' of the earth (cf. also Pind. frag. 54; Strab. 9.3.6). One of the sages of Archaic Greece, Epimenides of Phaistos (or Knossos), had inquired after the veracity of this myth at Delphi. He received an ambiguous oracle, which in due course prompted him to conclude that there was no navel of the earth (or sea), and if there was, that this was known to the gods alone. According to the narrator of the dialogue, the moral of this story is that it is unwise to investigate the truth of ancient myths (*De def. or.* 1.409F–410A). It is only after this short prelude that the dialogue proper begins and some of the participants are introduced.

De defectu oraculorum is the only Pythian dialogue that begins this way. One reason may be to do with introducing the quest for truth and knowledge as a guiding motif. In Plutarch's work, 'knowledge' and 'truth' are intricately connected to the gods, which is not to say that philosophical reasoning stands in a polar opposition to divine authority. Quite the contrary, as Frazier has suggested, for Plutarch, philosophy is a way of getting in contact with higher powers, and the search for truth is, in fact, seen as a service to the gods.[13] As Plutarch well knew, however, there were limits to what could be known and expressed in human terms, so every quest for the truth was possibly open-ended. This point is stressed by the structure of his dialogues, which usually end without a conclusive synthesis, leaving the recipients with the task of reflecting on the arguments brought forth.[14]

But, as I want to suggest, another reason can be found in the spatial-environmental dimensions that Plutarch's text establishes from the beginning. The passage that follows the story of the *omphalos* begins with the introduction of two participants in the dialogue, Demetrius, a grammarian, and Cleombrotus, a travelling philosopher. We learn that both had come to Delphi on the occasion of the so-called Pythian games, and that they had travelled from, as it were, opposing ends of the known world to get there: Demetrius from the British Isles and Cleombrotus from Egypt and Arabia (*De def. or.* 2.410A–B). Cleombrotus is characterized as a man who is driven by a thirst for knowledge, especially concerning theological issues. He relates a journey to the oasis of Siwa, site of the famous, seemingly age-old oracle of Zeus-Ammon. As he reports, there was a never-diminishing flame in this place, and he had learned from the priests that the lamp where this light was kept needed less oil every year, suggesting that the time intervals were unstable and that the years were in fact growing shorter (*De def. or.* 2.410B).

This observation prompts the first discussion, which takes place before the actual dialogue surrounding the main question begins; it also introduces the leitmotif, namely that the world is subject to change. As Cleombrotus argues, greater changes can be seen in 'small things' that indicate what will come to pass (*De def. or.* 3.410D). While this argument within the dialogue relates back to the practice of divination and the more general question of how to perceive and understand signs, it is also based on a long cultural tradition of empirical observations of the natural world for medicinal purposes and other prescriptive techniques such as meteorology.[15] Although Ammonius is not opposed to the idea of empirical observation, he points out that the fundamental issue lies in what kind of conclusions can be drawn from it (*De def. or.* 4.411A–D): if the oil lamp indicates anything, it certainly does not measure the sun's course from one solstice to another. Rather, he argues, one would have to ask whether the temperature of the air in Siwa had changed (which would affect the intensity of the fire); or inquire after the nature of the oil used for the flame (whether it was made from young or seasoned plants).

The important aspect of this discussion for our analysis is that *De defectu oraculorum* is, from the outset, concerned with offering explanations that revolve around the material dimensions of the world. Plutarch thereby establishes a causal relationship between the properties of matter and changes in the perceptible world. That there is a strong cosmological interest connected to this can be seen in Ammonius' discussion of celestial mechanics, an aspect that is taken up again in the course of the dialogue, and which entails a complex debate on the total number of worlds in the universe.[16] In general, however, it is not the point of the discussion to drift away from earthly matters. Rather, the trajectory of the dialogue is firmly rooted in a known geography, with the location and place names of oracles serving as a kind of mental map that helps to frame its setting. Around ten different oracles are named in the course of the conversation: while some formerly important sites in Greece have grown silent, there are other oracles, particularly in the eastern Mediterranean that are still working. Siwa, too, renowned for its ancient tradition, is struggling, as the reaction of Cleombrotus indicates when asked about its condition – an inquiry that finally prompts the discussion of the main theme of the treatise (*De def. or.* 5.411D–E). In this context, it is important that Delphi makes up the narrative centre point around which all of the discussions revolve.

The prominent role of Delphi can also be seen in the way mythological stories are embedded in *De defectu oraculorum*, most of which concern the founding legend of the site. Apart from the myth regarding the *omphalos* referred to above, this includes the account of how Apollo had to fight and kill a monster (a dragon or giant snake) living nearby. Ammonius first invokes this tale when he argues that the area surrounding Parnassos had not been desolate because of the beast dwelling there, but rather that it was its desolation that had attracted the monster in the first place (*De def. or.* 8.414A–B). Cleombrotus, who picks up the narrative in the subsequent sections, rationalizes the myth by suggesting that the slaying of the monster and the atonement of Apollo (which some of the stories report) point to a past human conflict, possibly over control of the site. He embeds this rationalizing idea within a larger argument about the nature of *daimons*,[17] supernatural beings, which he holds accountable for many of the acts that

Greek tradition attributes to the gods (*De def. or.* 15.418A–D). The implicit point he tries to make is that *daimons* are capable of both good and bad, and that they are not immortal, but perishable. He then relates a curious story about a holy man living in a desert near the Red Sea,[18] whom he recently met there. This man possessed great knowledge and, once every year, he was also a diviner, visited by powerful men who travelled great distances to see him. The man spoke of Delphi with great admiration, and taught Cleombrotus about *daimons*, insisting that they were also responsible for oracles (*De def. or.* 21.420F–421D).

There is another famous legend connected to Delphi, one related to the particular landscape features and properties of the earth in this place: Lamprias relates a local story about a shepherd named Coretas, who once came into this region and, upon breathing in the 'streams' sent up by the earth (usually referred to as *pneuma*, 'breath' or 'spirit'), became inspired and foretold the future (*De def. or.* 42.433C–D). This is an explanation of mantic inspiration (the technical term is *enthusiasmos*, *De. def. or.* 40.432C–D) that works quite differently from the one related above: it does not rely on invisible intermediaries, but rather focuses on material processes that affect the body – and, in a second step, the soul. According to Lamprias, the exhalations are a product of both the earth and the sun, whose heat is a necessary precondition for the specific mixture of vapours that finally rise to the surface (*De def. or.* 43.433E–F). He thereby draws on a long tradition that connects the prophetic power of the place to the physical landscape, specifically, to a chasm that was said to lie directly under the temple of Apollo and that emits the streams.[19] In philosophical debates surrounding oracular activity, there seems to have been some discussion about the shifting intensity of the *pneuma* and how it affected the oracle's (or rather the medium's) capacity to give prophecies before the time of Plutarch. In Cicero's *De Divinatione*, this theory is attributed to Stoic philosophers, who seem to have used it as an argument against rival schools that doubted oracular divination for the reason that it was not stable, such that prophecies had changed both in quality and quantity.[20]

In Plutarch's text, Lamprias picks up this idea and connects it to a more general observation, attributed to Aristotle, that exhalations in the earth are the root cause of many visible changes on its surface.[21] Thus, rivers and lakes that were known and frequented in the past, he argues, have suddenly disappeared (only to re-surface in other places); some mines, like Laurium in Attica, that were rich in precious metals and silver have run dry; and the rocks in Euboea have ceased to yield soft and thin filaments that could be found in many commodities that, in turn, could not be produced anymore (*De def. or.* 43.433E–44.434B).[22] In these lines, Lamprias describes a process that many of the other passages discussed so far have only hinted at, namely, the argument that the whole world is changing and that the oracles are changing along with it. Sometimes, this argument goes, this may be connected to violent convulsions within the earth itself, for instance when the exhalations within it cannot escape freely due to some obstacle, and their pressure leads to earthquakes. To underline his argument, Lamprias points to one such event when Delphi itself had been partly destroyed, traces of which can still be found in the cityscape (*De def. or.* 44.434B–C). This does not mean that the entire world is going to collapse at some point in the future, because, as Lamprias believes, it is everlasting. But it does mean that because of material processes there are changes occurring that will make themselves felt in one way or another. The inspiring vapour that he locates at Delphi is also subject to these changes, which he does not attribute to the agency of a god, but to an interplay of material forces.

This discussion of the material dimension does not exclude supernatural explanations for mantic processes per se. Even the *daimons* are not immune to the passage of time and are not, unlike the gods, immortal (*De def. or.* 10.415A–C) – a fact that is firmly established early in the dialogue.[23] In general, it is important to stress how the stories that Plutarch includes in the course of the dialogue paint a vivid image of the known geography of his time. They cover almost all of the parts of the Roman Empire, and there is a pervasive impression that the changes in oracular activity, on which the discussants reflect, are part of a much wider, all-encompassing development that does not solely involve oracles. These changes leave perceptible traces in the material world, including sounds, smells, layers of destruction in the built environment, and transformations in the natural environment. Moreover, they are inherently connected to both material and immaterial processes that are oftentimes hidden from plain sight, but can nonetheless make themselves felt in different ways and across vast distances in both time and space.

The materiality of divine inspiration

The passages discussed above make up the spatial framework of *De defectu oraculorum*. They function as kinds of coordinates, providing a counterpoint to the highly abstract debates that occur in the course of the dialogue, insofar as they are a reminder that the questions that concern the interlocutors take place in a physical, tangible realm. Lamprias, the main speaker, introduces this thought early on when he states that the gods are hardly responsible for the decline of oracles. While he does not deny that the gods truly were and are originators of the material world, he also believes that 'nature', or rather the materiality that makes up the non-human environment, functions independently of them – an argument that he relates to the mutability (and transience) of matter. Although he does not specify its exact workings, Lamprias attributes to the material world its own agency, a potential for changing its original (and by implication perfect) state into one of disintegration or corruption. This is also why he believes that mantic power itself is a transient phenomenon, one that decreases in strength and that could finally decay (*De def. or.* 9.414D–E).

The question of existence is important in this context, because the Middle-Platonist philosophy that Lamprias advocates firmly adheres to the idea that the act of creation follows a divine order and that god is good.[24] The moral qualities that Lamprias connects with this notion of goodness, for example, justice or friendliness, are decidedly social in kind, which, in turn, leads him to formulate an account of all things and beings in existence, which is based upon the principle of relationality (*De def. or.* 24.423D–E). Everything that exists gains its particular properties in relation to other things – it both shares characteristics with them and also differs from them. Similarity is a key feature of this understanding: 'For he who says that creation has but one land and one sea overlooks a matter which is perfectly plain, the doctrine of similar parts: for we divide the earth into parts which bear similar names, and the sea likewise. A part of the world (*kosmou*), however, is not a world (*kosmos*), but something combined from the differing elements in Nature (*all' ek diaforōn physeōn sunestēke*)' (Plut. *De def. or.* 24.423 E–F; trans. Babbitt).

This argument makes up part of a longer section on the possibility of multiple worlds existing side-by-side. Lamprias advocates this idea, while also reflecting on the individual properties that make each existing world unique. The possible multitude of worlds is, according to him, not based on duplication but rather variation. This is due to the materiality that shapes each world and that interacts with the forces of movement in nature. In this context, he argues against the notion of a fixed, and locatable centre of the world. As Lamprias posits, it is rather the dynamic interplay of co-constitutive elements that holds the world together (*De def. or.* 25–26.424A–F). If the gods take part in this interaction, this happens out of their free will and personal agency; what sets them apart from all of the other constituent parts is that they are not bound by any one world but can move between them. Lamprias pits these reflections against different ideas put forth by rival philosophical schools (the Stoics and, particularly, the Epicureans). What is even more important for our analysis is that the abstract ideas about the nature of the gods and the universe are thoroughly embedded in a coherent, natural philosophy that brings the discussion always back to the earth and the material interplay of matter, the physical landscape and the human body.

What Plutarch achieves in *De defectu oraculorum* is in many ways reminiscent of what Bruno Latour has, in his late work, referred to as a 'landing on Earth'.[25] Latour takes this metaphor from a modern worldview that is based on a technology that can, in fact, capture images of our planet from outer space and that is, at the same time, grounded upon the all too pervasive conviction that human systems can control the Earth's matter. Now, in an age of accelerating climate change and other ecological crises such as biodiversity loss and ocean pollution, Latour claims that the Earth's agency is forcefully re-entering humanity's attention in different ways: it suddenly becomes clear that material processes such as extreme weather events cannot be contained by human ingenuity. In fact, the Earth's agency poses a challenge to what he primarily sees as Western systems of knowledge and politics of power, which were closely linked in the course of history.[26] According to Latour, 'the intrusion of the Earth with a surprising shape, size, contents, and activity' triggers 'a triple feeling of *disorientation*; first, in *space*—where are we located?; then, in *time*—in which period do we find ourselves?; finally, in *identity*—who are we, what sort of agency do we possess (…)?'.[27] What Latour terms 'earthbound' is a reaction to this feeling of 'disorientation', one that he particularly speaks of in spatial dimensions. For instance, Latour has repeatedly referred to the double meaning of 'territory' as both an exact location on a map and a consciousness that humans depend on the ground upon which they live.[28] Indeed, it was the awakening of this consciousness of dependence on the land, its physical properties and the material processes that take place in a very thin layer above and below it, which drove his late work.[29]

I am not suggesting that Plutarch's *De defectu oraculorum* shares this outlook on the world. Plutarch writes from a very different position, one that was based on a completely different set of technologies and experiences of the world. Nonetheless, the 'existential crisis' that Latour perceives as a defining sentiment of our own era[30] is reminiscent of what Plutarch's interlocutors discuss, as they sit near the Apollo temple at Delphi and feel its material presence. The sense of crisis in this dialogue is palpable. It does not so much concern environmental stressors (and certainly no large-scale anthropogenic impacts on the natural world), but rather is entangled with a very concrete problem that Plutarch must have felt was real: the landscape of Greek oracles around the Mediterranean was shifting. The 'disorientation' that Latour alludes to in the quote above can also be found in *De defectu oraculorum*, particularly in the way the debate revolves around space and fixed locations, the lifespan of humans and supernatural powers, and the systems of knowledge related to both cosmology and divination. I want to suggest that part of Plutarch's answer to the many questions posed by these challenges was related to one we also find in Latour's notion of turning the attention back to earth – not the planet, but rather the very earth that the oracles (and particularly Delphi) depended on for their workings. It is also in this context of shared ideas, I argue, that we can find the most pronounced environmental arguments in Plutarch's dialogue.

Changing worlds: Plutarch's embodied perspective

Recent approaches in the environmental humanities, which have conceived the interrelationship between literary texts and worldly matter, can help us in this last stage of our environmental reading of Plutarch's text. As Iovino and Oppermann point out in their introduction to *Material Ecocriticism*:

> the world's material phenomena are knots in a vast network of agencies, which can be 'read' and interpreted as forming narratives, stories. Developing in bodily forms and in discursive formulations, and arising in coevolutionary landscapes of natures and signs, the stories of matter are everywhere: in the air we breathe, the food we eat, in the things and beings of the world, within and beyond the human realm. All matter, in other words, is a 'storied matter.'[31]

Iovino and Oppermann invite a practice of interpretation that perceives discourse and materiality as two sides of the same coin, entwined, as it were, in endless processes of signification. Latour's notion that non-human objects and things are to be thought of not merely as passive entities or resources, waiting to be extracted or used by humans, but rather as agents that stand in a dynamic interaction with human beings, is here brought together with a reflection on the role of literary representation. They argue that material configurations of the world form stories that can be read and interpreted in human discourse to ascribe meaning to material objects, thereby informing human relations to materiality. They also hold that literary texts possess a material dimension; not only because they are generally written down on a medium that stores information, but because they constitute cognitive responses to a concrete, material environment that is translated into human language.[32] While this act of symbolization is by no means to be confused with 'reality' as it presents itself at any respective moment in time, it builds on the biosemiotic notion that 'the natural world is perfused with signs, meanings, and purposes which are material and which evolve. (...) What goes *inside* an organism, and *between* an organism and its environment always involves what (..) we must call interpretations'.[33] As Iovino and Oppermann put it, this is 'an embodied process of understanding'[34] that, in general, finds a concrete expression in literary world-making.

Building on the idea that the process of making meaning of the world is both an embodied and a literary practice, I want to argue that *De defectu oraculorum* grapples with remarkably similar ideas as those brought forth in such recent, materiality-oriented approaches in the environmental humanities. In particular, Lamprias' ideas, referred to above, can be brought together with such new materialist theories that highlight the autonomous agency of material formations that provoke constant change in coupled social-natural systems. The overall point of Lamprias' long sections in the dialogue seems to be to argue that the only real constant in the world is change;[35] an argument that is intricately tied to how the material make-up of the world relates to other forces (be they divine or anthropogenic in kind), shaping and re-shaping the conditions that enable specific practices such as divination.

The last two monologues of Lamprias particularly underline this last point and combine his abstract philosophical ideas with a concrete, embodied perspective. Recent scholarship has referred to his account of how divination works as the 'theory of double causation' (see *De def. or.* 48.436D). Following Plato, he contends that everything in existence has two causes, namely, divine order, as well as physical materiality, which possesses agency (as we saw above), but which is at the same time devoid of reason.[36] This is why Plato, according to Lamprias (Plut. *De def. or.* 47.435F–436A), assigned

> to God (*theō*), on the one hand, the origin of all things that are in keeping with reason (*tēn archēn apodidous tōn kata logon echontōn*), and on the other hand, not to divest matter (*hylēn*) of the causes necessary for whatever comes into being, but to realize that the perceptible universe, even when arranged in some such orderly way as this, is not pure and unalloyed, but that it takes its origin from matter when matter comes into conjunction with reason (*alla tēs hylēs symplekomenēs tō logō lambanei tēn genesin*).

Lamprias underlines his point by drawing an analogy to painting: every painting is made up of small pigments of colour with various properties, many of which are mixed together in the process of creation. But, at the same time, a painting needs an artist that sets all of these different elements in motion and makes them work according to an overarching principle (*De def. or.* 47.436A–C). Lamprias' main aim is to show that his firm materialist position can be reconciled with accounts that attribute everything (including the workings of divination) to divine reason.

He eventually brings the argument full circle by focusing on the oracular medium at Delphi, the Pythia, and presenting his listeners with an embodied take on divination.[37] He has laid the foundation for his argument earlier, by pointing to the natural, physical conditions of the site and particularly the exhalations of the earth. He sees this *pneuma* as one central precondition for bringing about the inspiration, the *enthusiasmos*, necessary for prophecy. It has a divine origin, he argues, insofar as the material properties connected to the sun's rays that warm the earth, and the processes that act themselves out below ground were first produced by the gods – and are now supervised, as it were, by shapeless *daimons* who can influence the mixture of elements that make up the vapours for inducing inspiration. These exhalations act upon the soul of the Pythia, which, in a recurring metaphor, is described as an 'instrument', *organon* (De def. or. 48.436F–437A). The material forces arising out of the earth impact her soul (or rather a part of the soul, particularly receptive to the inspiring vapours), which sets her in the right condition for prophecy. According to this account, divine inspiration is characterized by a material, prelingual dimension: the Pythia's body is part of an environment whose very conditions must be in the right balance in order to induce prophetic power. This relational balance concerns both the exhalations of the earth, which must be in the appropriate mixture, and also the Pythia's body.[38]

In these lines, Lamprias serves as a focalizer for the author: Plutarch advocated a very complex theory of divination, one that adhered to Plato's concept of the soul, but that integrated many Aristotelian elements.[39] The metaphor of an 'instrument' should not be misleading here, because the Pythia is not seen as a passive recipient of inspiring elements (whatever form they may take). As Lamprias puts it, the Pythia's temperament, which makes her fit for prophecy, may change – just as may the exhalations rising up from below (De def. or. 50.437D). That emotions can affect mantic processes is an idea Plutarch takes from Plato (Ti. 47d, 69b–72d; Resp. 571c-d), while the strong emphasis he lays on the body's role is Aristotelian in origin (especially when it comes to the perception of signs, Arist. Parv. nat. 1, 450a22 and 459a8-22; Div. somn. 464b 30; also De an. 3.4-5). It can, for instance, be seen in the way Lamprias draws an analogy to dreams (Plut. De def. or. 50.437E):

> But especially does the imaginative faculty of the soul seem to be swayed by the alterations in the body, and to change as the body changes, a fact which is clearly shown in dreams (*malista de to phantastikon eoike tēs psychēs hypo tou sōmatos alloioumenou krateisthai kai symmetaballein, hōs dēlon estin apo tōn oneirōn*).

While Plutarch does not deny the divinatory potential of dreaming per se, he argues that bodily processes have to be taken into account when explaining what actually happens in divination. In the same way, as a living organism, the Pythia is susceptible to outside influences that affect her in multiple ways. Her body stands in an open, dynamic interrelationship with her environment. And only when both are attuned in the right way can true prophecy occur. In this context, Lamprias also explains why preliminary sacrifice happens before consulting the oracle: the trembling of the sacrificial animal when libations are poured is to him an indication that the time is right and that all elements are set in place.

There is one point to be made here to round off the essay: Plutarch's account of divination as embodied also offers an explanation of why prophecy can sometimes go wrong. Lamprias' concluding passage contains the story of a recent, disturbing event when the Pythia gave her prophecy only unwillingly and eventually worked herself into a wild frenzy from which she did not recover and died as a consequence (*De def. or.* 51.438A–B). There is a strong possibility that this really happened.[40] It may have influenced Plutarch's decision to write his dialogue in the first place, addressing the disorientation (and shock) that such an experience would bring. The way Plutarch talks about the Pythia and the medium's body is, in some ways, reminiscent of Iovino's and Oppermann's claim that 'bodies, both human and nonhuman, provide an eloquent example of the way matter can be read as a text. Being the "middle place" where matter enmeshes in the discursive forces of politics, society, technology, biology, bodies are compounds of flesh, elemental properties, and symbolic imaginaries'.[41] For the Greeks, the Pythia had stood in a metonymical relationship with Delphi. For centuries, verses attributed to the different Pythias that had lived in this place were recited at festivals and were part of elementary education. Plutarch was, of course, well aware of this and his Pythian dialogues engage in a long discourse on the 'symbolic imaginary' of her oracle. But in *De defectu oraculorum* he did more: by focusing on the 'elemental properties' of the place and how they interact with the 'flesh' and finally the soul of the Pythia, he brought the debate to focus on the material properties of mantic inspiration and the environmental dimension of all communication.

Notes

1. Since the Renaissance, there has been much written about Plutarch and his works. A comprehensive and profound introduction to his life and thinking can still be found in Sirinelli 2000. See Roskam 2021 for a brief, up-to-date account of his philosophy and writings. The essays in Beck 2014 tackle various subjects, including aspects of reception.
2. On the culture of knowledge and miscellanism in the literature of the early Roman Empire cf. König 2009: 66–8 and 70–2.
3. For a general discussion of these texts see Ziegler 1964: 190–202.
4. See Brouillette 2014.
5. For a comprehensive discussion of the dialogue form in Plutarch and his 'zetetic approach' see Roskam 2021: 22–8.
6. For a discussion of the question of continuation of divinatory practice at oracles from Hellenistic to Roman imperial times see Bowden 2013: 47–9.
7. Bendlin 2011: 211.
8. Ibid.: 210.
9. Ibid.: 210.
10. For a general discussion see Alcock 1993.
11. Cf. Roskam 2021: 23–4 and, with a brief overview of positions of how to read Plutarch's dialogues, Brenk 2005: 28–9.
12. See ibid. for a discussion of Plutarch's Middle Platonism.
13. Cf. Frazier 2005: 115–16.

14. See Ziegler 1964: 254.

15. Cf., for instance, Cic. *Div*. 1.12, 121, Hes. *Op*. 679–81, Theophr. *Hist. pl*. 1.10.5–6. On 'signs' as a topic of philosophy see Allen 2010.

16. See Plut. *De def. or*. 22-37.422A–430F with the discussion in Miller 1997.

17. Plutarch's demonology is very complex and, as some scholars have underlined, inconsistent. In *De defectu oraculorum* the viewpoint prevails that *daimons* are intermediaries between gods and humans and that they function as a kind of overseers of oracles. For a comprehensive discussion Brenk 1977: 49–183.

18. On this story and its later reception, Dörrie 1983.

19. Cf., for instance, *De def. or*. 50.437C as well as Diod. 16,26. For a discussion of foundational stories and how they relate to landscape features, including the problematic question of the chasm and vapours arising from the earth, see Scott 2014: 18–41.

20. Cf. Cic. *Div*. 2.117-18.

21. Aristoteles' theory explained earthquakes as a natural cause, inviting a different take on material processes that need not involve divine agency. Cf., for instance, *Mete*. 1.343a–b (also 344b and 2,368a–b).

22. Plutarch here, in fact, describes an ancient use of asbestos.

23. Cf., for instance, *De def. or*. 10.415A–C or the story of the death of 'great Pan' (18.419E–F).

24. Plutarch was particularly inspired by Plato's *Timaeus* and interpreted the text literally: obscure matter and an irrational soul had existed before creation. As Roskam summarizes (2021: 19): 'The Demiurge then gave this precomsic soul a share in his own rationality by ordering it according to numerical ratio, thus turning it into World Soul. The World Soul then ordered precosmic matter.'

25. Latour 2020.

26. Ibid.: 13.

27. Ibid.: 13; emphasis original.

28. Ibid.: 38–40 and 251–67.

29. See, for instance, Arènes, Latour and Gaillardet 2017.

30. Ibid.: 13.

31. Iovino and Oppermann 2014: 1.

32. See ibid.: 2–10.

33. Wheeler 2006: 279; emphasis original.

34. Iovino and Oppermann 2014: 4.

35. See, for instance, *De def. or*. 44.434B. This idea is not made explicit by Lamprias, but it can be inferred from his constant reflections on transformation. The saying itself was ascribed to the philosopher Heraclitus in the Greek tradition.

36. See Simonetti 2017: 97–105.

37. See further Timotin 2022: 46–67.

38. For a recent discussion of these aspects see Simonetti 2021.

39. Cf. Timotin 2022: 46.

40. Cf., for instance, Maurizio 1995: 70 and 74 (with further references).

41. Iovino and Oppermann 2014: 6. For discussion of integrating perspectives on the role of the body in divinatory processes see Eidinow 2013: 25–8.

PART III
CONTACT

CHAPTER 7
POSEIDON'S MODE OF ACTION: DIVINE AGENCY AND THE HELIKE DISASTER
Michiel van Veldhuizen

In the year 373 BCE, the city of Helike in Achaea was struck by an earthquake and subsequently overwhelmed by a tidal wave.[1] The city was said to have completely disappeared: Marcus Aurelius would later compare Helike and Pompeii as dead cities.[2] The ancient sources agree that the divine agency behind this catastrophe was the god Poseidon (Strabo 8.7.2, Diod. Sic. 15.49.3, Paus. 7.24.6). This follows a familiar pattern in ancient religious attitudes that is by no means restricted to the Greek world: environmental upheaval was – and still is – often interpreted as an indication of divine anger.[3] For the ancient world, Walter Burkert has distinguished four characteristic steps that mark this pattern: first, the experience of disaster; second, the intervention of a special mediator, such as a priest or seer; third, the diagnosis that defines and localizes the cause of evil; and fourth, the acts of atonement.[4] For Burkert, the opening of the *Iliad* provides a typical example: the Greeks experience a plague, which the seer Kalchas diagnoses as caused by Agamemnon's transgression against Apollo's priest. Agamemnon returns the priest's daughter, and the Greeks propitiate the god with song and sacrifice. The disaster is lifted.

My concern in this essay is with steps one and two, the experience of disaster and the identification of the god responsible for it. If we acknowledge that this is indeed a common pattern – and Burkert's wealth of evidence suggests that it is – the question arises how exactly the special mediator, or anyone for that matter, identifies the divine agency behind the disaster. The example from *Iliad* 1 offers some insights. The epic poet frames the identification of the divine agent responsible for the plague as a matter of course. Even before Kalchas, the religious specialist, arrives on the scene, Achilles wonders why Apollo is angry. It is clear to Achilles – and, presumably, the audience of the epic – that Apollo is the agency behind the disaster. How does the poet imagine that Achilles knows this? The answer must lie with this particular experience of disaster: the plague. In fact, the only time the word 'plague' (*loimos*) occurs in the entire *Iliad* is in Achilles' speech calling for a religious specialist (Hom. *Il.* 1.61). The question is not *who* is angry, but *why* he is angry. The experience of *loimos*, rather than any known religious offence, leads Achilles to assume the agency of Apollo.

Outside of the world of epic poetry, however, the historical disaster at Helike does not have the luxury of an omniscient master singer identifying Apollo or Poseidon beyond a shred of doubt. To be sure, the mythological pattern as witnessed in the *Iliad* continues to set expectations as to how a disaster will be experienced, at least in disaster discourse. There is ample research to suggest that storytelling – in oral traditions as well as literary societies – acts as a 'cultural safety net of context' to help make sense of future catastrophic events: disaster narratives influence the experience of actual disasters, and vice versa.[5] In the case of Helike, for instance, detecting a divine agent amidst environmental catastrophe is a matter of course, at least for most ancient authors. Attributing such divine agency, however, is more complex than simply matching up gods and disasters – there are reasons why particular gods are thought to be responsible for particular disasters. Thus, by analysing Poseidon's mode of action and the manner of his environmental intervention as presented in Helike's disaster discourse, we can gain insight into the nature of his agency, as understood by ancient authors. Namely, we learn about Poseidon's ability to hide things that are exposed or, alternatively, to expose things that are hidden. This mode of action can be traced to a variety of sources, including as early as Homeric epic. Thus, I argue, the discourse of the Helike disaster – specifically, as a Poseidon-induced disaster – is the product of a pervasive cultural and religious construct of disaster.

Agency and signs

Detecting supernatural agents in the environment appears to be, as the cognitive study of religion (CSR) has shown, a normal result of everyday theory of mind systems.[6] Agents, unlike objects, 'are beings capable of independently and intentionally initiating action on the basis of internal mental states like beliefs and desires.'[7] Humans have adapted to suspect the presence of other agents based on signs and traces: rustling leaves may indicate the presence of a predator; footprints in the sand may indicate the hunter's quarry.[8] Human and non-human animals are the most obvious examples of agents, but people tend to assign life and even human attributes, such as intentionality, to inanimate objects and events, too.[9] Peter Struck has described the ancient Greeks as inhabitants of an 'intentional cosmos', in which signs can be perceived as originating with a divine agent acting with purpose and volition.[10] This abundance of signs 'turns into a plethora of voices' as signs cross from unintentional signals (a thunderclap) into intentional communication (Zeus approves).[11]

Indeed, detecting divine agency also appears as a semiotic act, in which the presence of the supernatural agent can partially or exclusively be inferred from a sign. The cause, or agent, is hidden and must be inferred from its effects. Such a relationship between sign and object corresponds to C. S. Peirce's category of the index: a sign that is physically related to, connected to, or affected by, its object.[12] The relation is one of contiguity and may be causal or sequential: smoke is an index of fire and a footprint an index of the person who passed by. Extraordinary indices may point to extraordinary agents. Herodotus, for example, narrates that an enormous sandal appears every now and then in the sanctuary of Perseus at Chemnis (Hdt 2.91.3); when the sandal is seen, all of Egypt flourishes. The sandal, by virtue of its extraordinary size, indicates a hero, and, by virtue of its appearance in or around the sanctuary, indicates Perseus. Both facts are necessary for Perseus to be inferred as the one whose foot was attached to this sandal. For the religious observer, the sandal is an index of Perseus. Furthermore, the observation of the sign coincides with a period of prosperity, which enhances the inference of the sandal's supernatural ownership and intentionality.

My focus in this chapter, however, is neither on the divinity's physical manifestation (whether a full epiphany or just a sandal) nor, at the other end of the spectrum, on an awareness or sense of divine presence.[13] Rather, I focus on the signs, or *indices*, in the physical landscape and the environmental effects that reveal Poseidon's agency. Anthropologist Eduardo Kohn employs Peirce's semiotics for its non-dualistic system, stressing the continuity between human and non-human modes of representation.[14] For Kohn this means accessing processes of semiosis in dogs and forests; for the study of ancient Greek religion, this can mean the semiosis of human and divine modes of representation. Like the sandal, these indices or effects must be extraordinary to such a degree that they elicit an inference that explains their occurrence. Pascal Boyer's categories of supernatural concepts are instructive here: the sandal in Chemnis, for example, is an artifact that violates the intuitive-knowledge-domain of physics – it is too large, and it just appears and disappears.[15] Divine agency is inferred from the index of the sandal because of its intuitive-knowledge-domain violation. A famous example of a similar such violation – involving not an artifact but the environment itself – is the creation of the gorge in the Peneios Valley in Thessaly. Here, the environmental signs are such that they are indicative of Poseidon's agency.

The Thessalians say, so Herodotus reports (Hdt. 7.129), that Thessaly used to be a lake surrounded by tall mountains, until Poseidon split apart the mountain and created a passage for the Peneios River to flow out. According to Herodotus, the 'split' (*diastasis*) of the mountains is the 'work of an earthquake' (*seismou ergon*), and if Poseidon is believed to be the earthshaker, then it follows, through simple observation ('by looking,' *idōn*) – that 'Poseidon made it' (*Poseideōna poiēsai*). The split mountain is the index from which the cause (an earthquake) and its agent (Poseidon) are inferred. At first glance, in this example, nothing so extraordinary as to point to an intuitive-knowledge-domain violation can be discerned, nor is any motivation, like divine anger or beneficence, apparent. But the attribution of divine agency does not happen in a vacuum.[16] Established cultural and religious traditions prepare the observer's perception. Such perceptions of divine agency are, then, culturally specific – and the Greeks tended to associate earthquakes with Poseidon.[17]

We might stop there, and yet, I suggest a more detailed analysis of Poseidon's agency is possible than simply his association with earthquakes, by examining the manner of his interference, or mode of action. The result of Poseidon's action is that the lake drains out and the plain of Thessaly is revealed. Poseidon achieves this by breaking through the mountain barrier. In Philostratus' ekphrasis on this exact topic, the god's task is indeed described as 'uncovering the plain' (*anakaluptōn ta pedia*) by creating 'gates' (*pulas*) (Philostr. *Imag.* 2.14).[18] Poseidon's hand holding the trident is raised to 'break open' (*anarrēxai*) the mountain; the result, significantly, is that Poseidon rejoices 'looking at the plain, level and broad, just like the sea' (*ta pedia kai homala idōn kai eurea, kathaper thalattas*, Philostr. *Imag.* 2.14). Here, the emphasis is not on the split mountain but on the emergence of the Thessalian plain, a smooth and flat expanse like the sea itself. Poseidon has revealed something that used to be hidden. This environmental discourse about the Peneios Valley, then, tells us something about the manner in which Poseidon is imagined to operate and the effects his intervention has on the landscape. It is Poseidon's ability to 'uncover' and 'break open' that must inform our analysis of Helike's disaster discourse.

'God of brute force and chaos'

In the case of Helike, the disaster is of such proportions that intentionality is attributed to the event. Diodorus says as much when he writes that 'some divine agency' (*theias tinos energeias*) devised destruction and ruin (15.48.1). The ancient sources leave no doubt about Poseidon's perceived involvement in the disaster. Our earliest source, Strabo's testimony of Heraclides Ponticus, the fourth-century philosopher who was contemporary with the event, is worth quoting at some length (Heraclides F46a [Wehrli] = Strabo 8.7.2, tr. Jones, adapted):[19]

> Heraclides says that the disaster (*to pathos*) took place by night in his time, and, although the city was twelve stadia distant from the sea, this whole territory together with the city was hidden from sight (*kaluphthentos*) and two thousand men who had been sent by the Achaeans were unable to recover the dead bodies; and they divided the territory of Helike among the neighbours; and the disaster happened in accordance with the anger of Poseidon (*to pathos kata mēnin Poseidōnos*).

The disaster (*pathos*) is attributed to the anger of Poseidon – a clear attribution of intentionality to a supernatural agent. Strabo only uses this word for anger in the phrase *kata mēnin*, and always to express divine anger.[20] Pausanias, too, writes that 'the anger of Poseidon came without delay' (7.24.6). Diodorus, who is channelling Ephorus, reports that 'Poseidon, in his anger, brought ruin upon the offending cities through earthquake and flood' (15.49.3).[21] Accounts differ as to the exact nature of the offence, but presumably the Helikonians had maltreated or even killed their Ionian visitors, who, in accordance with an oracle, sought access to Poseidon's sanctuary at Helike for the benefit of their own cult of Poseidon Helikonios.[22] Above all, it was an act of 'impiety' (*asebeia*, Ael. *NA* 11.19). The religious diagnosis of the disaster points to Poseidon, which validates – and, in turn, may even have been influenced by – the experience of the disaster.

At the most basic level, there exists a superficial correspondence with the environmental manifestation of the disaster and the god's sphere of influence, or field of action. Diodorus makes this explicit when he comments that 'this god has authority (*exousian*) over earthquakes and floods' (15.49.4). Seneca, reviewing the theory that earthquakes are caused by trapped winds that slip under the earth through hidden passages under the sea, refers to the Homeric epithet 'Earth-shaker' to confirm that 'the power of the sea for moving [the earth]' (*maris movendi potentia*, Sen. *QNat.* 6.23.4) has traditionally been assigned to Poseidon. This notion is often echoed by scholars of Greek religion: Poseidon is 'a god who sends destructive storms at sea, earthquakes, seaquakes, volcanic eruptions and other natural disasters (*Naturkatastrophen*)', writes Erika Simon.[23]

Walter Burkert calls Poseidon 'an embodiment of elemental force'.[24] Similarly, Jan Bremmer designates Poseidon as 'the god of brute force and chaos', connected with the nervous energy of horses, 'the unpredictable strength of sea and earth', and perhaps even with 'springs which inexplicably emerged from the depths of the earth'.[25] The problem, however, is that other gods may equally be responsible for displays of elemental force: Athena, Zeus and Hera cause storms and shipwrecks, too. Nor is every earthquake a sign of Poseidon's wrath.[26] As with the example above from Herodotus, we must, then, attempt to be more precise in describing Poseidon's disaster agency at Helike.

To fully understand the role of Poseidon in ancient discourse about the Helike disaster, we cannot rely on Poseidon's supposed sphere of influence alone. One of the principles, as formulated by Georges Dumézil, for understanding polytheistic systems like that of the Greeks is that gods must be analysed in relation to one another.[27] Poseidon and Zeus the Suppliant (*Hikesios*) are both linked to the destruction of Helike in Pausanias' account. The god Dionysus, who in Euripides' *Bacchae* supervises the earthquake that shakes the foundations of Pentheus' palace, invokes 'Lady Earthquake' (*Ennosi Potnia*, 585). The epithet *Elelichthōn* ('Earth-shaker') is applied to Poseidon (Pind. *Pae.* 6.50) and Dionysus (Soph. *Ant.* 153). According to the scholiast, Dionysus is so called because the frenzied dance movements of his Bacchantes shake the earth. The power to shake the earth is not limited to Poseidon. It is the case that other epithets attest to Poseidon's ability to move the earth, including *Enosichthōn* and *Ennosigaios* (both 'Earth-Shaker') and the cult title *Asphaleios* ('Securer'). Pausanias (3.11.9) reports that Poseidon the Secuter had a sanctuary in Sparta together with Athena of the Marketplace. But Poseidon's epithet 'Earth-mover' or 'Earth-holder' (*Gaiaochos*) is also applied to Zeus and Artemis.[28] In the latter case, Artemis 'Earth-mover' is called upon to ward off the plague of Thebes alongside Athena and Apollo (Soph. *OT* 160). The polytheistic system of the Greeks suggests that a variety of divinities can be involved in causing, and warding off, disaster; the relations among them reveal a dynamic, rather than a static, picture of disaster agency.

As Marcel Detienne has argued, these instances of gods sharing sanctuaries or epithets – what Georges Dumézil refers to as 'the already-structural' – are only the beginning. For the analysist of Greek religion, 'the surest validation for an analysis of the relations between gods or the definition of the field of action peculiar to a divine power would stem from some native statement, particularly one of a theological nature: a statement produced by [...] the "administrators of memory" [...] who, down the ages, transmitted not only the most *conscious belief* but also, along with those, all that was abandoned to the *historical subconscious of the language* and the civilization that the language conveyed'.[29] While explicit native statements such as those of Diodorus and Seneca transmit the 'conscious belief' that earthquakes fall under Poseidon's *exousia* or *potentia*, narrative accounts of Helike's disaster reveal more than these conscious theological beliefs that identify the god's sphere of influence. What is more, a close philological analysis of Helike's disaster discourse can expose the 'historical subconscious of the language' transmitting the manner in which Poseidon intervenes. This leads to another one of Dumézil's principles, namely that 'the thing to discover is not *where* a god intervenes, but *how* he does'.[30] The god's field of action is thus distinguished from the god's mode of action.

A spectacle of absence

The first clue to Poseidon's mode of action is that the Helike disaster is characterized by the total disappearance of the site and its inhabitants. The singular most striking detail of Heraclides' account is that both city and territory are entirely 'hidden from sight' (*kaluphthentos*, cf. Poseidon 'revealing' [*anakaluptōn*] Thessaly, Hdt. 7.129 above). The 2,000 rescue workers are unable to recover any of the bodies. The place is rendered invisible, conspicuous only in its absence. Pausanias' account emphasizes this invisibility as well (7.24.6, tr. Jones, adapted):

> But an earthquake struck their land at once and rendered the buildings and, along with them even the very foundation (*edaphos*) of the city invisible (*aphanes*) for posterity.

When Pausanias discusses the type of earthquake that levelled Helike, he notes that this type dives under the buildings and shakes up the 'foundations' (*themelia*), the only kind of shock to never leave any 'signs' (*sēmeia*) of habitation on the land (7.24.11). Even the foundation (*edaphos*) of the city has become invisible (*aphanēs*). The word *aphanēs* is not only associated with the underworld as epithets of Hades and Persephone, but it is also a technical term in Greek astronomy for the obscuration of the moon.[31] An *aphanēs kosmos* is an invisible, i.e., starless, sky, one that is utterly dark, lacking points of orientation (Vett. Val. 1.2). Topographically speaking, Helike has been erased from the map, without leaving a trace, and can no longer serve as orientation point. It has become an index of a missing city. This is the paradox of visible invisibility that dominates discourse about Helike and that points to the extraordinary circumstance that signals supernatural agency. The missing city is an example of what has been called the 'spectacle of absence', an image of disaster in which the mutual exclusivity of the visible and the invisible no longer holds.[32]

Diodorus Siculus splits the disaster into two episodes: first, the earthquake struck at night so that everything was dark, adding to the confusion and destruction;[33] second, a wave washed over the town the next morning, just when the few survivors thought they had escaped the danger (15.48.1–3). The result is what Diodorus describes as the *aphanismos* ('disappearance, effacement') of an entire city. The fate that both types of victims suffer, those caught in the earthquake as well as those who drowned, is, in fact, similar: the first group, 'cut off and enclosed' (*enapolēphthentes*) by the fallen buildings, 'disappeared' (*ēphanisthēsan*); in turn, the survivors of that event were then washed away by a towering wave and 'disappeared' (*aphanisthentes*) along with their native lands (15.48.3).

The extraordinary extent and totality of destruction are themselves indicative of divine origins: never before had entire cities been wiped off the map. The destruction of Helike is once again represented as a radical disappearance, a city being made unseen, characterized by the words *kaluptein* (Strabo) and *aphanizein* (Diodorus Siculus, Pausanias).[34] The scene also recalls Thessaly, cut off and enclosed by mountains, appearing rather than disappearing as the water flows out rather than in. The disaster itself is embedded in a dual landscape of the natural and the divine: the earthquake and tidal wave are manifestations of Poseidon's anger. But in the aftermath of the disaster, the spectacle of absence oscillates between invisibility and lingering visibility. Despite the emphasis on the radical disappearance of the town, several accounts mention that underwater traces remained visible.[35] From a cognitive perspective, the sign keeps drawing attention to itself as an index pointing to a city that once was here, but is now covered over.

Poseidon's mode of action

The meaning of Helike in ancient discourse is bound up with the agency of Poseidon. Considering the disaster as a sign, the identity of the agent is revealed through its effects. As Helike is covered over, Poseidon is revealed. Already the pattern identified by Burkert is clear, and no doubt informs the representation of the Helike disaster in discourse. But we can go further, analysing Poseidon's particular mode of action in his particular field of action. Diodorus Siculus points the way, because his account is unique in offering self-professed 'clear proofs' (*emphaneis apodeixis*, 15.49.4) that it was Poseidon who destroyed Helike. Diodorus Siculus presents four such proofs, the first of which we have already discussed (15.49.4–5):

1. earthquakes and floods fall under Poseidon 'authority' (*exousian*);
2. ancient belief has it that the Peloponnese was Poseidon's 'dwelling-place' (*oikētērion*);
3. the Peloponnese is considered 'sacred' (*hieran*) to Poseidon, and he is honoured above all by all its cities;
4. there are great caverns and bodies of water under the Peloponnese, including two underground rivers, one of which plunges into the ground and, in former times, completely 'disappeared' (*ēphanizeto*), while the second one plunges into a 'chasm' (*chasma*) from where it flows 'hidden under the earth' (*kekrummenos kata gēs*).

The list presents a mixture of theological, geographical and environmental proofs. First, that earthquakes fall under Poseidon's authority is a theological assumption, one that is transmitted by as old and theological a tradition as Homer. Second and third, the geographical location of the disaster (Helike, in the northern Peloponnese) is suggestive of Poseidon as well, because this space is both home to him and considered sacred to him by the inhabitants. These proofs are transmitted as conscious beliefs.

But the fourth proof is more intriguing: it is, at first sight, somewhat strange, since the underground rivers bear no direct relationship to the events at Helike at all. While Poseidon is no river god, we can understand subterranean rivers that can inexplicably emerge as springs, as being likely associated with his perceived control over the earth.[36] Indeed, there may be larger, eschatological implications as well, given the reputation of underground rivers such as the Styx. The presence of rivers 'hidden under the earth' (*kekrummenos kata gēs*), and their marvellous re-appearance on the surface, again exemplifies Poseidon's control over the earth to cover up or expose things, as we have seen before. This is what happened at Thessaly, and what happened at Helike, as the parallel language of disappearance (*aphanizein, kruptein*) testifies, subconsciously or otherwise. This environmental proof, then, turns out to be the most precise: Poseidon's agency over the earth becomes manifest, specifically, in his ability to make things disappear, and possibly re-appear, by covering over things that should be visible or exposing things that should be invisible. This fourth proof stands out because it tells us *how* Poseidon intervenes.

Supporting evidence for this interpretation of Poseidon's mode of action in afflicting disaster is found in Pausanias. As we have seen, here, too, Helike is wiped off the map by a divinely sent earthquake followed by a tidal wave. But Pausanias offers a *comparandum* in the utter disappearance of a Lydian city on Mt Sipylus, which 'vanished into a chasm' (*es chasma aphanisthēnai*, Paus. 7.24.13). Pausanias tells us that the mountain split, water welled up, and the chasm became a lake called Saloë. The resulting absence of traces is similar to Helike (*aphanizein, kaluptein*). In fact, Pausanias points explicitly to the environmental change that hides the visible ruins from view: the ruins of the town were visible in the lake, until the water of the torrent 'hid them from view (*apekrupsen*)' (7.24.13). This passage demonstrates, again, the characteristic of Poseidon's disaster agency to completely cover up, hide from view (*apokruptein*), and render invisible both those it seeks to punish and the very signs or traces of it. The reverse is possible, too, as we will see in the next section.

Breaking open the earth

In this section, I argue that Poseidon's environmental agency also becomes manifest in the reverse phenomenon, namely the sudden exposure of that which used to be hidden. Poseidon's ability to hide from view is complemented by his ability to expose and make visible. First, an historical example from Strabo, following the testimony of Posidonius, relates how a volcano erupted in the sea between Thera and Therasia in 197 BCE. The eruption created a new island – 'gradually elevated as though by levers' (1.3.16) – and when the Rhodians first set foot on this new island, they immediately erected a sanctuary to Poseidon *Asphaleios*, 'Securer'. Once again, Poseidon's mode of action allows us to be more precise than simply connecting every cult of Poseidon Asphaleios with earthquakes.[37] In the case of the sudden emergence of this island, I suggest that the agency of Poseidon must have been felt not just because of volcanic activity or the fact that it happened at sea, but precisely because something was exposed that used to be hidden, like the Thessalian plain, or Helike in reverse.

This mode of action can similarly be discerned in two episodes from the *Iliad*, in which Poseidon's agency can be analysed alongside that of other divine agents. The first occurs in the *Iliad*, Book 20, which may well be the earliest representation of an earthquake in Greek literature. A scene of divine strife pitches gods against gods before the walls of Troy (Hom. *Il.* 20.56-65, tr. Lattimore, adapted):

Terribly thundered he father of gods and men
from high above, while Poseidon from deep under shuddered
the boundless earth and the sheer heads of mountains.
And all the feet of Ida with her many waters were shaken
and all her crests, and the city of Troy, and the ships of the Achaeans.
He was terrified, the lord of the dead below, Aidoneus,
and sprang from his throne and screamed aloud, for fear that above him
Earth-Shaker Poseidon might break open (*anarrēxeie*) the earth
and the houses (of the dead) be exposed (*phaneiē*) to mortals and immortals
ghastly and mouldering, so the very gods shudder before them.

The scene portrays the three dominant cosmic powers – the brothers Zeus, Poseidon and Hades – in their respective fields of action, engaged in their respective modes of action. Zeus thunders from on high, while Poseidon shakes from down below. Poseidon's power to shake things is all-encompassing: from bottom to top and from earth to sea. In the realm below, Hades fears that Poseidon 'might break open' (*anarrēxeie*) the earth and the Underworld 'might be exposed' (*phaneiē*). Exposing the houses of the dead to the light of day, for immortals and mortals to see, is a prospect of unspeakable horror: the last line (20.65) contains a formula typically associated with Tartarus, the dark chasm underneath Hades ('ghastly and mouldering, so the very gods shudder before them,' cf. Hes. *Th.* 739, 810).

Poseidon has personal and structural connections to Tartarus. It is a place that should remain hidden away in 'a place of darkness', or *Erebos*. (cf. Apollod. *Bibl.* 1.1-3). A late Roman source suggests that the type of earthquake (namely, a *chasmatia* or 'gaping' type) that swallowed up Helike sinks its victims down 'into the deep abysses of Erebus, hidden in eternal darkness' (*ad Erebi profundos hiatus abactae, aeternis tenebris occultantur,* Amm. Marc. 17.13). It not only represents death, but also the containment of chaos in the service of cosmic order. According to Hesiod, Tartarus was the place that imprisoned the Titans, who posed a challenge to the cosmological regime established by the Olympian gods (Hes. *Theog.* 729, 814). The 'gates' (*pulai*, Hes. *Theog.* 811) that guarded the entrance to Tartarus were built by Poseidon himself, and were guarded by the Hundred-Handers, one of whom was Poseidon's son-in-law. The purpose of this enclosure was for the Titans to be 'hidden' (*kekruphatai*, Hes. *Theog.* 730) by a wall that surrounded them from all sides. In Thessaly, Poseidon displayed an identical mode of action regarding walls and enclosures but in reverse: by 'breaking open' (Hdt. 7.129, the same verb as in Hom. *Il.* 20.63, *anarrēgnumi*) the enclosing ring of mountains, he creates open 'gates' (*pulai*) in order to 'reveal' (*anakaluptein*) the Thessalian plain by removing its watery cover. Arguably, both the action of revealing the fertile Thessalian plain and concealing the monstrous Titans serve the purpose of promoting order and containing chaos.

Indeed, Poseidon's hypothetical ability in Homer *Iliad* 20.56-65 to expose Tartarus to mortals and immortals represents a direct threat to the established order. This is indicated by the epic formula 'shining upon mortals and immortals' (*Il.* 20.64), variations of which are typically reserved for the sun.[38] In fact, a similar threat of exposing the houses of the dead is uttered by Helios himself in the *Odyssey*. The context is the cattle of the sun-god, which Odysseus' companions have foolishly slaughtered. Helios tells Zeus that unless he is compensated for his cattle, he will go down to Hades and shine among the dead, a threat that would upend the cosmic order (*Od.* 12.382-83). Zeus responds that Helios should 'keep shining (*phaeine*) upon mortals and immortals' (*Od.* 12.385-86). As compensation for his lost cattle, Zeus promises to strike Odysseus' ship with lightning and shatter it to pieces. Helios' threat to expose is based on his control over the movement of the sun. Hades' fear in Homer *Iliad* 20.61-65, by contrast, is based on Poseidon's control over the breaking open of the earth as a way to expose what must remain hidden.

Levelling the Achaean wall

The power of Poseidon to break things open is attested in another context in the *Iliad*, which sheds further light on his mode of action in rendering things seen or unseen in the landscape. While the earthquake in Homer *Iliad* 20.56-65 threatens to *uncover* things by breaking open, the scene at the Achaean wall in Homer *Iliad* 7.459-63 (cf. Hom. *Il.* 12.24-32) displays Poseidon's ability to *cover* things by breaking open. The same verb *anarrēgnumi* ('I break up/open'), quite rare in Archaic poetry, is used in a passage describing Poseidon's desire to destroy the Achaean wall. The Achaeans, anxious to protect their ships beached on the shores of Troy, have fortified their camp with ramparts, ditches and walls (Hom. *Il.* 7.436-41). The gods take notice, and at an Olympic council Poseidon complains to Zeus that no appropriate hecatombs have been given. What is more, the fame of the great Achaean wall threatens to eclipse that of the Trojan walls, which were built by Poseidon and Apollo. While the latter argument seems more personal to Poseidon and explains his particular interest in the matter, both the failed sacrifices and the rivalry with the Trojan wall are ultimately threats to his honour. In his reply, Zeus addresses this concern explicitly, reassuring Poseidon that 'your honour (*kleos*) will last as long as the light of dawn is scattered' (Hom. *Il.* 7.458, cf. 7.451). Poseidon's honour is tied to the fate of the Achaean and Trojan walls. Zeus realizes this and tells Poseidon (Hom. *Il.* 7.459-63, tr. Lattimore, adapted):

Come now, after once more the flowing-haired Achaeans
have gone back with their ships to the beloved land of their fathers,
break up (*anarrēxas*) their wall and scatter (*katacheuai*) it into the salt sea
and again cover (*kalupsai*) the great beach with sand;
so let the great wall of the Achaeans be levelled (*amaldunētai*).

The mode of destruction employed by Poseidon (or at least so proposed by Zeus) is not only to break up and to scatter, but also 'to cover' (*kalupsai*) – the same verb Heraclides would use to describe what happened to Helike. In the *Iliad* passage, Poseidon's concern with the utter removal of any visible sign of the wall is motivated by the threat to his *kleos*. Breaking up the Achaean wall, scattering it into the sea, and finally covering the beach with sand ensures the total effacing of the wall's traces. The verb form *amaldunētai*, which the scholiast glosses as *aphanizētai* ('is made to disappear'), underscores this effect: literally, *amaldunein* means 'to soften or smoothen'; in the case of the wall, it is a disappearing by smoothening or levelling. The effacing of any sign of the Achaean wall renders its surface a blank slate, devoid of points of orientation and hence changing it beyond recognition.[39] This mode of action recalls the uncovering of Thessaly in my first example, insofar as the result is a smooth and level plain, 'just like the sea' (*kathaper thalattas*, Philostr. *Imag.* 2.14). In the case of the erasing of the Achaean wall, this is achieved through two elements exemplary in their disorienting uniformity: water and sand, that is, the sea and the beach. In this way, Poseidon's agency manifests itself by smoothening out and covering up the visual signs that threaten his honour.

This interpretation is strengthened by the opening of *Iliad* 12, when Homer returns to the ordained fate of the Achaean wall in more detail. The poet announces that in the tenth year, when Troy has been sacked and the Achaeans have returned home, 'then at last Poseidon and Apollo took counsel to level (*amaldunai*) the wall, letting loose the strength of the rivers' (Hom. *Il.* 12.17). Three gods are involved in the destruction of the wall: Apollo, Zeus and Poseidon (Hom. *Il.* 12.24-32, tr. Lattimore, adapted):

> Phoebus Apollo turned the mouths of these waters together
> and for nine days threw the flood against the wall, and Zeus rained
> incessantly, to break the wall faster and wash it seaward.
> And the Earth-Shaker (*Ennosigaios*) himself holding in his hands the trident
> guided them, and hurled into the waves all the foundations (*themeilia*)
> of logs and stones, which the toiling Achaeans had put in place,
> and made all smooth (*leia*) again near the hard-running Hellespont
> and once again covered (*kalupse*) the great beach with sand
> after levelling (*amaldunas*) the wall.

Apollo manipulates the landscape by redirecting the rivers, Zeus rains down heavily from above, and Poseidon, who is portrayed as the leader of the effort, attacks the very 'foundations' (*themeilia*) of the wall. This is consistent with his titles *Ennosigaios* ('Earth-Shaker'), *Asphaleios* ('Securer'), and *Themeliouchos* ('Upholder of Foundations,' *SEG* 30.93, *IDélos* 290.116), and his tendency to destroy, as we have seen, from the bottom up. Pausanias, too, emphasizes how Helike was destroyed from its very foundations. Furthermore, Homer mentions that Poseidon made the land all 'smooth' (*leia*) again, before concluding with a close variant on the lines in *Iliad* 7.462-63, both of which include covering with sand (*kalupse/kalupsai*) and levelling (*amaldunas/amaldunētai*).

In his joint effort with Apollo to destroy the Achaean wall, Poseidon's mode of action involves breaking up and overturning foundations not, as in the cosmic earthquake of *Iliad* 20, to expose things, but now to cover up that which threatens his honour.

Indices of Poseidon

I could cite here further examples of Poseidon's significant interventions, such as his threat to 'cover on all sides' (*amphikalupsai*, Hom. *Od.* 13.158) the city of the Phaeacians with a mountain; or the flood legend told at Argos and its cult of Poseidon *Prosklustios* ('of the Surging Water', Paus. 2.22.4). But one instance from the Gigantomachy is, by way of conclusion, especially revealing. The visual record of Poseidon's battle with the giant Polybotes underscores Poseidon's ability to reveal and conceal. Several Attic red-figure vases from the late Archaic and early Classical periods show Poseidon wielding an enormous rock looming over the giant as he is about to fall.[40] The rock represents the volcanic island Nisyros, which itself is a piece that Poseidon has 'broken off' (*aporrēxas*, Apollod. *Bibl.* 1.6.2) the island Kos. On two such vases, the artist has depicted several small animals on the rock, including a scorpion, an octopus, a snake, a hedgehog and a deer.[41] By depicting the animals, the artist makes clear that the rock is in fact an entire island, complete with indigenous fauna.

But the presence of the animals serves another function that has to do with Poseidon's ability to uncover things. The animals depicted on these vases are experts at deception and hiding, whether through cunning (octopus, hedgehog, scorpion), chthonic connections (snake, scorpion), or swiftness of foot (deer). An ancient proverb, for example, warns against the scorpion lurking under every stone (e.g. Praxilla 750); a drinking-song offers a particular interpretation: 'Under every stone, my friend, a scorpion lurks. Take care that it does not strike you: all manner of trickery accompanies what is unseen (*aphanei*)' (*PMG* 903). The gigantic rock hurled by Poseidon certainly represents the brute, elemental force with which he conceals his enemy; but the creatures depicted on it also suggest that the breaking off, or unearthing, of the stone reveals things that are usually unseen. Poseidon has not just broken off any rock, he has overturned something at its very foundations, bringing to light animals that excel at hiding, yet no longer remain hidden.

At the same time, the projectile cast by Poseidon's hand *becomes* the island (Strabo 10.5.16). The very presence of Nisyros is an index of Poseidon. Its concealment of a hostile force (Polybotes) parallels the punishment of the Helikonians who committed *asebeia*. There, the very absence of Helike is an index of Poseidon. At Troy, too, traces of the offending wall are effaced as the foundations are overturned and the lands made smooth again, like the level plain of the sea, or the Thessalian plain. These physical, environmental effects at Thessaly and Helike, on the one hand, and at Troy and Nisyros on the other, become typical indices that point to Poseidon's agency.

To be sure, the actions of the anthropomorphic god of myth and epic, who conceals Polybotes under an island and uproots the foundations of the Achaean wall, differ from those portrayed in the writings of Strabo, Diodorus Siculus and Pausanias. In Helike's disaster discourse, Poseidon's angry agency becomes visible indirectly through the environmental signs – or lack thereof. But I am not suggesting that the present analysis of Poseidon's mode of action accounts for all his interventions in myth, ritual and history, nor that parts of his mode of action, such as covering up, cannot be shared with other gods. What I do propose is that understanding the environmental upheaval of the Helike disaster requires a full accounting of Poseidon's agency along the lines sketched out in this essay. This, then, goes beyond the conscious beliefs, transmitted by Diodorus Siculus, which might lead us to identify the god's field of action only; it is on the subconscious level of language that beliefs about the god's mode of action become apparent. And indeed, a remarkable consistency in how Poseidon's mode of action is imagined to operate emerges: his agency can become apparent in his ability to cover things up (*kaluptein*) and render them unseen (*aphanizein*), effects that are accomplished by breaking open (*anarrēgnusthai*) mountains or the earth itself, overturning foundations (*themeilia*), and leveling surfaces to make them smooth (*leia*). If Helike's disaster discourse is informed by Poseidon's perceived agency, our understanding of the meaning of Helike depends on the way Poseidon is imagined to operate. In turn, Poseidon's disaster agency as reflected in myth reveals how historical disasters like that of Helike are remembered in discourse.

Notes

1. The main sources are: Ael. *NA* 11.19, Arist. *Mete.* 343b, 368a-b, Diod. Sic. 15.48-49, Ov, *Met.* 15.293-95, Paus. 7.24.6, 7.24.12, 7.25.8–9, Plin. *HN* 2.206, Sen. *QNat.* 6.23.4, 6.26.3, with reference to Callisthenes (= *FGrH* 124 F 19), Strabo 8.7.2, with references to Heraclides (= Wehrli F 46a) and Eratosthenes (= Berger F III B 103).

2. M. Aur. *Med.* 4.48.1. This is the Helike of the imaginary; in reality, life resumed, and excavations have shown activity again in the Helike plain as early as the third century BCE, see Katsonopoulou 2016: 137–52. On the cultural construction of the Helike disaster in Antiquity and lessons that may be drawn for our present debates about anthropogenic climate change, see Walter 2016: 31–43.

3. On the religious interpretation of natural disaster, see Sonnabend 2012: 261–6, Steinberg 2006, esp. xiii–xiv.

4. Burkert 1996: 103, 110–11 (Helike).

5. Cashman and Cronin 2008: 417, with bibliography.

6. For some of the recent contributions of cognitive approaches to the study of ancient religion, see Larson 2016, Eidinow, Geertz, North 2022, Mackey 2022. For agency detection, see especially Boyer 2001: 93–167. On divine agency in particular, see Pongratz-Leisten and Sonik 2015: 3–69.

7. Tremlin 2006: 76.

8. Larson 2016: 74–6; Tremlin 2006: 76.

9. Seminal works include Guthrie 1993, Barrett 2000: 31–2, Barrett 2011.

10. Struck 2007: 16.

11. Burkert 1996: 160.

12. Peirce's triadic sign 'is something which stands to somebody for something in some respect or capacity' (Peirce 2.228); or, 'to put it more precisely, something is taken as the basis for a process of inference' (Manetti 1993: 14). Technically, an index is not a type of sign, but a relation between the sign-vehicle (representamen) and the object: other signs in this trichotomy are icons and symbols.

13. Eidinow 2022: 73.

14. Kohn 2007: 5–6, Kohn 2013.

15. For intuitive-knowledge-domain violations, see Barrett 2000: 31. The sandal is thus a 'minimally counter-intuitive concept' (MCI), for which, in the context of Greek religion, see Larson 2016: 19–20.

16. Ibid.: 21.

17. In contrast, the Romans did not hold any god in particular responsible, consistent with their ideas of prodigies and the expiatory formula *si deo si deae* ('whether to the god or to the goddess,' Gell. 2.28). Waldherr 1997; for the epigraphic evidence, see Ehmig 2016: 37–59.

18. Whether the paintings Philostratus describes are real or not does not concern us here.

19. For Strabo on Helike, see Baladie 1980: 145–57.

20. *kata mēnin Athēnas sunebē* (13.1.40; shipwreck); *kata mēnin tēs theou* (12.8.9; disease). While *mēnis* is a Homeric word and the subject of the *Iliad*, the phrase *kata mēnin* is not attested until Aeschines and, if Strabo is quoting verbatim, Heraclides (both fourth century BCE). Still, the Homeric resonance of *mēnis* as not just an emotional state, but 'a sanction meant to guarantee and maintain the integrity of the world order' may still be felt (Muellner 1996: 26).

21. For Diodorus and his sources for Book 15, see Stylianou 1998: 25–132.

22. See Walter 2016: 37–8. For the cult of Poseidon Helikonios, see Katsonopoulou 2021.

23. Simon 1969: 69

24. Burkert 1985: 139.

25. Bremmer 2006.

26. Chaniotis 1998: 404–16.

27. See, for example, Dumézil 1966: 179, 229, and Dumézil 1973: 10–16, with critical analysis and application to Greek polytheism in Detienne 2008: 57–78.

28. The meaning of this epithet is uncertain because of the latter part of the compound: an inscription from Sparta (*IG* V, 1.213) has *gaiawochos*, which would suggest the epithet does not belong to *echein* ('hold'), but to the root **uegh-* 'to move, carry'. Chantraine has postulated 'to shake.' See Burkert 1985: 402 n. 21. For a different interpretation, see Thély 2016: 24–30.

29. Detienne 2008: 61. Emphasis is mine.

30. Ibid. Emphasis in the original. See also Vernant 1990: 109.

31. As divine epithet: Sapph. Fr. 55; Soph. *OC* 1566. As astrological term: Vett. Val. 1.14, 6.22.

32. Stubblefield 2015: 11, where the term is used to understand the visual representations of the 9/11 disaster.

33. On Greek conceptions of darkness, see Eidinow in this volume.

34. Aelian uses the same verb to refer to the disappearance of Helike (*NA* 11.19).

35. Pliny *HN* 2.94, Ov. *Met.* 15.293-95, Strabo 8.7.2.

36. A chorus in Aeschylus praises the water of the Theban River Dirke, which 'Earth-holder Poseidon' and the children of Tethys send forth (Aesch. *Sept.* 304). Cf. Pind. *Ol.* 6.58. Burkert 1985: 139 points to the Aeschylus passage to suggest that 'all springs are said to be sent by Poseidon', but that seems an exaggeration to me. There is, however, a clear connection between Poseidon *Hippios* (of the Horse) and fresh-water springs. The epithet Epilimnios (Poseidon of the Lake) may be connected to this aspect of the deity as well (*SEG* 28.690; 32.1273; Hesychius *s.v.* 'Epilimnios').

37. Simon 1969: 69–70

38. *athanatoisi phaeinoi / kai thnētoisi brotoisin,* Hom. *Od.* 3.2-3, cf. *thnētoisi kai athanatoisi phaneiē,* Hom. *Il.* 20.64. The line ending is similar, with active and passive optative of *phainein,* respectively.

39. The Achaean wall scene has been read as a naïve device to explain the absence of traces of this wall in historical times. This is the view taken by the scholiast, cf. Aristotle Fr. 162 (= Strabo 13.1.36).

40. *LIMC s.v.* Poseidon 177–8, 180; two black-figure vases depict the rock without animals or plants (*LIMC s.v.* Poseidon 174–5).

41. Attic red-figure column crater (fifth century BCE), Kunsthistorisches Museum Wien, Antikensammlung, IV 688.

CHAPTER 8
RIVER, AGENCY AND GENDER: AN ECOCRITICAL READING OF THE MYTHS OF THE TIBER

Krešimir Vuković

The Tiber is one of the most studied rivers in the ancient world*. The river of Rome has been explored from a variety of perspectives, literary, archaeological and religious.[1] However, scholars have failed to appreciate it as an entity in its own right – as a natural element with its own agency. Agency is defined as a relational quality between human and non-human things that has an impact on the real world.[2] Following recent calls to investigate the agency of non-human elements and the ways in which they actively shape the world, this paper studies the river of Rome as an agent that has made a substantial impact on Roman history.[3]

The river Tiber often shifted and changed the landscape of Rome. River flooding was at times so extensive that it covered all the low-lying areas of the city, sometimes reaching as far as the Forum Romanum, leaving destruction and sediment in its wake.[4] But the impact of the Tiber on the Roman landscape was not restricted to flooding alone, as new archaeological research in the area of the Velabrum and Forum Boarium indicates.[5] The river ran much closer to the Palatine hill in the sixth century BCE, when changes in the river course created the characteristic crescent-shaped bend around the Campus Martius,[6] and formed the Tiber Island itself through processes of alluviation and sedimentation. If these archaeological studies are correct, we should expect to find evidence of this great disturbance in the natural environment of Rome. This essay argues that, although the majority of our literary and artistic evidence is several centuries removed from the period in question, traces of an ecological understanding of these major changes survive in the form of myths passed down the generations, which put the environment centre stage.

My approach to eliciting this evidence combines traditional historical, literary and textual methods with a novel ecocritical appreciation of the power of myth to reflect social and environmental perspectives. Following the examples of Esther Eidinow and Christopher Schliephake, who have both recently analysed ancient myths as cultural forms that reflect ecological knowledge,[7] I argue that a whole range of Roman myths can be read as ways of understanding the natural environment and its relationship with Roman society. Using the paradigm of storied ecology to underline the ecological aspect of these stories, I call a number of Roman myths 'myths of the Tiber' in order to stress their fluvial dimension.[8]

The Tiber is not only a backdrop against which the action of a story is set, I argue, but also an active agent that shapes the setting and drives the action forward. In a number of

Roman myths, it would be impossible for the human protagonists to perform their acts of valour without the Tiber landscape, which naturally encompasses not only the riverbed but also the river valley and all the spaces that the river shapes by its ceaseless activity, including the variety of creatures which it sustains in the process (and that form the river ecosystem). Analysing ancient sources for the Tiber myths in their historical and literary context,[9] I argue that the notion of river fluidity is central to most imaginative recreations of the Tiber landscape, especially when it comes to gender diversity in the representations of river characters as well as the river itself.

Roman foundation myths

I start with the most famous myth of Rome, its foundation by Romulus and Remus. This was a charter myth in Roman imagination and fundamentally shaped Roman identity. As we will see, in the 'canonical' version of the foundation myth, Livy places the fluvial landscape centre stage; this is surprising, given that ancient historians had a habit of making the landscape a decorative background.[10] Indeed, most modern discussions of this ancient tale skirt over that fact and narrate the all-too-familiar tale of the she-wolf, the shepherd Faustulus and his wife Acca Larentia. But, as I will argue, it is no accident that the most famous myth of Rome, the birth of the twins, takes place during a flood.

In the myth, Romulus and Remus are placed in a basket and delivered to a she-wolf by the flooding river Tiber. Livy expatiates on this aspect of the story in two meandering, structurally complex sentences:[11]

forte quadam diuinitus super ripas Tiberis effusus lenibus stagnis nec adiri usquam ad iusti cursum poterat amnis et posse quamuis languida mergi aqua infantes spem ferentibus dabat. ita uelut defuncti regis imperio in proxima alluuie ubi nunc ficus Ruminalis est—Romularem uocatam ferunt—pueros exponunt ... cum fluitantem aluueum quo expositi erant pueri tenuis in sicco aqua destituisset ...

It happened perhaps by some divine providence that the Tiber having spread beyond its banks into stagnant pools afforded nowhere any access to the regular channel of the river, and led the men who brought the twins to hope that being infants they might be drowned, no matter how sluggish the stream. So they made shift to discharge the king's command, by exposing the babes at the nearest point of the overflow, where the fig-tree Ruminalis now stands ... when the receding water left the floating basket in which the children had been exposed on dry land ...

Livy's tangled web of constructions reflects the chaotic diluvial landscape. Romulus and Remus are saved from certain death by a river in flood and safely delivered to a she-wolf. Scholars agree that the appearance of the she-wolf is miraculous and adds an incredible element to the story.[12] But just as surprising as the monstrous mother she-wolf, is the monstrous father Tiber.

The myth conveys a profound truth about the foundation of Rome: without the river there would be no city. The floating basket slowly drifts on the shallow waters on the floodplain and reaches the Lupercal cave at the foot of the Palatine hill. The language of myth connects the flooding river with the first settlements on the hills. The Tiber is not simply a backdrop to the narrative action. Livy gives a detailed description of the river (overspreading its banks, sluggish stream, stagnant pools, river course, overflow) and even allows for the role of divine providence without specifically attributing it to any particular god.[13] Notably, in both sentences the subject is the river Tiber (*Tiberis*), once referred to as 'shallow water' (*tenuis aqua*) and then by his actual name and personified through the expression *spem dabat* ('gave hope'), a metaphor that makes the river an active agent. Livy's detailed account of a river in flood reveals a number of key fluvial elements that were familiar to the people of Rome from experience. But iconographic evidence presents an even more colourful picture.

An altar from Ostia (dated *ante* 124 CE) contains a relief depicting the scene of the foundation myth, giving a fascinating glimpse of the way in which the ancients perceived their environment.[14] Sacrificial ram heads and festoons frame the picture of a diverse fluvial landscape: in addition to the iconic she-wolf and the shepherds (here, Faustulus is given a doublet), Father Tiber occupies a prominent place in the foreground, next to the she-wolf. This is a typical depiction of the river as a masculine, bearded, semi-naked, muscular god in a reclining pose, holding reeds in one hand and a jar in the other, and wearing an undulating dress suggestive of waves. The proliferation of reeds in the background is a clear marker of the river's banks, and Tiber's grip on a reed stalk conveys his mastery of the fluvial setting. The protrusions on the left side suggest the elevation of the Palatine hill and the Lupercal cave (connected to the she-wolf). Though the relief is damaged, one can discern a whole range of other animals placed in the central plane between the Tiber and the eagle, including a goat, a snake, a mouse, a lizard, a snail and a hare.

This is an environment teeming with non-human life, illuminating Livy's remark that 'there was a vast solitary wilderness in these places then' (*vastae tum in his locis solitudines erant*),[15] where the defining feature of the wilderness is the lack of humans, a perspective that neglects the non-human richness of flora and fauna. The copious fauna on the relief stands in contrast to this view, revealing why the Tiber is usually overlooked in telling the story of the foundation of Rome. While our modern perspective tends to frame rivers as inactive 'natural' elements with no agency, the Tiber emerges as a living agent in these ancient accounts.

The vivid representation of the Ostia altar conceptualizes the river in religious terms. Tiberinus was a god in Roman religion, who (not which) takes an active role in the salvation of the twins.[16] This image contradicts the modern conception of a river as a random mass of inactive water. The fluvial landscape is a lush environment with all sorts of plant and animal species that the river sustains.[17] Contrary to the rational view, the myth represents the river as a living supernatural entity. Tiberinus is a god and the twins are only one item in the rich web of life that he facilitates. Far from being its defining feature, the human animal is only one piece in a larger system: the twins are the object (rather than the subject) of the action and the two shepherds, though very large figures, recoil from the scene.

The myth idealizes the flood as an act of divine providence, seen as extraordinary. The foundation myth is set in a fluvial landscape during a flood, a destructive event that could kill thousands. But one can hardly expect the myth to be a faithful representation of historical floods. Tiber's parental role in the story is as miraculous as the motherly care of the savage she-wolf. The myth is not a faithful representation of historical events, but an attempt to conceptualize Rome's natural environment in relation to the city and its founding. There are many other instances that feature flooding as a crucial aspect of coexistence with the river.

Flooding was a continuous problem affecting large areas of the city well into the imperial period. One of the most memorable floods took place in January 27 BCE on the night the *princeps* assumed his new name, *Augustus*.[18] Horace (*Carm.* 1.2) says that the floodwaters of the raging river reached the temple of Vesta. Though most historians have taken Horace's poem as referring to omens after the death of Caesar in 44 BCE,[19] Nisbet and Hubbard rightly point out that the poem was heavily influenced by Vergil's *Georgics* and must have been composed after it, most likely in response to the momentous flood of 27 BCE.[20] Horace deliberately inverts Vergil's *Georgic* 1 where Vesta and Romulus are asked to protect the Tiber and the Palatine.[21] The reader is left to wonder what to make of Horace's ambivalent flood, with its seeming lack of reverence for traditional Roman cults.

Of course, Horace need not be referring to any single event in particular, not least because the Tiber flooded about every five years on average. But the extraordinary extent of the recent flood and the immediacy of Horace's 'we have seen' (*vidimus*) suggests that his readers would share the memorable experience:[22]

> *vidimus flavom Tiberim retortis*
> *litore Etrusco violenter undis*
> *ire deiectum monumenta regis*
>   *templaque Vestae,*
> *Iliae dum se nimium querenti*
> *iactat ultorem, vagus et sinistra*
> *labitur ripa Iove non probante*
>   *uxorius amnis.*

We have seen the yellow Tiber, its waves
hurled back from the Tuscan bank, proceed
to wreck the king's monuments including
Vesta's shrine,
while the river boasted that he was avenging
the bitterly protesting Ilia, and without
Jove's permission, flowed far and wide over
the left bank, like a fond husband.

The poem starts with images of storm, hail and thunder before continuing with an exaggerated description of an ominous flood that makes sea creatures swim in the hills.[23] The flood is then explained through a mythic cause (*aition*): unhappy over the treatment of his wife Ilia, the Tiber spills over his banks and endangers Rome's eternal flame in the heart of the city. The impression of the catastrophe is even more powerful because Ilia was a Vestal Virgin, a priest of one of the most sacred cults of Rome. Raymond Clark suggests that the Tiber is angry because Vesta had failed to save her priestess.[24] Abandoned by her goddess, Ilia threw herself into the river after giving birth to the twins.

Tiber's anger seems excessive and unwarranted: 'to go against with force' (*violente ire*) implies a violent attack on the most sacred institution of Rome and 'wandering' (*vagus*) conveys the sense of an impetuous and uncontrollable river. These are not the normal workings of nature but an extraordinary event that needs explanation. Horace delays the final word used to describe the river, 'conjugal, like a husband' (*uxorius*), which, after all the acts of destructive violence committed by the river, seems a surprising epithet. The adjective seems to cast the Tiber in the mould of a familiar elegiac trope, that of a wronged lover or vengeful husband; and the poet deliberately contrasts the abnormal behaviour of the Tiber with that of cosmic Jupiter who reigns supreme over the universe.[25]

Horace gives the Tiber a forceful personality arising from his relationship with Ilia and manifested in excessive flooding. We have seen that Tiber was closely involved with the foundation myth, but his connection to Ilia is not immediately obvious. Ilia's coupling with the river may be a result of his parental care of the children that she had to abandon or of the structural composition of the myth, which consists of binary oppositions (fire and water).[26] In any case, Horace strikes at the heart of fluvial ambivalence permeating many Tiber myths, which often feature an interplay between male and female gender. As we shall see, Ilia (meaning 'nourishment') represents the feminine side of the river (typically represented as male) whose main characteristic is fluidity.[27]

The Tiber in the *Aeneid*

Horace is not the only poet to render the Tiber as a character with strong volition. Vergil famously casts Tiberinus as an active agent that shapes the fate of Rome even before Romulus: he appears to the wandering Aeneas in a dream at the beginning of *Aeneid* Book 8 and tells him to sacrifice piglets to Juno and go the site of Rome. Vergil has Tiberinus welcome and encourage Aeneas, but the river god also introduces himself as a powerful 'river in full force of a flood' (*pleno flumine*), with a threatening image of 'tearing his banks and slicing through fruitful fields' (*stringentem ripas et pinguia culta secantem*).[28] Words of consolation and the prophecy of victory are capped off with a mysterious warning: 'you too will have to pay due honours to me' (*victor honorem persolves*), a hint of Aeneas' death to come (on the riverbanks).[29] Aeneas awakes to find the river flood has subsided and makes his offering, invoking the Tiber as 'horned ruler of Hesperian waters' (*corniger Herperidum rengator aquarum*).[30] He and his crew then sail up the tranquil waters of the river, so placid that they reflect the overhanging trees like a mirror. As

Rebecca Armstrong recently noticed,[31] the sylvan landscape comes alive as the Trojans sail up the river: the waves and the trees stand in awe of Trojan warships.[32]

The Trojan invaders are the first to disturb the idealized landscape of primitive Italy with warships.[33] It would be wrong, however, to assume that it had previously been a golden age, as the natives are prone to violence and greed. Tiberinus' mixed message to Aeneas betrays a similar sense of ambivalence: the instructions for and promise of a peaceful passage upstream come with a warning of future sacrifice. The closing image of flooding, with the river tearing its shores and slicing fruitful fields is threatening and violent. The Tiber is fully in control of its waters and decides the fate of Rome. The seeming placidity of the Trojans' rowing up the river is broken by the image of oars cutting the trees in their aquatic reflection.[34] The various elements of the ecosystem blend in the image of trees reflected in the water. The mirror illusion renders the fleeting image in perspective: the Trojans may think they are in control as active agents, but it is in fact the fluvial landscape that takes them in and allows them safe passage.

Similarly, the landscape's sense of wonder at the Trojan ships is not merely a sentimental metaphor, but underlies the sense of fluvial agency that Vergil established in Aeneas' dream and in several scenes of *Aeneid* Book 7. The war starts when Ascanius shoots the beautiful stag of Silvia, the daughter of king Latinus' chief herdsman, and the animal returns home 'similar to someone imploring' (*imploranti similis*).[35] As I have recently argued, this crucial scene is set on the banks of the Tiber, which Vergil signals with the word *fluvio* (always used to denote the Tiber in Books 7–9, thirteen instances in total).[36] The stag's ambivalent human/animal status gains more significance because of his great horns, a characteristic shared by the river (*corniger*) and a sign of strength, because rivers were often depicted as horned bulls. Vergil twice denotes Silvia's relationship with the stag with the word *soror*, implying his adoption.[37] The blending of human and non-human associations is reinforced through the name of Silvia, a feminine of Silvius,[38] Aeneas' future son with Lavinia, who will found the Silvian dynasty of Alban kings. Finally, the first men to fall in the conflict that ensues between Trojans and Latins are named after Italian rivers: Almo and Galaesus are described as just men and are the first innocent victims of unnecessary carnage.[39]

Thus, Vergil gives the Tiber a crucial role in shaping the fate of Rome and casts Tiberinus as a god with a strong will and power. He associates the river with the stag of Silvia, whom he calls his sister, but she only plays a secondary role in the episode of the stag's death. It is time to explore other Tiber myths that feature female characters as protagonists.

River and gender

Vergil's poetic vision echoes iconographic representations of the river projecting masculine strength. In all depictions the Tiber is a strong bearded man with toned muscles.[40] In Vergil's telling of these myths, this 'macho' man is repeatedly coupled with an ill-defined female character: both Ilia and Silvia are fleeting presences that make a single appearance on the stage.[41] But if one looks beyond Vergil and the literary narratives, it is possible to uncover the full significance of gender in Tiber myths. The literary versions of Tiber's gendered relations were not mere poetic 'personifications' or products of pathetic fallacy.

In Latin, the river of Rome was usually called *Tiberis* but the god of the Tiber had a special cultic name, *Tiberinus*. Particularly interesting are religious concepts and stories that connect Tiberinus with female deities: Tiberinus and Gaia shared a temple on Tiber Island. The joint feast of these deities was celebrated on 8 December in the early Republican calendar. This festival has a counterpart exactly half a year earlier, the Tiber games (*ludi Tiberini*) celebrated by fishermen on 8 June, one day before the great festival of the Vestalia, which ended when the refuse from the temple of Vesta was ceremoniously thrown into the river.[42] The juxtaposition of the festival of Vesta with the games on the Tiber can hardly be accidental. As we have seen, the masculine river of Rome is repeatedly coupled with a female partner. Ilia's lament is not a mere poetic speculation, but has an older mythic background.

The identity of Gaia, Tiberinus' partner in the island temple, has puzzled scholars. Several years ago, I argued that she is best identified with Gaia Taracia, a Vestal who was remembered because 'she donated the Campus Tiberinus or else Campus Martius to the Roman people' (*quod campum Tiberinum sive Martium populo condonasset*).[43] The place name 'Campus Tiberinus' is only attested in Latin in Gellius (*a hapax legomenon*) and, unless we understand it as another name for Campus Martius, it is a complete mystery to what it refers.

But perhaps there is a clue elsewhere: this action of Gaia Taracia finds an unlikely parallel in the life of a prostitute, Acca Larentia, who was worshipped on the banks of the Tiber in the Velabrum. Cato the Elder says she also donated several fields to the Roman people, but their names are otherwise unknown.[44] It is clear enough, however, that the donations of Acca and Gaia focus on fields of land adjacent to the river. Both the Larentalia (on 23 December) and the joint feast of Tiberinus and Gaia fall in December, a peak time of seasonal flooding. Larentia had a tomb in the Velabrum and a later story tells of her love affair with Hercules, who had several temples to the south of this area, in the Forum Boarium.[45] Archaeological evidence suggests the valley of the Velabrum was filled in by the river through the process of alluviation and flooding; in the regal period the river ran much farther east than in the Republic and the change of course was accompanied by heavy sedimentation of the Forum Boarium.[46] Thus, Acca Larentia's cult and love story reflect ecological knowledge about the Velabrum valley as the product of substantial river activity at a time of great environmental and political change.

Theodor Mommsen proposed that we should see Gaia's tale as a later reinterpretation of Acca's donation of land.[47] But the Vestal's tale is consistent with her ritual coupling with Tiberinus and the myth of Gaia Taracia is fully embedded in Rome's topography, even shifting its narrative content under the influence of river flux. The name of Gaia's donation of land, *campus Tiberinus*, triggered a futile search for its location and most modern scholars simply explained it as a reference to the Campus Martius.[48] The Tiber field in the myth of Gaia Taracia is neither the field of Mars nor the Tiber Island, though it probably did refer to some of those areas at some point in the ecological history of the ever-changing river, meandering like a snake through its landscape.[49]

Scholars of Roman topography look for stable and specific places but the shifting waters of the winding river elude such endeavours. Any field created by river activity could have been called 'Tiber field' including – but not limited to – the Campus Martius. While we may not be able to solve the historical question, we can observe how ancient imaginations spun stories that ascribed the creation of these fields (which were in reality a product of the processes of flooding, alluviation and change of river course) to the generous benefactions of women, Gaia Taracia and Acca Larentia. We can also respect the natural fluidity of the river and the instability of river landscape by not insisting on identifying any fixed point as the definitive location of 'Tiber field.'

If one must look for Tiber fields on a map of Rome, the most conspicuous candidates are the Campus Martius and the Tiber Island. Both areas grew in size and height with the flooding and sedimentation triggered by the shift in river course in the sixth century BCE.[50] The name Taracia suggests an aetiological link with the Tarentum,[51] a sanctuary of the underworld gods placed on the bend of the Campus Martius. In the myth of the origin of the Tiber Island the grain sheaves reaped after the expulsion of King Tarquin are harvested on the Campus Martius and thrown into the Tiber.[52] Floating downstream on the river they mix with mud and accumulate at Tiber Island. This myth clearly reflects the processes of flooding, sedimentation and alluviation while stressing the changing nature of the landscape. The transformation of the environment is rendered in terms of an agricultural metaphor: the myth attempts to convey the river shift that moved sediment downstream to form the Tiber Island. Grain signifies both agricultural prosperity and expansion of land because grain expands in water. The interplay of political and environmental instability gives a sense of contingency that characterized the first days of the Roman Republic, under threat from all sides. The new island was also far from stable; river islands are 'of a nomadic nature'.[53] Hence Livy closes his account of the story by noting that humans must have raised the ground further and added embankments.[54] The river shapes the natural environment and people respond in kind, seeking with their own interventions to modify the landscape and make it more stable for human use. The story of interaction between human and non-human agents is never a one-way street.

Constructing gender

It is time to step back and attempt to connect the various strands produced by the effusion of river myths. One should do this with awareness of Heraclitus' famous saying that 'one can never step in the same river twice'.[55] Though the many images of the changing river are in constant flux, they present an emerging pattern when considered together: the masculine Tiber is a powerful river prone to flooding, conceptualized as an outburst of rage or a sign of divine displeasure. In this sense the Tiber is comparable with Jupiter, the staple image of Roman masculinity transposed onto the divine realm. In Horace, Tiber's rage seems excessive and uncontrollable as his waters cover large areas of the city, disrupt life in the centre and threaten civic cults. The Tiber often has a female partner, such as Ilia and Gaia. The role of the Tiber's female partners may seem small and shadowy,[56] but myths of land donation indicate that they had a larger role in conceptualizations of river activity. How does one account for the gendered aspect of these Tiber myths?

One possible solution comes from ecofeminist theory: women in patriarchal societies were treated as objects of power, traditionally concentrated in the hands of men. In many instances throughout history, women have been associated with nature as fertile and nourishing mothers (qua mother Earth), subjugated to male dominance.[57] Roman conquerors certainly perceived the natural world as separate from culture (with the exception of religious spaces such as sacred groves) and exercised male dominance over nature in a way similar to the male supervision of women.[58] While Roman elite culture was primarily a prerogative of men, we should not overlook several aspects of religion and mythology that may complicate a simple explanation that equates nature and the feminine. Representations of the Tiber align with the notion of Roman masculinity as a performative display of virtuous behaviour,[59] but the myths of the Tiber are not exclusively concerned with Tiber's power. They also contain tales of female empowerment, performed by divinized women who played an active role in Roman myth and cult.

Scholars of gender theory have argued that the female gender in Rome was constructed in terms of emotion/affection, 'softness' (*mollitia*) and lack of control, in contrast to the masculine ideal of *virtus*, performed through strength, control of one's emotions, and power over others.[60] In this register, the varied and rich span of river actions and states could not be encapsulated by the masculine image of father Tiber because it is inadequate for the ideas of life-giving, nourishment, and land donation, all of which are clearly in the river's conceptual domain. An ecofeminist reading of this situation may lead to the conclusion that female characters were invented to convey the river's 'feminine' traits and so align the natural landscape with the construct of female gender in terms of nourishment, 'softness', and fertility.

Although ecofeminist critique rightly draws attention to the shared elements in the artificial construction of female gender and the natural world, the female protagonists of Tiber myths do not entirely fit this model. Gaia Taracia and Ilia may seem to represent stereotypical Roman women, giving and nourishing but silent and obedient. Acca Larentia was coupled with Hercules and other lovers to domesticate her and take away the agency of a powerful woman who managed a large property herself.[61] But what does one make of Claudia Quinta, the protagonist of a Roman myth placed on the mouth of the Tiber in the Second Punic War? Claudia hauled the ship carrying the sacred statue of Magna Mater up the Tiber when it was stuck on a sandbar at Ostia. In Ovid's *Fasti*, the only surviving version of the complete tale, Claudia steps in only after all other options are exhausted, and men have failed to deliver.[62] This implies that Claudia was both chaste and strong, a character trait that aligns her more closely to the model of Roman masculinity than would have been considered appropriate for Roman matrons. Moreover, her prayer (as a public performance) and association with the cult of Magna Mater, the powerful goddess who required male priests to castrate themselves, completely inverts the traditional models of Roman masculinity and femininity. One should also note that the association between the feminine and nature is usually based on the concept of the earth as a nourishing mother (widespread in world cultures),[63] not on the element of water, which is by definition varied (lakes, seas, rivers, torrents, ice, etc.) and fluid.

Thus, I argue, it is only through the concept of fluidity that one can begin to understand the many images of the river in flux with its ceaseless array of mythical images. Though rivers in Latin are always masculine, Roman grammarians recalled a time when rivers (*amnis*) were feminine, and comparative evidence confirms this hypothesis.[64] In many Indo-European traditions the gender of rivers can be either masculine or feminine, and feminine became the default in Iranian, Slavonic and Sanskrit, famously the Ganga and the Yamuna, the sacred rivers of India.[65] The Roman tradition on the Tiber originally refers to its ancient name 'Albula' as feminine.[66] The male construct of the river as a bearded father stands in contrast to a female appellative that associates it with purity and mountain origins.[67]

The female characters in Tiber myths are not *ad hoc* constructs to explain the perceived femininity of the river; rather they can be traced to ancient traditions that conceptualized the river itself as feminine. A Roman man was required to display constant, stable and controlled behaviour and any deficiency in this regard could be construed as soft and effeminate. In other words, lack of stability, inconstancy and uncontrolled displays of emotion were the hallmarks of soft and fluid identity, in contrast to the constancy required of a man. For example, Horace in his moralist guise condemns those of an unstable character (*Sat.* 2.7.12-14), such as unreliable Priscus, who changes habits and roles daily. In a very interesting mythic metaphor, Priscus is said to have been 'born with unfavourable Vertumni' (*vertumnis natus iniquis*), using the plural of Vertumnus to encapsulate the notions of hypocrisy and volatility.[68] Horace uses Vertumnus to signal unmanly qualities because this figure best reflects fluidity, which distinguishes Vertumnus as a water deity.

Timothy Morton, one of the most influential scholars of ecocriticism, has argued that queer theory and evolutionary ecology offer compatible perspectives on the network of life as fluid and composed of mutually interdependent entities.[69] The multiplicity of various beings in an ecosystem finds a cognate term in fluidity, which Judith Butler contrasts to monolithic heteronormativity and situates at the crux of queer theory.[70] The fluidity of evolution can be seen as akin to the fluidity of various social identities, if one wishes to question the game that essentializes social roles arising as a result of performance. It is this very game that Vertumnus exposes by changing shapes and forms, crossing from male to female, and from soldier to girl, as Propertius says:[71]

> *opportuna mea est cunctis natura figuris:*
> *in quamcumque uoles uerte, decorus ero.*
> *indue me Cois: fiam non dura puella;*
> *meque uirum sumpta quis neget esse toga?*

My nature is suited to all shapes. I can turn into whichever you want and I will look suitable. Put Coan silk on me and I will be a soft girl. And who would deny me a man if I put on a toga?

From the perspective of queer ecology, Vertumnus is a queer divinity that uses his fluidity to expose the performative nature of Roman gender roles. Simply by donning the typical signs of masculinity (toga) or femininity (Coan silk), Vertumnus is able to assume normative gender roles. Vertumnus' ability to change his gender at will exposes the construction of Roman gender roles as artificial and performative, rather than natural and essentialist, following Butler's theory.

This fluid god had a statue in Vicus Tuscus, a liminal space on the edge of the Forum, frequented by merchants and prostitutes.[72] Vertumnus shared a common cultural memory with the nearby cult of the prostitute Acca Larentia in the Velabrum valley, which was named after *vela* ('sails'), a memory of a time when water flowed through this area. The very name Vertumnus is meant to convey the changing character of the river: Propertius and Ovid derived it from the river (*verso ab amne*, 'from the turned river') and said the god owes his name to the river turning back from the Forum valley.[73] The poets' etymologies are supported by modern linguistics: the name, derived from the verb *vertere* ('to turn') and the ending -*mnos*, means 'the one who turns himself', an appropriate description of a river in flux.[74]

Vertumnus embodies the quality of river fluidity, which is naturally transposed into the social world and its construction of gender roles. A notable example of Vertumnus' shifting gender roles, in contrast to Horace's derogatory view of fluidity, comes from Sulpicia, the only known female writer in Augustan Rome, who uses Vertumnus in a positive manner. She compares her position as a poet, subverting traditional gender roles, to the many faces of a happy Olympian, Vertumnus.[75]

Aside from their cultural importance, the myths of the Tiber contain precious ecological knowledge about the changing environment of the river. Though major floods of the Tiber could still reach as far as the Forum in the historical period (as Horace attests) the cultural memory of the myth of Vertumnus is likely to be much older and may even date to the time of major environmental and political change at the end of the regal period. The Forum became the city centre in the sixth century BCE after major construction projects that involved raising the ground level and building the channel of Cloaca Maxima to drain excess water.[76] The placement of the statue of Vertumnus directly on the channel of the Cloaca indicates a connection to the water course and may have prompted memories of the enormous efforts made to turn back the river. As we have seen, the myth of the origin of the Tiber Island is also traditionally ascribed to the expulsion of King Tarquin, and archaeological evidence suggests that the river significantly changed its course in this period.

Conclusion

One should exercise due caution in any discussion that attempts to relate myth and history. Myths are subject to constant changes in their retelling and Tiber myths appropriately reflect the fluidity of the river.[77] It is enough to conclude that major shifts in the fluvial environment of Rome were rendered in terms of mythic language, in stories about the Tiber and his relationship with divinized women, Gaia, Ilia and Acca. In contrast, the myth of Vertumnus needs no female character because the shapeshifter can easily turn into the opposite gender. The great transformational power of the river in its various aspects (flooding, alluviation, sedimentation, nourishment, watering, connecting and blocking access), only some of which I have broached in this essay, could not be encoded in any one story or metaphor, especially not the standardized type of river representation as a masculine father. Hence a number of women find a notable place in these stories of a river that eludes definition and so underscore the simplest and yet most remarkable feature of the Tiber, its fluidity, most evident in the myth of Vertumnus, the god of the river in flux. Thus, the fluid character of the river is transposed onto the social world of Roman gender where it exposes the performative and artificial character of gender roles.

Notes

*   I would like to thank the editors, Christopher Schliephake and Esther Eidinow, for their invaluable suggestions that greatly improved this essay. Thanks are also due to the Alexander von Humboldt Foundation for funding my research.

1. The only monograph on the ancient Tiber is still Le Gall 1953a, on religious aspects see Le Gall 1953b, on literary aspects see Jones 2005 and Vuković 2020a, with references. The literature on the archaeology of the Tiber is vast. See Brock et al. 2021, with references.

2. Agency does not imply intentionality as things (living and non-living) may act without the ability to make conscious decisions. See recently Graham 2021.

3. See Latour 2005.

4. Aldrete 2007.

5. Marra et al. 2018. See now also Brock, et al. 2021 on the shifting riverbank in the early period.

6. La Rocca 1984 gives the bend a more becoming Italian name, 'la riva a mezzaluna'.

7. Eidinow 2016: 47–52, Schliephake 2020: 29–31. See also Hawes 2017: 1–13.

8. It has long been recognized that 'Roman myths are myths of place' (Beard et al. 1998: 173).

9. For an excellent discussion on methodologies in ecocriticism and environmental history see Sessa 2019: 211–55.

10. See Woodman 2003: 128–59.

11. Livy 1.4.4-6.

12. Ever since Dion. Hal. *Ant. Rom.* 1.84.

13. Livy's *forte quadam divinitus* ('perhaps by some divine providence') is in line with his frequent reservations about the mythic in history. For a discussion see Levene 1993 and Davies 2007: 1–142.

14. *LIMC* 1992, 294, s.v. *lupa Romana* no. 15. Though the inscription and dedication to Silvanus come from 124 CE, this seems to be a rededication, and the original dedication to Mars probably dates to the Flavian period. See Simon 1969: 222–4. The image is available on the museum website: https://www.miaroma.it/palazzi-roma-massimo-terra/ostia (accessed 27 October 2023).

15. Livy 1.4.4.

16. *Pater Tiberinus* is a religious appellative that appears for the first time in Enn. *Ann.* 26. I find it also captures the active masculine presence in the story. Katherine Blouin's (2019) has also argued for the agency of Rome's river.

17. It is no accident that the altar comes from Ostia, a river port that connected Rome to the Mediterranean via the Tiber, and the figure in the upper left (Hermes or Palatine?) is holding a rudder.

18. Cassius Dio describes the event at 53.20.1.

19. Aldrete 2007: 21–3.

20. Nisbet and Hubbard 1989: 16–19.

21. *di patrii, Indigetes, et Romule Vestaque mater/ quae Tuscum Tiberim et Romana Palatia servas* . . . 'O native gods, divine heroes, Romulus and mother Vesta, you who guard the Tuscan Tiber and the Roman Palatine . . .' (Verg. *G.* 1.498-99).

22. Hor. *Carm.* 1.2.13-20.

23. The trope was a proverbial impossibility (*adunaton*). See Nisbet and Hubbard 1989: 23.

24. Clark 2010: 262–7.

25. Horace often uses Jupiter to express Stoic ideas about the order of the universe and divine superiority.

26. Other Vestal Virgins are similarly related to the river; e.g. Tuccia carried Tiber water in a sieve and miraculously did not spill a drop (Val. Max. 8.1.5, Plin. *HN* 28.12).

27. Dumézil 1988: 88–91 proposes the etymology of Ilia as nourishment based on the comparison with the Vedic figure of Ilā, daughter of Manu, who is interestingly said to change gender every month.

28. Verg. *Aen.* 8.63, *pleno flumine* at *Aen.* 8.62.

29. See Seider 2021.

30. Verg. *Aen.* 8.77.

31. Armstrong 2019: 88–9.

32. Verg. *Aen.* 8.91-93.

33. See Thomas 2004.

34. Verg. *Aen.* 8.96: *viridisque secant placido aequore silvas,* literally: 'they cut the green woods in the peaceful water'.

35. Verg. *Aen.* 7.502. The force of the verb *implorare* denotes a human imploring for help.

36. Vuković 2020a: 464–82.

37. Verg. *Aen.* 7.487, 503. Vergil's description also suggests the deer was adopted by Silvia's family as a small buck, reversing the trope of the she-wolf nursing human infants (7.483-93).

38. Silvia and Silvius are derivatives from Latin *silva* ('forest').

39. Verg. *Aen.* 7.531-39, 575. Almo is a sacred tributary of the Tiber, which received the statue of Magna Mater for its annual bathing. Galaesus is a small river near Tarentum, mentioned by Vergil (*G.* 4.126), worked on by a poor but happy Corycian, an old man enjoying his rural peace.

40. See *LIMC* s.v. Tiberis, Tiberinus.

41. Similar to Lavinia's silent blush at Verg. *Aen.* 12.64-70.

42. Keegan 2008: 91–8.

43. Gell. 7.7. Plin. *HN* 24.25 cites only Campus Tiberinus. For analysis and *Quellenforschung* of the myths of Gaia Taracia and Acca Larentia see Nečas Hraste and Vuković 2015: 319–38.

44. Cat. in Macrob. *Sat.* 1.10.16: 'the fields of Turax, Semurius, Lintirius and Solinius' (*agros Turacem, Semurium, Lintirium et Solinium*).

45. See Coarelli 2012: 75–83.

46. Ammerman 2018: 398–409.

47. Mommsen 1864: 1–22.

48. See references in Nečas Hraste and Vuković 2015: 322 n. 39.

49. The Roman augurs invoked the Tiber as a winding snake (Serv. *Aen.* 8.95), a precious piece of ancient ecological wisdom that has many comparative parallels from North America to Australia.

50. Marra et al. 2018.

51. Ogilvie 1965: 245.

52. Dion. Hal. 5. 13; Liv. 2.5; Plut. *Publ.* 8.6-7.

53. Lahiri-Dutt and Samanta 2013: 32.

54. Livy 2.5.4.

55. Diels fr. B12, B91.

56. Though both perform essential activities they remain silent. We do not hear what Ilia's lament really is (except in the fragments of Ennius). This tallies with Spivak's (1999) idea that the subaltern are denied a voice and with the Roman construction of language as a male prerogative. See Newlands 1995: 146–74 for the example of Lucretia.

57. See Plant 2008, Kaur 2012. While cultural ecofeminists tend to celebrate what they see as shared traits of nature and women, socialist ecofeminists criticize this as a social construct. See Carlassare, 2000.

58. See Descola 2013: 48–53, who points to the Roman distinction between the domestic and the wild as essential in the formation of the Western polarity of nature vs. culture.

59. In contrast to the construction of the opposite sex and of passive homosexuals as weak, soft, and uncontrolled; see Williams 2010: 137–76, Masterson 2013: 24–31.

60. See previous note.

61. Prescendi Morresi 2020: 66. The binary opposition virgin vs. prostitute is still used in patriarchal societies to box women into pre-assigned categories that reduce their character to stereotypes defined by their sexual relation to men; see Giovannini 1981: 408–26.

62. Varro *de vir. Ill.* 46.1-3, Ov. *Fast.* 4.247-348; Val. Max. 1.8.2, Tac. *Ann.* 4.64.

63. The notable exception is ancient Egypt; see Vuković 2020b.

64. Nonius 282L. On Roman grammatical gender see Corbeill 2020.

65. Saadi-Nejad 2021: 19–42.

66. Lutatius 32 F5, ap. *OGR* 18.1; Alexander Polyhistor *FGrH* 273 F110, ap. Servius Danielis Verg. *Aen.* 8.330; Livy 1.3.8; Varro *Ling.* 5.30. See *TLL, s.v.* 'Albula' for gender variation in later authors.

67. Perono Cacciafoco 2013: 7–24.

68. Bettini 2015: 89–95, 180–5. For the notion of constancy as a male virtue see Cic. *Off.* 1.111.

69. Morton 2010.

70. Butler 2011.

71. Prop. 4.2.21-24.

72. *CIL* VI.1.804.

73. Ov. *Fast*. 6.410; Prop. 4.2.10: 'I am called the god Vertumnus from turning back the river' (*Vertumnus verso dicor ab amne deus*).

74. See Devoto 1940: 275–80.

75. *App. Tib*. 3.8.13-14: 'As happy Vertumnus on eternal Olympus has a thousand garments, she becomingly wears a thousand' (*Talis in aeterno felix Vertumnus Olympo/ Mille habet ornatus, mille decenter habet*).

76. See Bianchi 2015.

77. For example, the myth of Acca has several versions but her association with the temple of Hercules cannot predate the construction of Hercules' temples in the Forum Boarium in the third and second centuries BCE.

CHAPTER 9
ECOLOGICAL GRIEF AND THE SAFAITIC INSCRIPTIONS OF ANCIENT NORTH ARABIA
Eris B. Williams Reed

A bronze plaque is currently affixed to a basalt rock near the crater of Ok, a glacier in Iceland that stopped flowing two decades ago. Okjökull (literally 'Ok-glacier') did not die from a sudden disaster, nor an extreme weather event: he was the victim of 'slow violence', identified by Rob Nixon as the initially invisible harms enacted on the world's environments by rising global temperatures.[1] Ok's mourners added the plaque when they gathered on 18 August 2019 to commemorate Ok's death with a funeral, complete with speeches and readings, a procession, and the declaration of the glacier's cause of death.[2] The plaque bears a 'letter to the future' written by the Icelandic writer and environmentalist Andri Snær Magnason, in which he describes Ok's loss and the likelihood of all other glaciers disappearing over the next 200 years.[3] He concludes, 'This monument is to acknowledge that we know what is happening and what needs to be done. Only you know if we did it.'[4]

The plaque, and its ceremonial installation, were crucial to making Ok's death visible and mourning him accordingly: embedding these words in a place that simultaneously embodied Ok's presence and absence created a conduit for articulating the ineffable emotions generated by the mourning of his passing. Ok's commemoration has since been understood as an expression of 'ecological grief', a concept defined as 'the grief felt in relation to experienced or anticipated ecological losses' and increasingly mediated by making tangible what has been lost.[5] The Okjökull plaque is a powerful example of how material texts can articulate the emotions arising from the lived experience of environmental change. My contribution to this volume is concerned with how modern ecological thinking might help us to identify and comprehend comparable instances of living with environmental change in Antiquity and how such experiences were articulated via inscriptions.

Scholarship on ancient environmental change has accelerated rapidly in recent years, particularly work that reconstructs climatic conditions to foreground environmental themes in historical narratives.[6] Yet the experiences of real people living through environmental change often remain in the background of such studies, typically emerging only to confirm the occurrence of an environmental event.[7] Scholarship that does engage with individual experiences often focuses on elite authors, whose works naturally explore environmental disasters from a place of privileged safety and use them as a backdrop against which to advance other agendas.[8] We might observe resonances between this history of scholarship and what Nixon describes as the modern-day 'bias towards spectacular violence' that obscures the experiences of 'poor communities' who are affected most inequitably by slow violence.[9] In what follows, I focus on non-elite communities who directly experienced ancient environmental change and recorded these experiences in material texts. I argue that drawing on new thinking about the impacts of ecological change in the modern world presents an opportunity to expand our understanding of human–environmental interactions in Antiquity, especially for communities with close relationships to their environment. The Safaitic inscriptions of the Harrah desert, whose authors' lived experience of the environment intertwined closely with their emotional wellbeing and religious worldviews, offer an appropriate testcase.

The Safaitic inscriptions: Texts, authors, worldviews

By ''s¹d son of S²ʿ son of Ḥg son of S¹wd and he fed the goats on dry fodder in the year of misery because Baalshamin (B ʿls¹mn) withheld the rain; but may he preserve the text thereafter; and may he who would read aloud have spoil but may he who would efface this writing go blind.¹⁰

This text is one of over 43,000 found on the rocks of the Harrah(ḥrt), the basalt desert stretching across ancient north Arabia (now modern-day southern Syria, north-east Jordan and northern Saudi Arabia). It is one of many that preserve their authors' lived experience of the landscape, and it offers a springboard to introduce the key characteristics of this epigraphic corpus. These texts mainly comprise graffiti carved and scratched onto the basalt rocks and rockfaces of the Harrah in a South Semitic script.¹¹ The corpus is traditionally dated between the first century BCE and the third century CE due to the occasional application of dating formulae that can be securely connected to other historical events. The term 'Safaitic' is actually a modern one (denoting the Safa region of modern-day southern Syria) and is thus a linguistic rather than ethnic or cultural signifier. We therefore cannot speak of the texts' authors as a 'Safaitic people', nor of a 'Safaitic identity' self-consciously expressed by a single community.¹²

Nevertheless, several details suggest that the texts' authors shared certain worldviews and concerns. Most texts simply record their author's name and lineage; but those that offer further details usually adopt the same structural formula employed by ''s¹d, namely: a summary of activities ('he fed the goats …') and an invocation to a divine figure ('but may he preserve …').¹³ Dating formulae, such as ''s¹d's 'year of misery' (s¹nt b ʿs¹), indicate a desire to reference events that presumably impacted the wider community. Visually, the texts are carved with varying degrees of regularity and some included images.¹⁴ ''s¹d's text is also one of many carved on a loose rock that has probably moved from its original location; but other examples preserve tantalizing glimpses into textual interactions, with some recording multiple inscriptions being added over time and others referring to additional inscriptions nearby.¹⁵

Despite their formulaic composition, the texts are not devoid of meaning and personal significance to those who inscribed them; indeed, their creation as graffiti may have increased their emotional immediacy. Through these texts, we see glimpses of real people who lived, loved, and died in the Harrah: ʾmyt, who lost his dog (OCIANA 0002984); ʾġny, who had sex with S¹lm (OCIANA 0005472); Ḥbbt, who longed for Nmn (OCIANA 0026154). Grief is an emotion that finds frequent expression throughout the corpus following the death of a loved one. The most common term in such contexts is *wgm* ('to grieve');[16] but the inscriptions also bear witness to a 'rich vocabulary for grieving', including *wgʿ* ('to grieve in pain'), *wlh* ('to be distraught'), and *ndm* ('to be devastated by grief').[17] Significantly, ʾʾs¹d draws on this vocabulary too: his 'misery' (*bʾs¹*) is experienced by others when faced with the loss of a relative, implying that he regards the emotions arising from environmental change as comparable to those associated with familial loss.[18] This repertoire encourages us to consider many of these texts as a medium for expressing the lived experiences of those who inscribed them, particularly when faced with loss (ecological or otherwise).

The theme of landscape is also prominent in numerous texts concerning the seasonal movements of their authors, as they pastured goats, sheep and, sometimes, camels across different zones to maximize available water and pasture.[19] The authors of the Safaitic inscriptions clearly drew on extensive environmental knowledge to move successfully through the landscape: S¹krn son of S¹ʿd records how 'he returned to a watering place' (*ṣyr*) and began clearing out a pond from which he later collected water (OCIANA 0031758). S¹krn not only knew where to find water at a certain time of year, but also what activities could be done to optimize its collection.

The Safaitic inscriptions also reveal the religious worldviews of their authors.[20] The texts record their authors' religious practices and honouring of several divine figures who were sometimes invoked in relation to their spheres of influence. The most common religious rite seems to have been animal 'sacrifice' (*ḏbḥ*), with seasonal activities constituting a significant theme in the worshippers' desired outcomes.[21] For example, Qrn son of Mġyr made a sacrifice to Gadd-ʿAwīd in hope of 'security' (*s¹lm*) after unseasonable cold had killed his cattle (OCIANA 0004065); and Mrṣʿ son of ʿqrb sacrificed before migrating to the inner desert (OCIANA 0030952). These texts, and others, indicate that sacrifices could be motivated by a desire to ensure good environmental conditions, for example, Qrn further expresses his hope to avoid the harsh conditions of earlier times. Other texts demonstrate that environmental factors were judged to be within certain gods' spheres of influence. As we have already seen in ʾʾs¹d's text, Baalshamin was consistently associated with rainfall and storms; and figures such as Allat (ʾlt) and Shayʿhaqqawm (*s²ʾhqm*) were also invoked to ensure productive and safe environmental conditions. Crucially, Al-Jallad's statistical analysis of the corpus' religious texts has revealed that many exhibit a clear connection between the secular activities related in an inscription's narrative component and the scope of the invocation that follows.[22] One example is a text by Mġyr son of Msk who 'pastured the camels so, O Shayʿhaqqawm, may pasturing bring abundance'.[23] As we will see, this connectivity can sometimes allow us to trace a link between environmental interactions and religious practices.

Whilst many of these texts centre on pastoral activities, this did not preclude their authors' involvement in the region's wider geo-politics.[24] Multiple authors narrate involvement in military conflicts with various regional powers: a certain ʿbd records his service with an army unit during 'the year Herod waged war' and another, by Lṭ, slave boy of Gʿd mentions he served with an army unit near the borders of ʾbgr, probably referring to the Kingdom of Edessa.[25] Others were attuned to wider political events and epigraphically expressed their views on them: one author, Zd son of Rgl, dated his text with reference to the year he 'heard' (s¹mʿ) and 'laughed' (s¹ḥr) about the death of a certain Philippus, possibly the Herodian tetrarch who ruled the Hauran in the early first century CE.[26]

These texts thus provide an essential counterpoint to the representation of the region's communities in contemporaneous classical literature. Building on precedents established by Herodotus, authors such as Diodorus Siculus, Strabo and Josephus presented the communities of northern Arabia as homogenous groups who raided caravans and settlements.[27] Creating an artificial dichotomy between 'nomadic' and 'settled' communities, these authors sought to characterize those who existed outside classical cities as uncivilized barbarians, many of whom worshipped bizarre gods and engaged in aggressive, irrational violence.[28] Environmental determinism underpinned this dichotomy: the *barbaroi* of Arabia were synonymous with the perceived wilderness in which they operated. This representation served different purposes for different authors, but it was fundamentally grounded in the justification of Roman imperial expansion.[29]

The Safaitic inscriptions clearly tell a different story, one that several scholars have endeavoured to narrate. Michael Macdonald has consistently stressed that the epigraphic corpus challenges ancient (and modern) myths about the inherently aggressive nature of these nomadic communities, not least because pastoral activities are a considerably more common subject in the texts than 'raiding' (ġzz).[30] Similarly, he has emphasized the advanced literacy of these communities, which stands in stark contrast to many of those who lived in the region's villages and towns. The modern study of these texts has allowed us to appreciate their authors on their own terms and recalibrate them as part of the ancient world, rather than on the fringes of it.

Such historiography matters because it can help us to comprehend why far less attention has been given to the relationships these authors had with their local environment, particularly emotional ones.[31] An exploration of the human–environment relationship in the Safaitic inscriptions risks drifting towards the same environmental determinism that characterizes classical literature. Even if we no longer seek to equate seemingly hostile environments with hostile people, it remains problematic to trace the intensity of human experiences within the landscape alongside the perceived extremity of ecological conditions. Likewise, emphasizing the intensity with which the texts' authors valued the landscape, and seeking to identify extreme emotional manifestations of such values, threatens to place them back on an excessively emotive plain of aggression and passion. And yet, these inscriptions are a clear expression of the emotional relationships their authors shared with this landscape. Our understanding of these authors remains incomplete if we do not engage with this element of their lived experience. I propose that revisiting these ancient texts through the lens of ecological grief will create a space in which we can foreground the emotional responses to environmental change, helping us to recover the lived experiences of their authors and appreciate them on their own terms.

Ecological grief

Although the lexicon to describe the emotional impact of environmental change has boomed in recent years, it has been in the making for several decades by those living and working on the frontline of the climate crisis.[32] Of all the terms and methodologies currently in circulation, 'ecological grief' centres most strongly on the lived experiences of those affected by environmental change and offers an appropriate theoretical framework for exploring this topic in Antiquity. The concept finds its origins in the work of Ashlee Cunsolo, a health geographer who led multiple research projects with several Inuit communities in Nunatsiavut (north-east Canada);[33] and Neville R. Ellis and Glenn Albrecht, who worked with farming families in the 'wheatbelt' town of Newdegate (south-west Australia).[34] These projects informed a 2018 working paper in which Cunsolo and Ellis together defined ecological grief as: 'the grief felt in relation to experienced or anticipated ecological losses, including the loss of species, ecosystems and meaningful landscapes due to acute or chronic environmental change (. . .) ecological grief is a natural response to ecological losses, particularly for people who retain close living, working and cultural relationships to the natural environment.'[35] Crucially, they stressed the remarkable similarities between the communities with whom they conducted their research, despite their differences in cultural and environmental contexts, and thus highlighted the potential cross-cultural application of 'ecological grief'.

How might an ancient historian engage with this concept? Ancient communities did not experience environmental change as a rapidly transforming climate driven by industrialization, nor should we transplant modern understandings of certain emotions (ecological or otherwise) onto those of the ancient world.[36] Yet, as our own modern relationship with the environment transforms, our understanding of the historic human–environment relationship ought to expand in new directions. Our approach to gender and sexuality in the ancient world has been enriched and accelerated by feminist and queer theories, and critical race theory has likewise enhanced and elevated our understanding of race and ethnicity in Antiquity. As much as we should avoid anachronism, socio-cultural shifts in the modern world have long had the potential to steer our scholarly focus towards ancient ideas and experiences that always existed in our material, but were often overlooked or misunderstood. I suggest that engaging with the concept of ecological grief presents an opportunity to deepen our understanding of ancient environmental change by foregrounding the lived experiences of affected communities.

I propose that two principles should underscore a cross-cultural methodology for identifying and analysing expressions of ecological grief across pre-modern communities. First, we must adapt the framework devised by Cunsolo and Ellis by centring on those components that transcend cultural, environmental and historical boundaries. They identified numerous experiences of ecological grief, which can be distilled into three cross-cultural 'pathways', which often overlap: enhanced emotional reactions; behavioural change; and erosion of personal or cultural identity. Crucially, the elasticity of these pathways allows us to analyse expressions of ecological grief within specific cultural contexts, whilst also enhancing our understanding of such expressions by bringing them into dialogue with those of other cultures. It follows then that, secondly, we should establish datasets that have their origins in distinct environmental and cultural contexts, and comprise evidence generated by real people about their lived experiences. Whilst we cannot interview affected communities, we can purposefully compile evidence produced by people in comparable circumstances, namely those 'who retain close living, working and cultural relationships to the natural environment', who Cunsolo and Ellis identify as being especially susceptible to ecological grief.[37] As raised by the Okjökull Memorial Plaque, inscriptions can offer valuable insights due to their materiality, making visible both invisible emotions and the landscape on which they reflect. Angelos Chaniotis' discussion of 'emotional community' in Greek epigraphy can extend this conclusion: he demonstrates inscriptions can be formulated in a way that assumes their readers will experience certain emotions in certain situations, with epigraphic interventions enhancing a 'shared emotional response'.[38] For our purposes, this notion goes beyond acknowledging that inscriptions can be emotional testimonies and instead emphasizes the centrality of material texts in expressing and *creating* the cultural contexts that give rise to different emotions. The Safaitic inscriptions offer an appropriate dataset, not only because the corpus meets these methodological parameters, but also because ecological grief will allow us to foreground the authors' previously problematized relationship with the environment.

Ecological grief and the Safaitic inscriptions of ancient north Arabia

The earlier introduction to the Safaitic inscriptions and their authors has given a sense of the lived experience of environmental change: ''s¹d's text revealed that, when faced with the absence of rain, he changed his behaviour to save his goats, attributed the lack of rainfall to the gods, and regarded the whole year as one of 'misery' (b 's¹). As proposed above, a cross-cultural methodology for ecological grief may examine three, often overlapping, experiential 'pathways': enhanced emotional reactions; behavioural change; and erosion of personal or cultural identity. In the Safaitic corpus, altering one's movement through the landscape appears to constitute the main behavioural change in the face of environmental shifts, especially 'a return to a place of water' (syr) in times of drought. One example, from an area known as Riǧm Qaʿqūl in southern Syria, records how Gmm son of 'nʿm made such a return 'from the inner desert the year Baalshamin withheld the rain from the Province' followed by a prayer to Allat to grant 'security' (s¹lm).[39] Here, Gmm suggests that he has had to alter his usual route because the anticipated rainfall has not materialized, with his comment about Baalshamin withholding the rain from the entire region suggesting that it was a particularly dry year. We also catch a small glimpse of the emotional dimensions underscoring such changes:

Gmm's final prayer is not to the storm-god Baalshamin, but the goddess Allat, perhaps implying that he no longer hopes for Baalshamin's intervention.

Other texts hint at the emotions arising from altering pastoral activities and behaviours. In some cases, this is explicit: an inscription of now-uncertain provenance describes its author, S²km son of S¹'d'l, as having 'suffered from lack of rains' (ṣwy) and another, again without secure provenance, records the 'despair' (y's¹) experienced by 'mn son of Ġnt whilst he waited for the rains.[40] This latter term, y's¹ ('despair') bears an additional layer of significance: the term is deployed both in light of not only absent rain, but also other personal events, such as familial loss, war and inter-personal conflict.[41] Similar to ''s¹d's 'misery' (b's¹), 'mn son of Ġnt is anchoring his emotional response to environmental change in an existing emotional vocabulary.

There are also many instances of authors calling on Baalshamin to grant 'relief' (rwḥ) from the adverse situation in which they find themselves.[42] One particular theme concerns authors lingering near permanent water sources and waiting for appropriate meteorological conditions. Many examples attest to individuals who 'waited for the rain' (tẓr h- s¹my) and prayed to Baalshamin for relief, including two texts from Zalaf, a large area of wells and trees in modern-day southern Syria. Several thousand Safaitic texts are known from the site, with some implying that their authors simply passed through Zalaf briefly, rather than stopping for part of the season.[43] By contrast, two (probable) brothers, Whb'l and ''s¹d, both sons of Mḥlm son of Rb'l son of 'n'm, individually described their unexpected waits for rainfall:[44]

By Whb'l . . . and he stayed near permanent water in {this} valley the year [----] {s¹}ṭrky and he waited for the rains {and so} Baalshamin grant relief from adversity and [give him] security and blind {whoever?} {may scratch out?} the inscription . . .

By ''s¹d . . . and he camped here at permanent water and awaited the rains during the heliacal rising of Scorpio (mid-December), so, O Baalshamin, [grant] relief; and blindness and scorching heat be upon him who would efface this writing.

In each case, the brothers have deliberately lingered close to the safety of permanent water sources because the rainfall remains insufficient to support their usual seasonal journey into the Hamad, where they would expect to support their livestock with wadis and pastures recharged by the winter rains. Both texts conjure a rather striking image of the author scanning the skies for the rainclouds that will prompt them to move on and then calling upon Baalshamin when these conditions do not materialize. Similar testimonies from modern-day Newdegate and Nunatsiavut can expand our thinking around these ancient texts: individuals in Nunatsiavut spoke of their fear of venturing out onto the land as their knowledge of weather patterns became obsolete, whilst farmers in Newdegate explained how they obsessively refreshed weather monitoring websites.[45] One thread between these ancient and modern experiences is the affected individuals' helplessness whilst awaiting desired conditions and the behavioural changes elicited. Whb'l and ''s¹d cannot use and experience the landscape in the ways to which they are accustomed, and their texts testify to that moment of realization. Both texts end by calling on Baalshamin and his rainfall, and this may constitute an expression of vulnerability and humility before the gods in the face of environmental instability. ''s¹d also requests that those who efface his text suffer 'scorching heat' (*wqd*), perhaps an allusion to what he is experiencing and what he perceives as therefore being a worthy punishment for those who might erase this record of that experience. These two texts show how behavioural alterations in the face of environmental change could become entwined with enhanced emotional reactions and, perhaps, shifts in personal identity.

Of further interest are several texts in which the author describes their activities using deliberately emotive language, a form of expression that contrasts noticeably with the texts' usual brevity. Significantly, many of these examples involve the authors being unable to provide satisfactory care for their animals, which is of course bound to their ability to traverse the landscape successfully. At the site of Al-'Īsāwī, Rb'l son of 's¹d draws on an evocative juxtaposition to describe the situation in which he found himself as 'he fed on dry fodder the animals born in a time of plenty' ('*lf h- mrb 't*); and, at an unspecified site in northern Jordan, S¹krn son of Ḥṭs¹t likewise records how his 'camels were without milk' (*s²ḥṣ 'bl*) and so he prayed to the gods to grant 'abundance upon [the] herds' (*ġyrt b- n 'm*).[46] Another example is a text found at Zalaf by Ṣrmt son of Ṣrmt, who 'fed some weakened new-born animals on dry fodder' ('*lf (w)ld wny*) and subsequently prayed to Baalshamin for relief.[47] This is a purposefully emotive and emotional text: Ṣrmt's efforts to describe his animals as 'weakened' (*wny*) and 'new-born' (*wld* – which can also denote human children) reflects his own emotional experience of environmental change. By feeding them with dry fodder, Ṣrmt has failed to lead his young herd towards suitable fresh herbage and he now must resort to less nutritious supplies; his description of the animals is thus an act of testifying to the distressing circumstances in which they have found themselves on account of his own failure. Once again, evidence from modern-day Nunatsiavut and Newdegate can broaden our interpretation of this text: individuals from both cultures described the erosion of their environmental knowledge as a personal failure and indicated a negative effect on their personal and cultural identity.[48]

Likewise, despite regarding Baalshamin's rains as the essential force needed to generate fresh pasture for his animals, Ṣrmt's description of this moment arguably reflects his own personal shortcomings and undermines his individual identity as a successful pastoralist. Of course, a key difference between the ancient and modern worlds is that Ṣrmt's ideas of how to mitigate this failure were bound up in religious mentalities, with his attempts to address the absence of rain focusing on appeals to Baalshamin. Yet meticulously inscribing these prayers to gods is a ritualistic behaviour that finds some common ground with the methodical, often obsessive, actions undertaken by individuals in modern-day changing environments, whether that be compulsively checking weather reports or monitoring the seasonal (un)synchronicity of flora and fauna. In all cases, what lies behind the descriptions of these actions is a real person living through environmental change, experiencing a negative impact on their emotional wellbeing, and attempting to mitigate the situation through actions and expressions grounded in their own identity and worldviews.

Thus far, we have examined texts that primarily focus on individual experiences of environmental change, although we have encountered details that speak to more collective experiences and cultural identities: for instance, expressions like 'the year Baalshamin withheld the rain from the Province' allude to a shared awareness of major droughts. Yet the corpus also suggests that individual pastoralists shared one specific religious experience in harmony with the ecological rhythm of the year, providing a potential example of the impact of environmental change on cultural identity. As is now clear, the authors of the Safaitic inscriptions attributed the presence or absence of rain to Baalshamin, a storm-god worshipped by both the authors and other religious communities in the more fertile lands around the edges of the Harrah and further afield. The sanctuary at Seia, close to the Decapolis city of Qanawat (Kanatha) in the Hauran, seems to have been the most significant to the authors of the Safaitic inscriptions.[49] One fragmentary text has been found at Seia;[50] and another, found in the Harrah, indicates that the god's connection to the sanctuary was well-known:[51]

By ʼs¹ son of {ʻm?} son of ʼs¹ of the tribe of ʻbs²t and he rebelled against the people of Rome; so O Baalshamin, god of Seia, [grant] security.

The text firmly connects Baalshamin with Seia and the mention of 'the tribe of ʻbs²t' finds a possible link with a bilingual (Greek and Nabataean Aramaic) inscription from the sanctuary, which records the involvement of a group called the Οβαισηνοι / ʻbyšt in the building and restoration of Baalshamin's temple.[52] As Michael Macdonald has stressed, both ʻbs²t and ʻbyšt are common personal names in their respective languages, but it is possible that a group who inscribed Safaitic texts across the Harrah was also heavily involved in the establishment of a sanctuary to the storm-god on whom their pastoral activities depended.[53] The remains of the sanctuary at Seia certainly suggest that it would appeal to the authors of the Safaitic texts, as sumptuous vegetation adorns the sanctuary's extant architecture and a statue base of Seia herself.[54] For those who relied so intensely on Baalshamin's rains, the sanctuary at Seia offered an exemplar space in which to show their devotion to the storm-god.

One Safaitic inscription indicates that Seia was a place of pilgrimage (ḥg) for the pastoralists of the Harrah:[55]

By Qʻṣn son of {S¹ly?} ... and he escaped {by fleeing?} the year the pilgrimage to Sia had no effect.

The precise timing of this pilgrimage is unknown, but it was probably synchronized to the pastoralists' seasonal movements. One text, by Dʼy son of Ns²l, describes washing (rḥḍ) in preparation for a pilgrimage when the sun was in Virgo, thus between August and September and before the first rains.[56] Seia lies on the western edge of the Harrah on the fertile lower slopes of the Jebel Arab and is surrounded by the lush fields of the Auranitis that have a long history of agricultural productivity. The area around the sanctuary was therefore unsuitable for long-term grazing and the authors of the Safaitic inscriptions probably pastured their livestock there for only a short time. Nevertheless, this was long enough for them to visit the sanctuary at Seia, where they may well have made offerings to Baalshamin for their imminent seasonal journey into the Harrah and beyond to the Hamad.

For our purpose, this inscription by Qʿṣn son of Sʾly offers an important insight into the overlap between religion and environment in the pastoralists' worldviews and it is worth examining it alongside another text that mentions Seia, found at Al-ʿĪsāwī:[57]

By Ḍb son of Sʾḥr . . . he waited for the rains but {the water?} did not come the year the images/idols left Seia. So, O Allat, [grant] security {and} . . .

The first inscription, by Qʿṣn son of Sʾly, introduces the notion that a pilgrimage could have no effect (bṭl) and the second, by Ḍb son of Sʾḥr, clarifies the consequences of this inefficacy: the rain does not come, precisely because the gods have 'left' (brḥ) the sanctuary where they are worshipped by the texts' authors. Although Ḍb's individual experience of waiting for rainfall prompted him to inscribe this text, he also seems to acknowledge that this is a collective failure, as does Qʿṣn, whose use of the unsuccessful pilgrimage as a dating formula implies that what transpired was known across the community. Both authors' language choices hint at some of the emotions surrounding this event: the term bṭl captures not just inefficacy but failure and futility, and brḥ is commonly applied to the departure of pastoralists from different landscape zones, or even complete abandonment.[58] Although the emotional impact is not explicit, these language choices speak to the perceived gravity of this situation.

We can also consider the impact this alleged abandonment may have had on any sense of shared cultural identity recognized by these affected communities. Even though individuals and small family groups would encounter other members of the community throughout the year (either directly, or indirectly through their epigraphic communications) these movements through the landscape were otherwise relatively solitary activities, with different groups probably following certain routes based on familial knowledge shared intergenerationally. By contrast, the pilgrimage to Seia probably involved many members of the community converging on one place over a particular period, thus constituting a rare moment of social cohesion in the seasonal calendar when religious activities were performed for individual and shared benefit. If the benefits did not materialize and the activities were judged to have failed, then the value of this communal action is undermined and so too are the intertwined collective identities. At Nunatsiavut and Newdegate, the erosion of these collective identities – and the ways of life that reinforce them – has precipitated poor emotional wellbeing. As someone from Nunatsiavut said, 'Inuit are people of the sea ice. If there is no more sea ice, how can we be people of the sea ice?'[59] Ḍb son of Sʾḥr chose not to describe the emotions arising from the situation in which he found himself, but it remains significant that he chose to bear witness to his present circumstances and attribute them to the abandonment of Baalshamin, something that is perhaps reinforced by his invocation of Allat. Did Ḍb hope his ineffable emotions would find expression through the materiality of his text, rather than the words that had perhaps failed him? For Ḏb, and the many other authors discussed, the production of these material testimonies affirmed their participation in and creation of an epigraphic community, where experiences of environmental change found expression through common religious worldviews and emotional vocabularies. By foregrounding these expressions, ecological grief prompts us to recognize more than just the importance of the environment to these authors: it elevates the experiences and emotions arising from their human–environment relationship and takes seriously the value of carving these expressions into the very fabric of the landscape itself.

Inscribing consolation

I hope to have demonstrated the value of modern ecological thinking to our understanding of human–environment relationships in Antiquity through this example of ecological grief and the Safaitic inscriptions of ancient north Arabia. By way of conclusion, I wish to offer some initial thoughts on how we might elicit a multi-directional dialogue between ancient and modern expressions of ecological grief, and ask: what might ancient material texts teach us about expressing ecological grief and developing new modes of consolation in the face of modern environmental change?

Fundamentally, these ancient texts demonstrate the significance of making visible personal testimonies of ecological grief within a landscape where environmental change is directly experienced. Even if common worldviews underscored much of the content and form of the Safaitic inscriptions, these texts were still personally meaningful to those who inscribed them and reflected individual circumstances. Whilst the Okjökull Memorial Plaque was a communal expression of ecological grief, the Safaitic inscriptions demonstrate the value of articulating individual experiences too. The physical production of these texts is likewise key to their individuality: these inscriptions are found almost exclusively on basalt, with their authors deploying a variety of techniques and a significant degree of force to carve their texts. Statistical analysis on the production of Safaitic rock-art and inscriptions has suggested that 'pounding' or direct hammering was the most common method, which involves hitting the rock with a hammerstone of equal or higher hardness.[60] The process of inscribing one's text was thus physically strenuous and mentally absorbing. Could this activity have been a positive outlet for distressing emotions, with authors both giving material expression to their emotional state and processing those emotions through the creation of a tangible text? Just as tactile activities (such as colouring) are increasingly recognized today as effective strategies for reducing anxiety, so too might the physical creation of these inscriptions have offered their authors a way to process troubling thoughts.[61]

The placement of these inscriptions within the landscape was likewise crucial, both for making visible what was absent (particularly rainfall) and for rooting their authors' experiences within a particular place. Finally, these personal testimonies arguably contributed to the creation of contexts in which ecological grief could be expressed; or,

145

put another way, these individual expressions nurtured an 'emotional community'. For the challenges faced by modern communities – particularly 'poor communities' affected by slow violence – the Safaitic inscriptions hint at the benefit of making visible individual testimonies of ecological grief within an affected landscape and the potential for this visibility to build collective resilience. By working across disciplines on the topic of ecological grief, perhaps ancient epigraphers can offer new insights on how to create and articulate 'climate testimonies' and thus contribute to the collective thinking and action needed as we live through the climate emergency.[62]

Notes

1. Nixon 2011.

2. Howe and Boyer 2020.

3. The text is bilingual (Icelandic and English). See Howe and Boyer 2020 for the full text and images.

4. Ibid.

5. Cunsolo and Ellis 2018: 275, and Cunsolo Willox 2012: 137–64, building on Butler 2004.

6. The *Geodatabase of Historical Evidence on Roman and Post-Roman Climate* was a key project that drove this shift (McCormick et al. 2013).

7. E.g. Harper 2017 and McConnell et al. 2020: 15443–9; with the critique of Sessa 2019: 211–55.

8. E.g. Keitel and Closs 2020, and König in this volume.

9. Nixon 2011: 4.

10. Adapted slightly from OCIANA 0009306: *l ''s¹d bn s²' bn ḫg bn s¹wd w 'lf h- m'zy s¹nt b's¹ w ḫgz h b'ls¹mn 'kd h- dṣn w ġnmt l- ḏ d'y w 'wr l- ḏ 'wr h- ḫṭṭ*. Unless indicated otherwise, all Safaitic inscriptions discussed here follow the edition and translation presented in OCIANA, in conjunction with Al-Jallad and Jaworska 2019. The anglicization of divine and geographical names is a key exception. Note that uncertain readings of letters and words are enclosed thus: { }.

11. Al-Jallad 2022a: 99–104 and Macdonald 2022a: 327–33.

12. Thus, Al-Jallad 2022b: 13, building on Macdonald e.g. 1993: 303–403.

13. Al-Jallad and Jaworska 2019: 8–18.

14. Della Puppa 2022 and Østerled Brusgaard 2019.

15. E.g. 'n'm son of 'm recorded that he found the 'writing' (s¹fr) of his uncle and felt longing (ts²wq) for him (OCIANA 0029242).

16. Eksell 2005: 163–72.

17. Al-Jallad and Jaworska 2019: 14–15.

18. E.g. OCIANA 0008330 and 0028601.

19. E.g. Macdonald 1992: 1–11.

20. See now Al-Jallad 2022b, building on e.g. Eksell 2002 and Bennett 2014: 43–52.

21. Al-Jallad 2022b: 17–26.

22. Ibid.: 10–14.

23. Adapted from OCIANA 0022515, with Al-Jallad 2022b: 10: *r ʾy h- ʾbl f h š ʿqm ġnyt m-r ʿyt*.

24. E.g. Macdonald 1993: 303–403 and 2014: 145–63.

25. OCIANA 0021652: *s¹nt qttl hrd* (which Herod is unclear); and OCIANA 0005280, with Macdonald 2014: 145–63.

26. OCIANA 0030127, with Macdonald 2014: 151.

27. E.g. Bosak-Schroeder 2020.

28. See also Macdonald 2022b: 397–401 on related problems surrounding the terms 'Arab' and 'Arabia'.

29. E.g. Strabo *Geography* 16.2.20.

30. E.g. Macdonald 1993: 303–403 and 2022a: 332.

31. See Head 2016: 22–3 on how perceptions of emotion as the 'antithesis of rationality' hinder tackling the emotional dimensions of the climate crisis.

32. E.g. Albrecht on 'solastalgia' 2005: 41–55, informed by Mitchell 1946. See also Craps 2020: 1–7.

33. E.g. Cunsolo Willox et al. 2012: 538–47 and 2013: 14–24, and Cunsolo Willox 2012.

34. Ellis and Albrecht 2017: 161–8, building on e.g. Albrecht 2005: 41–55.

35. Cunsolo and Ellis 2018: 275.

36. Thus, e.g. Chaniotis and Ducrey 2013: 9–14 and Cairns and Nelis 2017: 7–30. Gallegos-Riofrío et al. 2022 have highlighted the damaging prevalence of Western-world bias in studies on nature and mental health, encouraging us to discuss ecological grief with reference to culturally constructed emotions, rather than clinically determined mental health conditions.

37. Cunsolo and Ellis 2018: 275.

38. Chaniotis 2016: 95.

39. OCIANA 0004663: *m- mdbr s¹nt hgz -h b ʾls¹mn ʾl- h- mdnt* (trans. adapted).

40. OCIANA 0010516 and 0019615.

41. E.g. OCIANA 0032254, 0030496 and 0015894.

42. In some cases, the author specifically asks Baalshamin to 'grant relief with rain' (*rwḥ b- mṭr*, e.g. OCIANA 0021862, 0022111, 0023051).

43. For example, Ṣ ʿd son of S²rḥm just notes that he was migrating to the inner desert (OCIANA 0005159).

44. OCIANA 0005130: *l whb ʾl . . . w ḥḍr {h}- nḥl s¹nt ----{s¹}trky w tẓr h- s¹my (f) (h) b ʾls¹mn rwḥ w s¹lm w ʾwr {ḏ} {y} ʾwr h- s¹fr*; and OCIANA 0005131: *l ʾ ʾs¹d . . . w ḥḍr h- dr w tẓr h- s¹my b- rhy ʿqbt f h b ʾls¹mn rwḥ w ʾwr w wqd l- ḏ y ʾwr h- s¹fr*.

45. Cunsolo Willox et al. 2013: 19–20; Ellis and Albrecht 2017: 165.

46. OCIANA 0029974 and 0021389. Al-Jallad and Jaworska 2019 also note that the term *s²ḥṣ* ('to suffer from scarcity') is commonly juxtaposed with a prayer for 'abundance' (*ġnyt* or *ġyrt*).

47. OCIANA 0005922.

48. Cunsolo Willox et al. 2013: 19–20 and Ellis and Albrecht 2017: 165.

49. Dentzer-Feydy 2015: 313–25.

50. Macdonald 2003: 278–80.

51. OCIANA 0015351: *l ʾs¹ bn { ʾ}m bn ʾs¹ ḏ- ʾl ʾbs²t f mrd ʾl- ʾl rm f h b ʾls¹mn ʾlh s¹ ʿ ʿ s¹lm*.

52. *CISem.* II 164 and Wadd 2366.

53. Macdonald 2003: 278–9.

54. Dentzer 1979: 325–32.

55. OCIANA 0035859: *l q ʿṣn bn s¹{l}y . . . w ngy n[[]]fr s¹nt bṭl ḫg s¹ʿʿ.* On pilgrimage in the wider region, see e.g. Lightfoot 2005: 333–52.

56. OCIANA 0013968. Another text (0018595), discussed by Al-Jallad 2022b: 42–3, suggests a springtime date.

57. OCIANA 0026968: *l ḍb bn s¹ḫr . . . w tẓr h- s¹my w ṣlf h- {m}l s¹nt brḥ h- ʿṣlm s¹ʿʿ {f} h lt s¹lm {w}.*

58. Al-Jallad and Jaworska 2019 *sv. bṭl* and *brḫ.*

59. Cunsolo and Ellis 2018: 277, Table 1.

60. See now Østerled Brusgaard 2019: 105–13 and Della Puppa 2022: 107–29.

61. E.g. Khademi et al. 2021: 1437–44 found mandala colouring to be an effective strategy for reducing anxiety in hospitalized Covid-19 patients.

62. I warmly thank the editors, Alison Cooley, and Jason König for their thoughtful comments on this chapter. Any remaining errors are my own.

PART IV
CHANGE

CHAPTER 10
ECOLOGICAL GRIEF IN AELIUS ARISTIDES AND PHILOSTRATUS
Jason König

Ecological grief, ancient and modern

In 178 CE the city of Smyrna was destroyed by an earthquake.[1] That incident[2] is described by the orator Aelius Aristides in a series of surviving works, which include a lament for the city, accompanied by a request for aid, addressed to the emperors Marcus Aurelius and Commodus. Remarkably we have an account of Marcus Aurelius' reaction to reading that text, from Philostratus' *Lives of the Sophists*, written about half a century after the event (Philostr. *VS* 2.9, 582):

> And it is not boastful praise to say that Aristides was the founder of Smyrna, but very just and truthful. For when this city was obliterated by earthquakes and chasms that opened up in the ground Aristides lamented over it to Marcus in such a way that the emperor often groaned over the other parts of the lament, but when he came to the phrase 'the west winds blow over a desert' the emperor actually shed tears over the text, and in response to this prompting from Aristides agreed to the rebuilding of the city.[3]

My aim in this chapter is to set that passage in the wider context of Philostratus' text, and similarly to set Aristides' portrayals of the Smyrna earthquake against the background of the rest of his writings, in order to explore the range of ways in which these two authors represent human–environment relations, especially but not exclusively in relation to natural disaster. In the process I am particularly interested in assessing the ways in which their images of mourning for the city of Smyrna – both on the part of the emperor and on the part of Aristides himself, who talks repeatedly about his own experience of sorrow – compare with present-day notions of ecological grief.[4]

Recent research on ecological grief[5] in modern contexts has often focused on communities living close to landscapes affected by climate change. Glenn Albrecht's concept of solastalgia, as 'the lived experience of negative environmental change',[6] has been particularly influential.[7] Building on Albrecht's work, Ashlee Cunsolo and Neville Ellis have studied ecological grief in relation to 'experienced or anticipated ecological losses, including the loss of species, ecosystems and meaningful landscapes due to acute or chronic environmental change'.[8] They view it as a natural response for those who live close to damaged environments. And they see it as a form of 'disenfranchised grief', in the sense that it tends not to be publicly acknowledged,[9] and to be more pronounced in populations with existing vulnerabilities.[10] They argue that acknowledging ecological grief can illuminate our relations of mutual dependency with complex ecosystems, and our ethical and political responsibilities to them.[11] Their research has emerged against the backdrop of a situation where more and more people are exploring the possibilities for redirecting human emotions of love and grief towards more-than-human objects, for example in recent high-profile cases involving public expressions of mourning for shrinking or vanished glaciers.[12]

By contrast, another strand in recent research on ecological grief gives attention to the emotional responses of individuals and groups who are much further removed from the objects of their mourning. Timothy Clark contrasts 'ecological grief', which he sees as a response to the loss or damage of particular places, with a more generalized experience that he calls 'anthropocene horror', which involves a less clearly defined and less firmly anchored anxiety about ecological damage on a much wider scale.[13] Equally widespread, if not more so within Western cultures not on the front line of climate change, is the phenomenon of anxiety about the risk of extinction for certain high-profile, 'flagship' species,[14] or the desire to maintain certain special wild places in a pristine condition. These kinds of reactions are the consequence of a situation where the causes and effects of climate change are massively difficult for us to understand and to envisage.[15] On some accounts, localized responses like these can distract from environmental initiatives that would have a more widespread effectiveness. Alternatively, one might argue they can be used as powerful starting points for environmental education and for emotional and imaginative engagement, or as spurs to beneficial action and investment.

My goal in what follows is to ask how far these phenomena are paralleled in ancient Greek and Roman culture. As we shall see in the first section on Philostratus, there is a risk of anachronism if we try to force the ancient evidence into a modern template: sometimes the exercise of examining ancient and modern environmental thinking together can reveal the differences between them as much as the similarities. I also argue, however, in turning to the work of Aelius Aristides in the second half of the chapter, that these modern perspectives on ecological grief do have some powerful resonances with their ancient equivalents, and that they can help us to see aspects of ancient environmental engagement that might otherwise be hidden from view.

Philostratus

How does Philostratus' representation of Marcus Aurelius' response to the Smyrna earthquake relate to those modern ways of thinking about ecological grief? And how does it relate to Philostratus' representation of human–environment relations in the *Lives of the Sophists* (VS) more broadly? In many ways the passage quoted at the beginning of the chapter seems closest to the last of the responses outlined in the previous section. Marcus Aurelius is a member of the wealthy elite (an understatement) not directly affected by the disaster or required to live day to day with its consequences.

Philostratus' mention of his 'rebuilding of the city' hints at the possibility that he is concerned as much with the architectural beauty of Smyrna as with the fate of its people (as we shall see, that impression is reinforced by other sections of the *VS*, and in various passages from the works of Aristides himself). At the same time those emotions are leveraged by Aristides to generate beneficial post-disaster investment.

There seems to have been a widespread expectation that emperors would act decisively and generously to help cities affected by earthquakes and other natural disasters,[16] but even so one of the striking things here is the abruptness of the emperor's decision to give financial assistance: he moves from tears to investment in the space of just seventeen words in Philostratus' Greek ('the emperor actually shed tears over the text, and in response to this prompting from Aristides agreed to the rebuilding of the city', *kai dakrya tō bibliō epistaxai ton basilea synoikian te tē polei ek tōn tou Aristeidou endosimōn neusai*, *VS* 2.9, 582). Philostratus makes it clear that it was the phrase 'the west winds blow over a desert' that moved the emperor to tears. If we look at Aristides' speech (discussed in more detail below), we can see that that phrase comes right at the end of his relatively brief catalogue of the former charms of Smyrna, immediately before he launches into his much lengthier plea for assistance.[17] It is as if the emperor's tears have come right on cue, at exactly the right moment to make him well-disposed to Aristides' proposals, and in a way that demonstrates Aristides' skills of rhetorical manipulation. What follows in the speech is focused above all on the emperor's obligations to the city: the evocation of grief is a means to an end. We might see that as an ancient equivalent of the way in which environmental campaigners today will use (say) the fate of flagship species or landscapes, without reference to human populations, as a means of encouraging donations and investments that bring broader benefit.

At the same time, however, and despite those similarities, I also want to argue that this passage can provide us with an intriguing example of the risks of anachronistic reading in relation to ancient environmental thinking. That becomes clear when we read this passage in the context of the text as a whole. Philostratus almost entirely neglects the issue of human–environment relations in the rest of the work (unlike Aristides, where they are a major theme). He seems to be interested in this incident above all as one of many examples where persuasion, benefaction and grief are important components in imperial and sophistic self-definition, and in that sense the initial impression of resemblance with modern varieties of environmental grief may be quite misleading.

For one thing, it is striking that the primary purpose of this passage for Philostratus seems to be as part of a much wider reflection on the power of sophistic rhetoric. The emperor is explicitly said to 'shed tears over the text' (*kai dakrya tō bibliō epistaxai*) – the Greek suggests that he is reading the text and that the tears drop on it physically – rather than over the event itself, as a consequence of the power of Aristides' writing.[18] It is also part of a series of scenes where sophists request favours from emperors on behalf of cities, not always with the same level of success. For example, when the father of Herodes Atticus writes a letter to Hadrian asking him for a water supply for the city of Troy the emperor is initially enthusiastic but then expresses his disapproval, guided by officials who object to the favouritism being shown to Troy (*VS* 2.1, 548). Aristides' letter after the earthquake is implicitly measured up against this example, as part of Philostratus' reflections on different styles of sophistic influence: he succeeds in guiding the emperor towards precisely the kind of one-sided investment that Herodes' father attempts but ultimately fails to extract.

Running through all of this is a set of assumptions – which as we shall see are closely paralleled in Aristides' work – about the quasi-erotic attraction exercised by certain cities over their elite admirers. Many of Philostratus' sophists proclaim their love for particular cities. In some cases that is a two-way relationship, whereby sophists can be objects of desire for whole cities in turn. The result is that we are often left with the impression of a special, exclusive connection between sophist and city. Some of the most prominent examples of that kind of relationship are in relation to Smyrna.[19] That is the case especially for the sophist Polemo. We are told that 'many cities were in love with him, and especially Smyrna' (1.25, 530). Polemo, too, represents Smyrna in embassies to the emperor, as well as heaping benefactions on the city on his own account (1.25, 531-32). By showing Marcus Aurelius mourning for the city and then investing in it, Philostratus thus makes it clear, for any reader paying attention to the wider context of the work, that the emperor is part of this sophistic world of quasi-erotic entanglement between great individuals and certain very special communities.

The scene is also part of a long series of reflections on the workings of grief in sophistic contexts. The text gives us positive and negative images of sophists both refraining from grief,[20] and indulging in it.[21] Herodes Atticus, for example, was criticized for excessive grief in response to the deaths of his wife Regilla and his daughters (2.1, 557-58). We are invited to measure up Marcus Aurelius' response against those precedents. The fact that Herodes uses building as a response to grief, in the magnificent theatre he constructs in honour of Regilla (2.1, 556), hints at the possibility of a negative reading of Marcus Aurelius' reaction, as if the emperor's response to the earthquake is an even more extravagant version of the kinds of behaviour that are associated elsewhere with sophistic excess.

Philostratus' primary interest, then, is in characterizing Marcus Aurelius not so much as an individual with an especially acute environmental sensibility, but rather as a figure whose responses, as emperor, are closely parallel to standard features of sophistic behaviour, and also exemplary of the Stoicism that Marcus Aurelius espoused in his own writings, with its commitment to channelling one's initial, involuntary emotional reactions into action. That fact should make us pause before we seek to characterize Marcus Aurelius' response and Philostratus' characterization of it, as ancient equivalents of modern ecological grief reactions. Details which have superficial similarities with modern environmental discourse sometimes turn out on closer inspection to have rather different significance when we view them within their own contexts.

Aristides' *Sacred Tales*

How do Aristides' representations of the Smyrna earthquake compare? And how do they relate to his representations of human–environment relations in the rest of his work? I want to look first at some of the distinctive features of Aristides' *Sacred Tales*, his first-person diary of his illness and his treatment under the guidance of the god Asclepius, before turning to his Smyrna orations.

It is immediately clear, when we turn to the *Sacred Tales*, that the theme of human–environment relations has an importance far beyond its role in Philostratus. The *Sacred Tales* offers us some of the ancient world's most powerful images of the openness of the human body to environmental forces, although it is only recently that that phenomenon has begun to be explored from a new materialist and ecocritical perspective. That is clear especially in Aristides' repeated descriptions of bathing, where he represents his own immersion in water as an experience of permeability between his own body and the more-than-human world.[22]

One of the fascinating things about these bathing descriptions is the way in which Aristides appropriates the idea of corporeal immersion in landscape as something to be celebrated, in contrast with many other imperial texts where it is associated with low status or with foreignness, for example in ethnographic portrayals of barbarian communities who live closely intertwined with their environments.[23] One might even expect that this would make Aristides more inclined to sympathize with the perspective of non-elite populations dealing with their own experience of being overwhelmed by environmental forces, not least in the Smyrna earthquake, but in fact the opposite turns out to be the case. Aristides' interest in his own immersion in the environment, under the guidance of the god Asclepius, is paralleled by the god's ability to protect him from exposure to harmful environmental forces in other contexts. That very distinctive and to modern eyes even quite odd feature of Aristides' representation of human–environment relations has not to my knowledge been discussed in detail before. In many passages of his work Aristides has an acute awareness of the differential impact of environmental disaster, and in that sense his writing has superficial overlaps with postcolonial approaches to environmental crisis, which also take an interest in that theme.[24] Aristides is aware of the elemental threat of dangerous nature, and of the way in which it does not affect everyone equally. His version of that concern, however, is in most respects quite alien to its modern equivalents: there is no awareness of the way in which that might be related to, for example, structural economic and geographical inequalities, and indeed no sense even that it might be a bad thing; instead Aristides uses it as a way of recording and celebrating the presence of the divine.[25]

That impression of Aristides' insulation from harmful environmental forces is clear especially in his representation of the earthquakes in Smyrna and elsewhere in Book 3 (Ael. Arist. *HL* 3.43):

I became so bold that, almost in the midst of the earthquakes, as I was returning from the warm springs to the city in accordance with my dreams, and saw men in supplication and distraught, I intended to say that there was no need to be afraid, for there would be nothing harmful. For under these conditions, I would not be summoned to the city [i.e. by the god]. Then I stopped, so that I might not seem to be some demagogue, but I asserted to those who were with me, how I had 'obtained safe conduct', using these very words.

Here, in contrast with his later orations on the earthquake, there is nothing that at all resembles emotions of grief. There is also very little empathy with the experience of the populations who have been subjected to the terrifying natural forces of the earthquake at first hand. If anything, the tone is celebratory: Aristides is aware of his position of privilege and safety by contrast with the desperately supplicating inhabitants of the affected cities. He is at least tactful enough not to draw attention to his own sense of immunity to others at the time. He is also keen to spread his good fortune: he claims in a passage just before this one that he has stopped the earthquakes for everyone himself through his sacrifice of an ox to Zeus, performed under the guidance of Asclepius. But in the end, he does seem primarily interested in exulting in his own freedom from being exposed to environmental disaster. This detached self-positioning could hardly be more different from the immersive character of the bathing incidents and of the other cures prescribed by the god in his dreams. And it could hardly be more different from the despairing experience of ecological grief among modern populations dealing with the degradation of the environments they live close to.

Aristides' Smyrna orations

How do Aristides' Smyrna orations compare? I want to focus here especially on *Oration* 18, which is presented by Aristides as a spontaneous outpouring of emotion composed immediately on hearing the news of the earthquake, and *Oration* 19, the letter to Marcus Aurelius and Commodus already referred to above. In these texts the theme of grief is much more consistently prominent than in the *Sacred Tales* or the *Lives of the Sophists*. They also have some important features in common with both of those other texts, however, especially in their lack of attention to human suffering. Up to a point, those features are typical of other surviving ancient speeches in response to earthquakes,[26] which tend to draw heavily on the images of architectural beauty that were so important for the widespread genre of speeches in praise of cities,[27] and of reports of earthquakes in ancient historiography, which tend to take much less interest in victims and survivors than their modern equivalents.[28] Aristides, however, is unusually uncompromising in his manipulation of those traditions.[29] Libanius, for example, in his lament for the destruction of Nicomedia (Lib. *Orat.* 61) in an earthquake 200 years or so later, follows some of the same pathways as Aristides, whose work he knew well, but supplements them with regular and vivid descriptions of the fate of the city's population,[30] for example at 61.17: 'Where are the young? Where are the old? ... Where is the senate now? Where are the people? Where are the women? Where are the children?'

Why do Aristides' expressions of grief in these two texts shut out almost any reference to the population of the city? One answer might be just that he was not very interested in their fate, as if his account replicates the invisibility of marginalized populations, and of their disproportionate exposure to environmental harm, that characterizes even some modern accounts of natural disasters, as approaches from postcolonial ecocriticism have increasingly made clear.[31] No doubt Aristides' shared with his fellow members of the

Roman elite many of the same blind spots about human suffering in certain segments of the population. Certainly, his account seems very far removed from the kind of non-elite, lived experience of environmental harm discussed by Cunsolo and Ellis.[32] There are even moments when Aristides' persona resembles the persona he had adopted in his account of the Smyrna earthquake in *Sacred Tales* Book 3. For example, he also mentions in *Oration* 19 the story that the god prompted him to leave the city just in time, side by side with the suggestion that the task of speaking on behalf of the city is one to which he is especially suited, as if he has been spared by the god precisely for this purpose: 'thinking that the matter spoke to me, if to anyone at all, I appointed myself to this service, even if for nothing else, at least to bewail the misfortunes of the city' (19.6). In these passages, Aristides' expressions of grief seem to be very much tied up with a sense of privilege – both his own and that of the city. Those details raise the possibility that Aristides' lack of attention to human suffering in *Orations* 18 and 19 may be simply a consequence of a privileged, detached, elitist way of responding to environmental disaster, paralleled perhaps by the very partial and selective responses to environmental crisis that are prevalent within many sections of contemporary Western culture. Perhaps we too are inclined to express grief in response to environmental damage from a position of detachment (as discussed already above in the introduction to this chapter), in relation to places and objects that are represented as exceptional or beautiful or unique, and with insufficient attention to the impact of environmental damage on disadvantaged human populations.

There is, however, surely a risk of overstatement in that explanation, not least because Aristides' other works do sometimes give more attention to human victims in similar situations. His *Rhodian Oration*, in response to an earthquake that destroyed the city of Rhodes nearly thirty years before, in the early 140s CE, is a case in point (assuming it is right to ascribe it to Aristides, as most scholars now do).[33] It shares many of the standard themes that we find in the Smyrna orations – for example in its repeated focus on the beauty of the city – but it supplements that, as Libanius also does in writing about Nicomedia, with a sustained interest in the human victims and survivors.[34] Aristides also talks at length about the population of the city in his two later Smyrna orations (*Orat.* 20 and 21), both of which were composed later once the reconstruction of the city was well advanced. With that evidence in mind we might suspect that Aristides' exultation in his own self-preservation and his corresponding lack of interest in the fate of others around him in Book 3 of the *Sacred Tales* may be shaped more by genre and context – in other words by his wider goal of praising the god Asclepius – than by some inflexible set of underlying attitudes.

In what follows, therefore, I want to explore two alternative explanations for Aristides' lack of interest in mourning the human populations in Smyrna in *Orations* 18 and 19. My first explanation, picking up on my reading of Aristides' rhetorical virtuosity in extorting tears from Marcus Aurelius in the *Lives of the Sophists*, is to see the architectural, non-human focus of Aristides' grief – especially in *Oration* 19 – as a pragmatic ploy for rhetorical influence.[35] According to some modern theorizations, ecological grief can be productively redirected, in order to generate a focus on concrete solutions and responses.[36]

On that account, missing out any mention of the human inhabitants is a way of attracting the emperors to invest in a way which will have broad benefit for the population of the city. It might also be designed to emphasize the emperors' potential as benefactors: they are represented as having a superhuman stature, individually equal in prestige and power to whole cities and so able single-handedly to bring the relief to Smyrna that it needs.

Those strategies take as their starting point a set of assumptions about the capacity for the city to inspire love that Aristides had explored already in *Oration* 17, another of his speeches in praise of Smyrna, this one probably delivered around twenty years before the earthquake:[37] Aristides refers back to that earlier text repeatedly in *Orations* 18 and 19. Much of *Oration* 17 is taken up with discussion of the quasi-erotic impact of Smyrna on the viewer,[38] and the construction of the city as an entity more or less equivalent to a human person.[39] Some of it draws on motifs that were quite conventional in praise of cities, especially the theme of visual impact, and the motif of the city's intimate relationship with the hills and the seashore around it;[40] nevertheless Aristides uses those conventions in quite intense and original ways.[41] He tells us that the city 'itself recommends a love of itself among all mankind' (*Orat.* 17.8). The city is 'consistent in appearance, harmonious, its parts compatible with the whole, like the human body' (17.9). The city is like an embroidered gown or a necklace (17.10). 'Delight never forsakes it' (17.13). It impacts on its viewers like a magnet (17.17) or like a snake bite (17.18). These passages are particularly extravagant manifestations of the theme of love between emperor and city that we have seen already in the work of Philostratus.[42]

Those are the kinds of assumptions Aristides goes on to exploit powerfully in *Oration* 19, where love turns to grief, which is then in turn converted, at least according to the hopes Aristides expresses throughout the second half of the text, into energy and investment for the future. Aristides starts by reminding the emperors of their passionate response to the city in the past (*Orat.* 19.2)[43] before moving on to the loss of the sights and architectural wonders they enjoyed: 'The harbour, which you saw, has closed its eyes, the beauty of the marketplace has gone, the adornments of the streets have disappeared' (19.3). There is also brief attention given to the human population here in the detail that the 'gymnasia together with the men and boys who used them are destroyed', and in his passing mention of 'ruins and corpses', but those are very much more cursory than the equivalent passages in Libanius and in the *Rhodian Oration*. Aristides then describes the intimate relationship between the emperors and other cities they have benefited in the past: 'you restored those cities which long ago were sick' (19.10). Even other cities, he says, are not strong enough to help Smyrna in the way that the emperors can, and in the way that Smyrna itself assisted other cities in the past: 'There is no city now sufficient to assist it in the way in which one city then aided other peoples' (19.12). In *Oration* 19, then, Aristides presents the emperors' love for the city and their grief, and also their capacity to benefit it, on a vast scale, from a zoomed-out perspective where the concerns of individual humans are likely to register only in passing, in a way that emphasizes the emperors' unique ability to solve the problem.

I also want to explore, however, a second and perhaps more surprising way of approaching the question of why Aristides pays so little attention to the inhabitants of Smyrna. My argument here is that the sidelining of human populations stems from Aristides' interest in exploring the difficulty of expressing grief for a more-than-human object, especially in what is represented as his spontaneous outpouring of emotion on hearing the news, in *Oration* 18.[44] How do we express grief for a city – or indeed for whole ecosystems or a whole planet – when those things are beyond human proportion, on a vaster scale than the objects our language of mourning is designed for? Might one see the omission of the human in *Oration* 18 as a starting point for Aristides' attempt to envisage large-scale environmental destruction; in other words, as a way of dealing with precisely the problems of scale that on some accounts are such powerful barriers to environmental action for us in the present? By choosing to avoid references to the suffering of the human inhabitants of the city Aristides forces himself to explore the difficulty of imagining and articulating human grief in relation to a more-than-human entity, and so opens himself and his readers to new ways of thinking about environmental destruction as something that cannot be straightforwardly encompassed within the commonplace language of human experience.

The opening of *Oration* 18 immediately foregrounds the idea that Aristides' grief is inexpressible, or barely expressible (Ael Arist. *Orat.* 18.1):

> Oh Zeus, what am I to do? Am I to be silent when Smyrna has fallen? Have I such an adamantine nature or such self-control? But am I to weep? What mode am I to use? How can I be so bold? For if all the voices of the Greeks and the barbarians, those still upon the earth and those of every age, I say if all came together, they would be too little for this calamity, even to undertake the task, not to mention maintaining its true proportion.

That dilemma recalls the opening of Aristides' *Sacred Tales* (which postdates *Oration* 18), where he says that even if he had all 'human strength, speech and wisdom' (*Sacred Tales* 1.1) he could not do justice to the deeds of the saviour god Asclepius. Aristides' experience of loss thus has a certain amount in common with his experience of the divine in that later text, in being beyond the power of any individual human to articulate. The image of inexpressibility then resurfaces a little later in relation to the magnificence of the city as it was before the earthquake: 'There was that which cannot be expressed in words or firmly grasped by seeing it, but is somehow elusive, yet ever afforded us the desire to comprehend it … a thing such as earth and sun never before revealed to humankind' (18.4). The indescribable quality of the city's beauty – like the indescribable sense of loss and grief Aristides feels on hearing of its destruction – has a quasi-sublime quality, in its capacity to overwhelm human understanding.

In what follows Aristides repeatedly describes features of the city in terms one might use for a body: that is not in itself an unusual thing to do, but Aristides does it with what Janet Downie has called 'unconventional intensity'.[45] For example, he tells us that 'the sights were beyond description. Immediately upon approaching there was a sheen of beauty, and there was proportion, measure, and stability in its magnitude, as it were in a single harmony' (*Orat.* 18.4). Later the bodily imagery is even blunter, with its focus on specific body parts: 'Such is the head that you have taken from our people, such is the eye which you have plucked out!' (18.8); 'The whole continent ought to have cut its hair in mourning, for its fair lock is wholly gone' (18.9). He also describes features of his own mourning experience in language one might use for landscape features or natural forces of various kinds, in an attempt to articulate the barely describable experience of emotional engagement with a non-human object vastly beyond the scale of his own human body. 'What kinds of springs of tears', he asks, 'are suitable for such a great disaster' (*poiai pēgai dakryōn hikanai tosoutō kakō*) (18.7). At other times he imagines various natural objects expressing their grief (as other ancient writers had before him, for example famously in Vergil, *Eclogues* 5), as if acknowledging the inadequacy of his human perspective on its own to lament the city's destruction: 'All the earth within and without Gadira! The orb of the stars! Sun who beholds all things! What a spectacle did you endure to see!' (18.7); 'The rivers ought to have flowed with tears' (18.9); and then in the final lines of the text: 'Now it is time for the trees themselves to mourn you, O most gracious of cities' (18.11). Here Aristides' own grief is joined with a bigger and more powerful chorus of lamenting voices from nature, as if in acknowledgement that this is the only way for him to mourn the city's destruction sufficiently.

Conclusions

My aim in this chapter has been to ask how far a comparative approach to ancient and modern notions of ecological grief can be used to open up new perspectives on a series of works by Philostratus and Aelius Aristides, and on the potential for those texts to serve as resources for environmental thinking in the present. Some aspects of their engagement with ideas of grief in relation to the destruction of Smyrna seem quite alien to their modern equivalents: Philostratus, for example, uses the emperor's tears primarily to advance his exploration of a range of different themes connected with ideas of imperial and sophistic self-definition that are ultimately very far removed from any kind of sustained ecological concern. I have also suggested, however, that there is a range of ways in which we might productively draw connections between these texts and contemporary manifestations of sorrow in relation to environmental degradation and disaster. That might involve seeing them as negative models that can help us to perceive more clearly the prevalence of ways of thinking that are more heavily rooted in liberal Western society than we are inclined to acknowledge, where expressions of environmental grief are still often made from a position of detachment, and still often sideline the perspectives of human populations, and especially marginalized communities. Alternatively, we might appropriate them opportunistically and selectively as powerful images of the way in which intimate, passionate, even anthropomorphic descriptions of love and grief can help us to break through our complacency and apathy in relation to the fate of threatened environments and the communities that inhabit them. We might see Aristides' *Oration* 18, too, as a powerful reflection on the challenges we face in trying to adapt our human emotions of grief in order to make them adequate for the kind of more-than-human objects and environments whose loss we are increasingly having to come to terms with in the present.

Notes

1. I am grateful to Eris Williams Reed and to the editors for comments on a draft of this chapter.

2. For dating see Franco 2005: 471–4.

3. Translations are based on the latest versions in the Loeb Classical library series, or in the case of Aristides on Behr 1981, but with some significant adjustments.

4. Cf. Williams Reed in this volume, but focusing on marginal communities rather than cosmopolitan, elite responses as I do here.

5. For a survey of recent publications, see Craps 2020.

6. Albrecht 2020: 9.

7. See Albrecht 2005; also 2020 for a survey of later publications by Albrecht and others.

8. Cunsolo and Ellis 2018: 275; cf. Cunsolo and Landman 2017a for a collection of essays along similar lines.

9. Cunsolo and Ellis 2018: 275.

10. Ibid.: 279.

11. Ibid.: 276.

12. See Cunsolo and Landman 2017a, Craps 2020: esp. 1–2 on glaciers, Burton-Christie 2011, Craps and Olsen 2020: esp. 115, Bruns 2021 on the Okjökull glacier funeral. On the problems associated with anthropomorphic thinking in these contexts, see Garrard 2012: 54–60 and 64–6 and Jensen 2019.

13. See Clark 2020; cf. Lertzman 2015 on 'environmental melancholia'.

14. See Lorimer 2015; Craps and Olsen 2020: 129.

15. On the difficulty of envisaging climate change on a global scale, see, among many others, Heise 2008, Morton 2013, Ghosh 2016, Clark 2019: 38–110; also Cunsolo and Landman 2017b: 16: 'although it is hard to imagine the loss of a human, it is harder still to think through the loss of non-humans, particularly if the non-humans we are mourning are large assemblages or systems, such as a body of water or an ecosystem or a forest'.

16. See Deeg 2019; also Jones 2012 for caveats; other important studies of responses to earthquakes include Borsch 2018 and 2021, and Walter 2019. See also Woolf 2020: e.g. 88–9, 314, 354–5 and 415–16, on the vulnerability of ancient cities, especially large ones, in the face of natural disaster, and the importance of imperial intervention for ensuring resilience.

17. As Downie 2017: 70 points out; see also Webb 1997: 115 on other factors contributing to the impact of this phrase.

18. See Webb 2009: 161–3 on this passage as a rare example charting an emotional reaction to epideictic rhetoric; also Civiletti 2002: 568 n. 20 on this incident as formative moment in Aristides' career.

19. E.g. see 1.21, 516 on Scopelian.

20. E.g. absence of tears represented positively at 2.16, 596; negatively at 2.25, 610.

21. See 2.10, 587 for a positive example of grief associated with sophistic commemoration.

22. I have learned a lot from Artemis Brod's not-yet-published work on that topic; cf. Petsalis-Diomidis 2008, who shows not only that Aristides draws attention to his bodily immersion in the act of travel, but also (139–40) that he envisages his body as a kind of landscape in itself;

also Petsalis-Diomidis 2010: 101–21 and 148–50 for further discussion along similar lines; Downie 2013: 110–13 for the full series of these bathing cures; Holmes 2008: 110–11.

23. See Bosak-Schroeder 2020.

24. E.g. see Huggan and Tiffin 2010; Clark 2019: 137–59.

25. E.g. see *Sacred Tales* 4.32-37 and 5.27, where Aristides describes threatening weather events while also stressing his own invulnerability.

26. On earthquake speeches as a category in ancient rhetorical theory, see Franco 2008: 233.

27. Cf. Webb 1997: 115 and 2009: 162, who points out that *Oration* 19 corresponds to the category of 'ambassador's speech', which according to Menander Rhetor (*Treatise* 2.12, 423-24), was supposed to include an account of the destruction inflicted on the city, with special attention to impact on the city's monuments (although it is important to stress that Menander is writing after Aristides, and was presumably very much aware of his work).

28. See Newbold 1982 on earthquake reports in ancient historiography; cf. Toner 2013: 114.

29. See Demoen 2001: 114 on the absence of references to the human victims of the earthquake.

30. See Watts 2014 for discussion of Libanius, *Oration* 61, along with his other descriptions of the Nicomedia earthquake, against the background of Aristides' work.

31. E.g. see Clark 2019: 138.

32. Cf. Williams Reed in this volume.

33. On *Oration* 25, see Franco 2008, including discussion of arguments for ascribing the text to Aristides.

34. E.g. see 25.22-23 for vivid description of the range of different fates suffered by the city's inhabitants as their buildings collapsed around them; and Franco 2008: 235 on Aristides' mention of human bodies in Rhodes in *Oration* 25, explaining the difference by its different goals: *Oration* 18 aims at winning the emperor's support for rebuilding, whereas *Oration* 25 is a speech of consolation aimed at the survivors.

35. Cf. Franco 2008.

36. That phenomenon is discussed in many of the essays in Cunsolo and Landman 2017a, e.g. Cunsolo and Landman 2017b: 14–15; however, see also Sideris 2020 on the way in which grief is represented by one strand of 'climate humanists' as incompatible with solutions-focused thinking.

37. Dated by Behr 1981: 356 to 157 CE.

38. Cf. Downie 2017: esp. 54; also Yatromanolakis 2005: 278–82 on Aristides as one of many Greek authors who represent the city as an object of desire.

39. See Downie 2017: 59 and 61–2; also Petsalis-Diomidis 2008 on body imagery in Aristides' praise of Smyrna, and on the way in which the city is likened to a fragmented body after the earthquake.

40. On the way in which the Smyrna speeches adapt standard rhetorical formats, see Downie 2017: 56 and 66, with extensive further bibliography.

41. Cf. ibid.: 57 on the way in which the speech focuses intensively on 'the visual impression made by the city – to the near-total exclusion of its history, its mythological past, its institutional and intellectual life, and the virtues of its citizens'; and see also Demoen

2001: 113–16 on the way in which Aristides' Smyrna texts relate to a long tradition of lamenting ruined cities in Greek literature from Homer to the Byzantine period.

42. See above on Polemo and Smyrna, with reference to *VS* 1.25, 530.

43. Cf. Downie 2017: 66–72 on the way in which *Oration* 19 inserts the emperor into the role of lover of the city.

44. E.g. see 18.2 side by side with 17.3.

45. Downie 2017: 59.

CHAPTER 11

AN ALLEGORY OF THE ANTHROPOCENE: ENVIRONMENTAL AND TEXTUAL DISORDER IN CLAUDIAN'S *DE RAPTU PROSERPINAE*

Marco Formisano

History is a nightmare from which I am trying to awake.

James Joyce, *Ulysses*, p. 34

Allegory is concerned with founding myths and their disjunctions.

Elizabeth D. DeLoughrey, *Allegories of the Anthropocene*, p. 49

Reading the Anthropocene in ancient texts

Close reading – undoubtedly the most unquestioned approach taken by classicists, whatever their methodological agenda, in order to read ancient Greek and Latin texts – is not unrelated, as it may appear, to the discourse of the Anthropocene. As recently stated by Helena Feder in the introduction to a volume significantly entitled *Close Reading the Anthropocene*, 'close' indicates a proximity of the reading subject to the read material object.[1] But what are some implications of close reading the Anthropocene? As Feder astutely argues, 'depending on its use (*scil.* of the Anthropocene), its turn in a text, it may signal a resistance to false holism, an awareness of our stratified humanity and damaged planetary ecology, or the shiny, technical face of domination'.[2] In the same volume, Graham Huggan reminds us that the Anthropocene 'registers the *limits* of the human as much as it acknowledges the *influence* of the human'.[3] Huggan, referring to Rosi Braidotti, emphasizes that the human subject is actually not at the centre of the Anthropocene, although the term is literally derived from the Greek word for 'human' (*anthropos*). Rather, the discourse of the Anthropocene systematically sheds light on the enmeshedness of human and non-human or more-than-human agents. Thus, following Timothy Clark's concept of 'scalar critique', Huggan contends that the Anthropocene requires 'a drastic readjustment of our reading practices in order to accommodate both human and non-human life' within much broader spatial and temporal scales.[4]

What are or might be the implications of this new kind of close reading caused by its generative encounter with the Anthropocene within the field of literary classical studies? At a first glance, the encounter between the Anthropocene and the study of ancient texts might appear problematic for the hermeneutic tradition within which the discipline operates and is situated, because environmental criticism cannot be considered as just another hermeneutical tool that can be added to the discipline's long methodological tradition. Rather, I understand it to be a totalizing approach generated by the radical breakthrough in perspective which comes with the abandonment of human primacy and a full acknowledgement of the centrality of the environment and other more-than-human agents. As Dipesh Chakrabarty teaches us, history as a human construction yields to natural history: geology surpasses history.[5] From the humanistic and anthropocentric perspective, the hermeneutic implications of this change of scale might be perceived as dangerous and destabilizing. This is especially because it can lead to anachronism, i.e. to ignoring the immediate historical context, and to a split between author and text, since the latter is not seen as a direct emanation of an individual human poetic project but rather as a 'force of nature',[6] that is, as an element that generates its own agency in relationship to the environment. But it must be equally emphasized that classical studies, precisely in virtue of their mastery of close reading, have the potential (perhaps more than any other literary field) to make a significant contribution to environmental criticism, provided that classicists are ready to move towards forms of criticism that are able to 'disidentify from the potentially all-encompassing tropes of Man and Anthropos'.[7] In this chapter, I explore the strange textuality of a mythological poem from the end of the fourth century CE.

The late Latin epic poem *De raptu Proserpinae* by Claudius Claudianus famously comes to us incomplete, ending abruptly before bringing the story to its well-known conclusion.[8] In this chapter I consciously try to follow the unfinishedness and fragmentariness of the poem rather than to furnish a unitary vision of the text in its entirety. Jean-Louis Charlet, editor of Claudian's poetic corpus, discusses the range of interpretations of *De raptu Proserpinae* that he describes as 'literary, religious, political, and symbolical or allegorical'.[9] All these approaches are generated by the firm, though implicit, conviction that Claudian had a project that he realized in such a way as to keep it hidden from his readers, who are thus invited to solve a mystery: what precisely did the poet want to tell us? Instead, in what follows I would like to look at the text *as it is*. I try to make sense of the broken narrative style and the incompleteness of this poem (whose relationships with its immediate historical context are particularly unclear) by fully embracing them.

Allegories of the Anthropocene: Claudian's *De raptu Proserpinae*

The myth of Proserpina's abduction narrates an unstable universal order preceding the advent of agriculture in human civilization, an event that can be seen as the foundational act of the Anthropocene, profoundly changing relationships between the soil, the landscape and human work.[10] Yet the connection between agriculture and Anthropocene in this text is problematic for two reasons in particular. The first is that Ceres' gift to humanity which follows her daughter's abduction by Pluto into the Underworld and, consequently, the agreement established by Jupiter according to which Proserpina can divide her time between her new infernal husband and her mother, is entirely lacking from the narrative in Claudian's poem. The introduction of agriculture is only alluded to in the opening of Book 1 where the poet seems to summarize the content of his poetic project in an appeal to the gods of the underworld (1.25-31):[11]

> Disclose to me the mysteries of sacred matters and the secrets of your world: with what torch Love made Pluto bend; how high-spirited Proserpina was stolen away and came to possess Chaos as her dowry, and over how many shores her anxious mother wandered on her troubled course; whence grain was given to the nations and, with the abandonment of acorns, the oak of Dodona gave way to the discovery of corn.

Perhaps the clearest illustration of this poem's discourse of incompleteness is the famous description of Proserpina creating a tapestry which represents, precisely, the cosmos in its making (1.246-75). Weaving the tapestry intended to be a gift for her mother, Proserpina is interrupted by the arrival of Venus, Pallas and Diana which causes her to 'leave her work incomplete' (*imperfectumque laborem/deserit*, 1.271-72). The reader encounters not only the image of incomplete work but also the unfinishedness of the universe contained in the tapestry. Both *textus* ('woven artefact' and 'text') and the cosmos are framed by the incomplete and virtually never-ending boundary of the water: *Coeperat et vitreis summo iam margine texti/oceanum sinuare vadis* (1.269-70, 'She had even now begun to curl the Ocean with its glassy waves round the very edge of the weaving'). More generally, incompleteness is not only a structural but a narrative feature of this poem. Descriptions of tormented and broken landscapes and of other natural elements marked by incompleteness seem to represent or prefigure what is happening with the divine protagonists.

The second feature that complicates any interpretation of this late antique poem is that it evidently invites being read as an allegory. The sharp contrast between this traditional pagan myth and the triumphant Christianity of Claudian's time is evident. Yet readers are given no clue as to what this poetic rendering of the pagan myth might be an allegory *of*. In the wake of the theorization developed by Walter Benjamin in his influential study of German baroque drama, allegory is one of the textual features which most emphasize disruption and incommensurability;[12] Frederic Jameson writes that an allegoresis which establishes a neat correspondence between two different levels is a 'bad allegory', since 'genuine allegory does not seek the meaning of a work, but rather functions to reveal its structure of multiple meanings, and thereby to modify the very meaning of the word *meaning*'.[13] Elizabeth DeLoughrey, discussing how natural disasters appear at key moments in such a way that they represent the 'planet as a system', has explored the deep and intimate connection between allegory as a textual function and the Anthropocene. Allegory emphasizes moments of disjunction and rupture between humans and their more-than-human environment; 'the Anthropocene is both forward-looking and a future retrospective', and allegory is characterized by an 'anticipatory logic'.[14]

One thing any reader will quickly notice in the *De raptu Proserpinae* is the massive presence of environmental factors, often presented within independent ecphrases, and their violent functioning. More than fifty years ago Alan Cameron in his pathbreaking book on Claudian declared the continuous insertion of ecphrastic and descriptive scenes in this poem to be an aesthetic failure, since they hold up 'the flow of narrative'.[15] An aesthetic criterion which privileges a logical and harmonious narrative structure that flows smoothly from beginning to end will simply not be met by this Late Antique poem.[16] Landscapes and natural elements in this poem are by no means stable. Land and sea, mountains, rivers, lakes, meadows, and groves *move around*: all is unstable and in constant motion. It is as if these landscapes, like the text, are not entirely under the control of author or readers. We might say that both the landscapes and the text itself have a certain agency, which is marked by motion and incompletion.

Land and sea

Elsewhere I have discussed the *praefatio* to the *De raptu Proserpinae*, which has often been read as Claudian's declaration of intention in terms of his poetic career, i.e. his planned progression from less worthy literary genres to a major epic poem.[17] I have suggested the limitations of this approach, arguing that it is insensitive to the very content of the poetry which – beyond any metapoetic interpretation or search for intertextual relationships – simply describes the first human being sailing the ocean using *ars* to provide what *natura* denies, namely the ability for humans to travel on the water:

> He who first (*primus*) cut the deep (*profundum*) with the ship he had invented and disturbed the waters with rough-hewn oars, who dared to commit his vessel of alder-wood (*alnum*) to the unreliable blasts and made available by his art ways which nature denies, at first trusted himself trembling to the calm waves, coasting along (*legens*) the edge of the shores on a safe course; soon he began to try out vast bays, to leave the land (*linquere terras*) and spread his sails to the mild south wind; but when, little by little, his impetuous boldness grew and his heart forgot sluggish fear, roving now far and wide he burst upon open water, and, following the sky, mastered Aegean storms and the Ionian Sea.

Formally, this little poem in six elegiac couplets consists of a single sentence, as if to emphasize its independence from the epic itself, in hexameters. The content is not placed in a historically defined time nor is it explicitly located within any particular mythic narrative. Rather, it is about a primordial time or before the historical becoming itself: *primus* ('the first') here is all we know of the sailor, to whom the only specificity conferred is actually his gender. Nor is there any identification between the sailing man and the poet; the learning of the art of navigation is narrated in the third person. Even more surprising is the fact that the prefatory poem does not contain any reference to the theme of the poem itself, the rape of Proserpina and the consequent birth of agricultural cycles. The sailor and his voyage are usually interpreted as an allegory of the epic journey undertaken by the poet, but I suggest that we can consider the sailor as an allegory for the reader: just as that first sailor gradually distances himself from the shore (v. 6 *litora summa legens*) and, on the strength of his 'art' (v. 4 *praebuit arte vias*), 'unlearns his fear' (v. 10 *dedidicere metum*), so the reader departs from a literal reading to embrace an allegorical interpretation of the mythological event narrated in the poem. The *littoral* thus becomes an allegory of the *literal*, from which the reader-navigator learns to detach himself. Significantly, the sea is in the first line named through its attribute, *profundum*, 'the deep': going into the sea can be allegorically read as a way of reading (v. 6 *legens*) which goes to a *depth*, in tension with a journey which moves superficially, i.e. on the water. Like this sailor, the reader's activity is in constant tension between a superficial and a deep reading.[18] The narrative of the sailor en route to the high seas can thus assume not only a new meaning, but becomes itself an allegory of allegory, or, more precisely of allegoresis itself – a reading which a mythological poem written in a period of triumphant Christianity clearly invites.

Focusing on this territorial configuration of poetic language, my reading places the coast itself, described in the central verse as *summa litora* (v. 6), at the centre. It thus assumes the fundamental role of demarcating the physical and conceptual boundary: the man leaves the coast to venture to the high seas. Note how the adjective *summa* is somewhat pleonastic in that it describes a quality that the very coast, as such, already possesses in its essence as a boundary line and edge, so much so that its rendering in modern translations fails. Indeed, at the end of the 'coastal verse' (v. 6) we find what I consider to be the key term: *legens*. The centrally located participle not only represents a conceptual turning point and border but also its materialization: until the end of v. 6, the sailor – as well as the reader – *reads* the coast, but thereafter he distances himself from that 'literal' shoreline. *Legens* in its insoluble ambiguity is a syllepsis that compels the reader, especially because of its prominent position at the heart of this prefatory poem, to reflect on the duplicity of meaning: 'skimming' the coast but also inevitably 'reading' it. It should be noted, however, that in this case *legens* is not only a syllepsis but perhaps *the* syllepsis par excellence, because it is precisely in the experience of *reading* that the phenomenon of syllepsis manifests itself. *Legens*, to borrow the title of a famous essay by Gilles Deleuze, represents the *pli*, the 'fold' made by the text.[19] Shane Butler, in *The Matter of the Page*, invites us to consider ancient texts in their very materiality, that is, in the elementary *mise-en-page*, considered as 'a plot available for plots'. The page represents the physical space in which the reader's eyes move in different directions and not necessarily diachronically. The text always confronts the readers with an elementary truth: 'All these words are here together, at the same time'.[20] Following these suggestions, we can appreciate how *legens* becomes an allegory of its own dual meaning and as such demarcates both the conceptual and material boundary on the written page between land and sea, between letter and allegory, between verbal signification and aesthetic perception, between symbolic meaning and the materiality of the text, between the land of the text, finally, and the sea of its reception.

Not only does this preface depict a displacement defined by the presence of the natural elements, land and sea, and the movement from one to the other, but prefaces are arguably by their very nature liminal. As Laura Jansen notes, 'paratexts are neither fully attached to nor detached from the text, but they conform to a liminal zone between its inside and outside'.[21] Considering the preface to *De raptu Proserpinae* as a liminal zone creates a number of interpretive possibilities. First, the sailor is depicted in the act of moving away from the land toward the deep sea. The two spaces between which the protagonist moves, hypersemantically 'skimming the coast' (*litora legens*), are precisely land and sea, two kinds of space as described by Deleuze and Guattari: the 'striated' and the 'smooth'.[22] Striated space is characterized by the continuous traces imposed by structures of power, state, police and authority in general and is therefore 'homogeneous', while smooth space is the nomadic space of continuous movement that perpetually shifts boundaries, set from time to time only to be crossed. If the land is the striated space par excellence, the sea is the smooth space, whose only internal boundaries are the perpetually moving waves, never fixed or firmly determined,[23] yet threatened by human control, as in Claudian's *praefatio*, whose sailor subdues (v. 12 *domat*) the waves through his technique (v. 4 *arte*).

Suggestively enough, the sailor's actions in the smooth space of the sea are described with *striating* imagery: *secuit*, prominent in the first verse. Like *legens*, this verb is a syllepsis, compressing within itself the meanings of 'to cut' and 'to cross' (defined by the *praefatio*) but also that of 'to incise' (as a medical term) and 'to wound', which is what the plough does in ploughing the earth (used in this sense by Claudian himself shortly afterwards at 1.186-87). And, as Butler observes, in Latin some agricultural terms are used as metaphors for writing, for example, *exarare* can signify writing.[24] But since *secare* implies drawing a line, on sea or on land, it is not difficult to think of the stylus marking the character on wax or papyrus. Next, with his still inexperienced oars (v. 2 *rudibus remis*) the sailor beats the waters (v. 2 *sollicitavit*) and with his technical knowledge succeeds in imposing 'roads' precisely where nature had denied them (v. 4 *quas natura negat praebuit arte vias*), thus 'streaking' the expanse of the sea. Roads are imposed on sea, but by their very definition they exist only on the land, which in turn displays an order determined by human 'striation'. In short, one can read Claudian's preface as the description and material representation of the process of signification itself, imposed by language on nature.

A further detail supports this observation. In the first part of the poem no proper nouns appear, and until the end of verse 6, which closes precisely with *legens*, temporality remains expressed only implicitly by the perfect tense of the verbs (*secuit*, *sollicitavit*, *praebuit*, *credidit*). The boundary crossing is determined by temporal markers (*mox*, *paulatim*, *iam*) while there is a progression from the past to the present tense (note *domat* prominently at the end of line 12, closing the poem itself). Proper nouns appear at verse 8 (*Noto*) and then more prominently right at the close: *Aegaeas hiemes Ioniumque* (v. 12), as if to mark how signification has now been definitively accomplished and settled through the imposition of geographic and climatic nomenclature: from the *Ortung*, then, to the *Ordnung* imposed by naming.[25] The sailor, now skilled in his art, not only traces roads in the open sea, imposing the striated on the smooth, but also rules the stormy waters, which the poet delimits within precise toponyms which were altogether absent in the first part of the poem, when he was about to embark on his voyage.

In the topographical constellation of the *praefatio*, the coast is thus charged with different meanings and takes on various functions. The first is that of the boundary between land and sea, between the 'striated' land, habitable, measurable, cultivable and controllable by human beings, and the sea, the realm of the 'smooth', of the unknown, without fixed boundaries, not yet controlled by *techne*. Furthermore, if the land can be defined as a place of signification, the sea, which bears no recognizable human mark, could be said to be uninscribed, representing the absence of language or the asymbolic.

Thus John Hamilton, commenting on a novella by Theodor Storm, suggests that 'the coast is defined as the place where the sea denies itself'.[26] This leads me to see a second function in Claudian's preface. By representing the coast as a boundary and concretizing it in a territorial image, it exhibits its own liminality: the coast is the paratext itself as the 'liminal zone between the inside and the outside' (Jansen 2014) of the text. And there is a third function, one that creates a deep connection between an intellectual and a perceptual level. Insofar as it is placed at the centre of the poetic preface (v. 6 *summa litora*), the coast demarcates an inner boundary of the *praefatio* itself, inviting the reader to simultaneously 'read' and 'skim' (*legens*) it.

Reading an unorderly environment: Analogy or allegory?

Seismic movements are a notable characteristic of Claudian's text and they often function as a prefiguration – or allegory? – of human actions or events. A passage from Book 1 exemplifies this feature. In the account of why Ceres decided to keep her daughter hidden in Sicily, and therefore protected from possible offenders, Claudian describes the geological circumstances that caused the island to be detached from the Italian continent (1.141-47):

> Trinacria was once a conjoined part of Italy, but sea and time have changed the lie of the land. Victorious Nereus burst his boundaries (*rupit confinia*) and washed between the severed mountains with his waters (*abscissos interluit aequore montes*), and a small division keeps apart these kindred countries (*parvaque cognatas prohibent discrimina terras*). Now Nature has set against the sea that three-pronged island that is broken (*raptam*) from its related ground.

In a thought-provoking article Wolfgang Fauth sheds light on the representations of seismic activity appearing throughout *De raptu Proserpinae* 'as expression of an elementary threat, invoked by chthonic and cataclysmic forces'.[27] Concentrating on passages that express in an exemplary way the chthonic thematic that decisively marks this poem, Fauth is mainly interested in determining whether Claudian was original in his poetic project, or rather re-used material and images already present in the literary tradition, above all in the Homeric *Hymn to Demeter*, Callimachus, Vergil and Ovid. Like many, Fauth's discussion gives primacy to the author's intentions and to human agents in the text. But Fauth's argument also hints at ways in which considering the role of the environment along with other more-than-human factors can reveal the text as a 'natural force', not wholly under the control of its author. On this passage, for example, Fauth notes that the sea (*Nereus victor*) and the now separated but 'related' Italian regions (*cognatas terras*) are personified and, above all, that *rapere* (*raptam*) powerfully alludes to the central event of the poem: the *raptus* of Proserpina by Pluto.

More recently, Elizabeth Heintges has discussed the crucial role of the Sicilian landscape within the narrative of Claudian's epic poem, noting that its presence in each of the three extant books articulates the focus on cycles of death and rebirth. On the passage from Book 1, Heintges notes how Sicily presents in itself 'seemingly incompatible components', i.e. the cycles of destruction and production characterizing the interpretation of the Greek myth offered in this poem,[28] and she points to the 'analogy between the young goddess and the island' emphasized by *illam raptam* (1.147). The *raptus Siciliae* (as we might call it) presents the relationship in terms of the tension between land and sea seen in the preface, as discussed above, and it powerfully visualizes the sense of breaking and interruption of various kinds that is thematized within the poem, at the level of both content and form (*pace* Cameron).

But this passage is important from a further perspective. This description of such an abrupt geological event is not so much an analogy (as for instance Heintges describes it) as it is a *strange* allegory, embodying what will happen in the central scene of the abduction, when the earth will be disrupted by the furious arrival of Pluto from beneath, when he tears Proserpina away from her divine relatives Diana and Minerva. Why a *strange* allegory? It is as if the geological situation, that is, Sicily's abrupt division from the continent, is foreshadowing the mythical event narrated, but at the same time it creates its very setting. For the 'abducted' Sicily is the place where the abduction of Proserpina takes place, when she in turn is dramatically separated from her relatives (*cognatas*). This foreshadowing disturbingly assimilates a violent geological event (the division of Sicily from Italy) and a narrative of rape: what happens to the earth, raped by Nereus, also happens to Proserpina, raped by Pluto. And it is this violated land, Sicily, that provides the very setting for the event of the girl's rape. The geological prefiguration of the abduction also shows the power of a 'deep time', that is, of temporal arcs in which humanity does not participate, yet which profoundly influence our life on the planet. There is no rational or narrative connection between Sicily's *raptus* and Proserpina's; the text establishes a relationship that is disturbing precisely because it is associative, i.e. metaphorical or, better, allegorical, rather than cause-and-effect.

Yet such foreshadowing is difficult to classify according to the usual rhetorical categories: on closer inspection, it is neither a metaphor, nor an allegory, nor an actual prefiguration, since in all three of those techniques the comparison remains external to the narrative and acts on another conceptual level. Here Sicily is the very place where Proserpina's abduction occurs, suggesting a deep identity between the human protagonist and the environment that contains her. The mechanism of classical allegory does not work either, because in this case it cannot be determined which one, Sicily or Proserpina, is an allegory of the other: the one cannot be separated from the other. The two entities are placed on the same level, they are co-present, one contains the other.

Illuminating in this regard are the considerations of Deborah Danowski and Edoardo Viveiros de Castro, who, commenting on the transformation of humans into a geological force as active protagonists of the Anthropocene, write:

> In an ironic and deadly (because recursively contradictory) inversion of the relationship between figure and ground, the *ambiented* becomes the *ambient* (or 'ambienting'), and the converse is equally the case. It is effectively the collapse of an ever more ambiguous environment, of which we can no longer say *where* it is in relation to us, and us to it.[29]

Along these lines, Sicily and Proserpina can be read as 'ambienting' and 'ambiented' agents, each influencing the other, so that human readers cannot distinguish them in terms of a mutual relationship between two different things. In other words, the allegorizing agent, the Sicilian territory and its peculiar landscape, and the allegorized story, Proserpina's rape, are not only conceptually linked but physically joined, such that the one literally contains the other. Both humans (or anthropomorphic gods) and landscape are part of the universal mesh.

The relationship between the two dimensions recalls the ubiquitous presence of a hyperobject: 'The more I struggle to understand hyperobjects, the more I discover that I am stuck to them. They are all over me', as Morton writes.[30] More interestingly still, consideration of hyperobjects can 'provoke *irreductionist* thinking',[31] that doesn't keep human agents separate from their more-than-human environment.

Trees, really. The matter's other story

Pourquoi est-ce que je me souviens de ces lectures?

Pourquoi faut-il travestir la forêt de mes vieux symbols?

Pierre Moinot, *Le Guetter d'ombre*, p.51

Undoubtedly the most acknowledged reading technique inspired by environmental criticism is the identification within a text of a subterranean or superficially invisible network of correspondences between various factors and elements that represent and exalt the kind of interconnectedness characteristic of the functioning of the environment. Natural phenomena are never graspable in their entirety; they might have been generated in completely different contexts and under circumstances remote from the place of their manifestation, so that humans can perceive them only locally and partially. Timothy Morton famously coined the term of *hyperobjects*, i.e. entities (such as climate warming) which, although very real and concrete, manifest themselves to human beings only partially, but in such a way that they thoroughly affect their very perception.[32] An ecocritical approach reveals complexities that cannot be controlled or resolved, and the kinds of connections explored by ecocritics are fundamentally unsettling, undoing the tacit pact between author and reader by presenting not an orderly universe where everything neatly refers to something else, but rather a series of incongruities that ultimately have the potential of fragmenting and breaking the text as well as of exalting its fundamentally unfinished nature. Incommensurability, differences of scale, and lack of logical connections are the most significant features of texts that ecocriticism invites us to consider. In this final section, I identify a particular kind of hidden connection that goes through the entire poem, that is represented by trees and the material they provide, wood.

Towards the end of the third book of the poem, Ceres, desperately searching for her lost daughter, travels to the peaks of Mount Etna where she enters a grove (3.332 *lucus*) that contains the spoils of the rebellious Giants. The goddess in her fury eradicates several trees in order eventually to turn them into torches which she uses, permanently burning, to illuminate her way through the dark night in her search for Proserpina. The passage has a density that mimetically parallels that of the grove itself. In particular, the trees take on a variety of attributes and functions. First, they symbolically represent the Giants, proudly bearing their very names: *nullaque non magni iactat se nominis arbor* (3.344, 'there is no tree which does not boast of some great name'.) The trees become linguistic symbols of the Giants they literally enclose: these trees are tombs testifying the deadly outcome of the Giants' insurgency against Jupiter: *Phlegraeis silva superbit / exuviis totumque nemus victoria vestit* (3.337-38, 'The wood exults in the spoils of Phlegra and victory clothes all the forest'.).

Although this grove is considered a sacred space by others, precisely the holiness attached to it (3.358: *religio loci*) enflames Ceres' furious quest of her daughter. The goddess then begins to uproot several kinds of trees in order to test their individual qualities: *pinus* (3.359) and *cedros* (3.360), as well as *fagos et alnos* (3.365). She eventually chooses two cypresses: (*cupressus* 370): *haec placuere faces* (3.376, 'These won her approval as torches'.) Ceres is here depicted as an expert engineer testing different kinds of woods and trees that she might use in order to create torches destined to light her search through the Mediterranean Sea, as described in last extant lines of the poem (3.437-48). During her spasmodic activity Ceres is, quite surprisingly, compared to a sailor in these terms (3.363-69):

> So when a man, intending to transport merchandise (*merces*) over remote waters, constructs his vessel on dry land and makes ready to expose his life to gales, he measures up beeches and alders (*fagos metitur et alnos*) and adapts the timber in its raw state to various uses (*et varium rudibus silvis accommodat usum*): the long one will provide yard-arms for the swelling sails; the strong one is better for the mast; the pliant one will be good for oars; the one that puts up with swamp water should be fitted to the keel.

This sailor parallels the one presented in the preface (*praef.* 1, *primus qui*). There are a number of interesting points to be made. First, while the sailor of the preface is by no means presented as a *comparandum* – even though almost every modern scholar in fact reads the preface as a comparison with the poet – this sailor is introduced in comparison with Ceres. It is as if the reader, having already met the sailor of the preface, is now invited to compare the goddess with that specific sailor. We see the material with which the sailor's boat is made, alder, both times at the end of the line: there *alnum*, here *alnos*. The reader now learns what the first sailor, previously depicted in the act of preparing to go out with his boat on the high seas, had done even earlier: building his boat after identifying alder as one of the most suitable materials. More importantly still, the reader now comes to know the real goal of the sailor's enterprise: business. What has been previously presented as a unique adventure into the open sea aimed at launching the art of navigation becomes here a much more common enterprise determined by a purely economic reason (*vecturus merces*) which colours that event in utilitarian terms: building a ship is functional to earning money, a goal that is distant both from Ceres' frantic actions as well as from the courageous cultural project of the sailor in the preface. This mercantilist detail adds a normalizing nuance within the mythological context of the poem, revealing what turns out to be a standard motivation for human beings to exploit natural resources: their own economic advantage. Finally, a comparison of Ceres and the sailor draws attention to the point that, while the goddess will be using trees in order to make torches from their wood, the sailor made use of wood in order to cross the sea. In other words, a discrepancy emerges between natural elements, fire and water as well as land and sea.

Joshua Hartman has recently interpreted the violation of the sacred grove by Ceres as an image for destruction of the literary tradition, considering her eradicating fury 'as a metaliterary commentary in which the goddess represents the secondary poet who must destroy and repurpose the existing canon'.[33] Hartman sees confirmation of his hypothesis precisely in the comparison with the sailor of the preface, a passage which he considers to be an allegory of the creativity of the epic poet. Thus the trees appearing in Book 3 as described above 'are as overburdened as the poet's own mind'.[34] Reading the trees as testimony of the literary tradition, Hartman then argues that the poem itself results from a poetic negotiation between the heaviness of the classical models and their destruction by Ceres in order to create something new: 'When the grove is ultimately destroyed, it is transformed into both the torches of Ceres and the ship that the preface presents as a symbol of literary boldness.'[35]

Hartman's reading is characteristic of a long-standing form of criticism that exalts human language and semiotic activity above non-human elements. As observed by ecocritic Pierre Schoentjes, in many hermeneutic traditions since Romanticism nature becomes an abstraction and a bookish reality through which humans speak about themselves in the first place, while an ecocritically inspired reading aims at privileging the natural worlds in its own terms by approaching texts as concrete experiences rather than symbolic abstractions.[36] Following this path implies perceiving Claudian's trees in their concreteness rather than as purely literary symbols, and a different set of implications emerges. The wood of the trees becomes a vehicle for suggesting the inconsistency and the fundamental instability of the meanings attached to matter by human beings. As Ceres sets out on the long journey through the whole world searching for her daughter, she exclaims (3.407-10):

> It was not such torches as these, Proserpina, that I hoped to carry for you, but I had the wishes common to all mothers: of marriage-bed and festal torches and a wedding-song to be sung in heaven before everyone's eyes.

Ceres first tests different trees, but in order to fabricate her torches she does not select beeches and alders (as does the sailor to whom she is compared) but another kind, namely cypresses. Soon after, she regrets that these torches are not the ones she would like to bring to Proserpina for her wedding. While the material is the same – wood (though from different trees) – the meaning constantly changes, in a revelation of the inconsistency of the process of human signification itself.

At the same time, the presence of one species of tree in particular, the alder, allows the reader to identify an intra-textual interconnection in material terms. *Alnus* appears three times throughout the poem, always as an accusative and in all three occurrences in a prominent position at the end of the verse, highlighting its inherently excellent quality for navigation.[37] After first appearing at the end of line 3 of the preface, the term returns in the second book in a passage full of telluric tension, namely, when the boatmen navigating the Po hear the rumbling of the opening of the ground in Sicily caused by Pluto's arrival in the central scene of the abduction (3.176-78):

It was heard by those shut in by Alpine ice, and him who swam you, Tiber, when you were not yet circled with a crown of Latin trophies, and him who rowed an alder-wood boat launched upon the River Po (*missamque Pado qui remigat alnum*).

In this exemplary passage the interdependence of different factors is explicitly thematized: what happens in Sicily is felt in the Alps, in the Tiber, and by those who are sailing on the Po in the boats made of alder. The *alnus*, generally associated with crossing a water surface, in its very materiality sustains the narrative at three crucial moments in all three books of the poem, with different accents. While in the preface the sailor uses this tree for the first time ('he dared to commit his vessel of alder-wood to the unreliable blasts'), in the passage from Book 2 just quoted, the men crossing the river Po seem to be habitual users of this kind of wood. And in the comparison presented in Book 3 the sailor-merchant is depicted in the very act of testing it ('he measures up beeches and alders and adapts the timber in its raw state to various uses'), transferring the reader to a time that occurs even before the first voyage narrated in the preface.

This situation configures within the framing narrative – the rape of Proserpina – another story that is mediated through the materiality of the *alnus*. This other story not only undoes the chronological sequence of the main narrative but also installs the meaning of the wood of the tree in itself and in doing so emphasizes the role of matter as such. Writing about 'storied matter', Serpil Oppermann describes how 'matter slides through human "express ways" often unnoticed but always exerting its influence in conceptual and material habitats', adding that 'storied matter compels us to think beyond anthropocentricity and about our coexistence and coevolution in the story of the earth itself'.[38] It is worth recalling here that the Latin *silva* is not only the word for 'wood' or 'forest' but also translates the Greek *hule* (which also signifies 'matter') and that both terms are used to refer to textual 'material' used by writers.[39]

Imperfectus labor, or the enmeshed text

In both content and form Claudian's poem represents a particularly fortunate field for the environmental critic. The very myth of the rape of Proserpina tells of the birth of agriculture, a fundamental anthropocenic event. But, in fact, the text blurs an overly neat distinction between form and content. This is done, first, by its sustained enmeshment of various human and non-human actors (gods, landscapes, mountains, trees, sea, lakes, etc.) and, second, by two features of the form in which we read it: its evident openness, due not least to its incompleteness, and its highly allegorical potential.

As we have seen, in the final part of Book 1 (246-70) Proserpina is depicted weaving a tapestry representing the birth of the cosmos still in the making, and her tapestry is left incomplete, broken off. Similarly, the poem depicts a universe in constant motion, and the geographical setting of the story, Sicily, is a territory ruptured, broken and still *in fieri*. Proserpina's tapestry returns in Book 3, when Ceres enters the palace where she was keeping her daughter hidden (3.153-58):

> And, opening the doors, as she passed through the empty rooms and deserted halls, she recognized the half-ruined weaving with its disordered threads (*semirutas confuso stamine telas*) and the work of the shuttle that had been broken off. That wonderful task of the goddess had gone to waste and the bold spider was completing the gap left behind with her sacrilegious web (*audax sacrilego supplebat aranea textu*).

The cosmos that the young goddess was depicting now turns into a confused tangle of threads that continues to be worked on by a non-human actor: a spider weaving in accordance with its own pictorial program. Nothing is said about the content of this 'sacrilegious web' (or 'text', *textu*), but the agency of humans or anthropomorphic deities is now excluded. The tapestry initially woven by a goddess is now enmeshed with the 'supplements' of a spider. For us readers, this tapestry has become a truly *textual* hyperobject. The entire poem itself, which (regardless of Claudian's intentions) we read in an incomplete form, parallels Proserpina's *imperfectus labor*. This is not only because both are incomplete, but because they both testify to the fundamental chaos of a world subject to a rampant and unorderly materiality that the work of both poet and weaver ultimately cannot evade.

Notes

1. Feder 2021: 4.
2. Ibid.: 11–12.
3. Ibid.: 132.
4. Huggan 2021: 134.
5. Chakrabarty 2009.
6. Zapf 2016.
7. Huggan 2021: 141.
8. See Formisano 2018 for further discussion of the poem's incompleteness as a matter of its form and its discourse.

9. Charlet 2000.

10. Ruddiman 2003 sees in agriculture the original moment of the Anthropocene.

11. Latin text and English translation from Gruzelier 1993.

12. Benjamin 1998.

13. Jameson 2019: 10. See Formisano 2018 for allegoresis as one of the most characteristic features of Late Antique literature.

14. DeLoughrey 2019: 89

15. Cameron 1970: 264.

16. See Roberts 1989 for the influential concept of the 'jeweled style' as characteristic of Late Antique literature, a style which includes a diffused fragmentariness (Roberts 1989).

17. Formisano 2021a and Formisano 2021b. In what follows I summarize the main arguments of these articles, and then enhance and reframe within the critical agenda of this chapter.

18. For this tension see Huggan 2021 ('In defense of deep reading', in particular 132–3).

19. Deleuze 1988.

20. Butler 2011: 9.

21. Jansen 2014: 5.

22. Deleuze and Guattari 1988: 479.

23. Lysen and Pisters: 'The sea is a smooth space par excellence: open water always moved by the wind, the sun and the stars, nomadically traversable by noise, colour and celestial bearings. Increased navigation of the open water resulted in demands for its striation' (2012: 1).

24. Butler 2011: 8 (see note 17 for the references).

25. Westphal evokes the assonance in German between *Ortung* and *Ordnung*: the process of spatialization and 'localization' automatically generates and imposes a human 'order' (2011: 56).

26. Hamilton 2015: 170.

27. Fauth 1988: 69.

28. Heintges 2021: 427.

29. Danowski and Viveiros de Castro 2017: 14.

30. Morton 2013: 28.

31. Ibid.: 19.

32. Ibid.

33. Hartman 2021: 95.

34. Ibid.: 99.

35. Ibid.: 117.

36. Schoentjes 2015: 25 and 28.

37. See Charlet for various poetic attestations of *alnus* as an apt kind of wood for ship building (2002: 83). Gruzelier 1993 notices the reference to Verg. *G.* 2.451-42 *torrentem undam levis innatat alnus / missa Pado*.

38. Oppermann 2018: 412.

39. See for instance Butler 2011: 17–19.

CHAPTER 12
THE ENVIRONMENTAL ETHICS OF DELPHI: BACK-FILLING LATOUR'S *FACING GAIA*
M. D. Usher

The Oracle at Delphi will be familiar to most readers and modern visitors to Greece as the possession of the god Apollo. It was not always so. Aeschylus, at the beginning of the *Eumenides*, the final play of his *Oresteia* trilogy, first produced in 458 BCE, recounts a traditional genealogy that traces control of Delphi back to Earth (Gaia), the Oracle's first sovereign, and to her avatar and successor, Themis (*Eum.* 1–8). Themis, a traditional metroac deity,[1] like Gaia, and a personified first principle governing humans' relationships to one another and to the environments in which they live, covered considerable moral ground for the Greeks. Her name, as Moses Finley once noted, is 'untranslatable' ... '[a] mark of civilized existence, sometimes it means right custom, proper procedure, social order, and sometimes merely the will of the gods';[2] 'custom, tradition, folk-ways, *mores*, whatever we may call it',[3] Finley adds, '*themis*' – which we might translate as 'what has been laid down', from the verb *tithēmi* – represents 'the enormous power of "it is (or is not) done"'.[4]

As implicitly described in Aeschylus' account, and explicitly in various other versions of the myth,[5] Apollo wrested Delphi from Earth, Themis, and the Oracle's protecting serpent Pytho by force, effecting a mythological ascendency of male rulers over primordial female powers. That mythic scenario fired the imaginations of Johan Jakob Bachofen[6] and Robert Graves,[7] both of whom saw in the mythological progression a historical, paradigmatic shift, posited a pre-patriarchal phase of Matriarchy (*das Mutterrecht*) in human cultural development, supposedly presided over by 'The Divine Feminine'. Their thesis was influential in some circles (and indeed still is), but unfounded vis-à-vis the historical and archaeological record, as Roller and Borgeaud have shown, charitably, and in detail.[8] But the notion of a transition from the self-organizing parthenogenesis of the natural world in Hesiod – Gaia, or Earth, produces her own consort Ouranos, 'Sky', spontaneously (*Theog.* 126–7) – to a male-dominated, differentiated cosmo-political order is on full display in a different Succession Myth that Hesiod recounts. In that story (*Theog.* 154–210 and 453–506) Ouranos is supplanted by his son Cronos, who is in turn overthrown by his son, Zeus – in both instances, paradoxically, with assistance from their respective mothers. Ancient visitors to Delphi would have been shown the 'navel' of the world (*omphalos*), as was the Greek travel writer and antiquarian Pausanias in the second century CE. The spot was marked near to where the stone coughed up by Cronos was located, in the ruse devised by Zeus' mother Rhea, as related in Hesiod's tale (*Theog.* 498–500). Navels, of course, were once umbilicals; which makes Delphi something of a womb of Earth, from whose crevices arose, according to some ancient accounts, a vaporous steam that inspired Apollo's seer-priestess, the

Pythia (named after the vanquished serpent), to issue divine, oracular pronouncements that were deemed binding – i.e. *themis* – for both the individuals and states that consulted her (see, e.g. Plut. *De def. or.* 437c as well as Diod. 16,26).

Facing Gaia

The late Bruno Latour rehearses Hesiod's accounts, as he mines the depths of Gaia in eight sermons, originally delivered in 2013 as the Gifford Lectures in Natural Theology, expanded and published in French in 2015, and, in 2017, in English, as *Facing Gaia*.[9] Latour finds Hesiod's Gaia 'dangerous', 'sombre', 'savvy', even 'monstrous'; 'What is certain is that she is not a figure of harmony', he writes, and 'there is nothing maternal about her.'[10] The Gaia that ultimately concerns him, however, is not Hesiod's, nor Delphi's original proprietary deity, but Lovelock and Margulis's scientific model of a self-regulating biosphere – the living superorganism that Lovelock dubbed 'Gaia', our dynamical planet Earth.[11] Despite its unscientific associations with a pagan deity, Gaia is a term and concept Latour finds more apt for describing our new climatic regime than, say, 'The Anthropocene', which reinforces a dangerously false distinction, he thinks, between humans and the non-human world.[12] He eschews, too, the very word 'Nature.' For Latour, Gaia is preferable because it is, ironically, 'wholly secular'[13] and '*much less* a religious figure than Nature is'.[14] 'We have to do for the scientific theory of Gaia', he argues, 'what the magnificent work of the Hellenists has taught us to do for the mythological characters such as the ancient Ge [Gaia] . . . We have to replace what gods, concepts, objects and things *are* by what they *do*.'[15] We need, in other words, to understand reality as consisting of processes and agents, not substances or essences.

Latour's own emphasis on processes and on interrelationships amongst objects, agents and events marks every page of *Facing Gaia*, much of it, like the Oracle at Delphi, in the paradoxical mode. But the crux of his argument about Gaia is well represented in these sentences:

> The climate is the historical result of reciprocal connections.[16]
>   Gaia is a *power of historicization*.[17]
>   There is nothing inert, nothing benevolent, nothing external in Gaia. If climate and life have evolved together, space is not a frame, not even a context: *space is the offspring of time*.[18]
>   Gaia is *an injunction to rematerialize our belonging to the world*.[19]
>   The concept of Gaia captures the distributed intentionality of all agents, each of which modifies its surroundings for its own purposes.[20]
>   In the face of what is to come, we cannot continue to believe in the old future if we want to have a future at all. This is what I mean by 'facing Gaia'.[21]

In this essay I would like to backfill a bit around these foundational statements with some additional ancient material. Given Latour's mercurial penchant for mythology and his admiration for the Greeks, it is an *hommage* of which I hope he would approve.[22]

There is no disputing Latour's observation (not his alone, of course) that agents modify their surroundings for their own purposes. The ancient Greeks and Romans also impacted the ecosystems in which they lived, often negatively, as is catalogued in a bevy of publications like J. Donald Hughes's *Pan's Travail* from 1994.[23] Yet ancient thought and practice, even that encoded in ritual and myth, still has much to offer by way of fostering environmental awareness today. As far as human-induced climate change is concerned, the ancients have bequeathed to us both the enigma and its solution. Pre-industrialized, pre-digital, pre-capitalist, pre-reductionist, pre-postmodern, pre-posthuman, ancient peoples necessarily lived closer and with greater sensitivity to both the perils and prospects of their environments. As inheritors of their estate – and in today's Westernized world we are all in some sense inheritors – we have much to re-learn from them, and not only from their mistakes.[24] If solutions to our contemporary environmental problems must be driven by science, not mythology, that is no impediment, insofar as 'myth and science', as Latour himself emphasizes, 'speak languages that are only apparently distinct; as soon as we approach the metamorphic zone . . . they begin to exchange their features.'[25] Or as Karl Popper once noted, 'Historically speaking all—or nearly all—scientific theories originate from myths ... a myth may contain important anticipations of scientific theories.'[26]

If, as Latour puts it, Gaia is 'an injunction to rematerialize our belonging to the world', and 'a power of historicization', what then might be *themis* in that world? The world that we currently inhabit is overdeveloped, overpopulated and environmentally precarious. Many species are teetering on the edge of extinction, including perhaps our own. While there is no turning back the clock, Hesiod, as it happens, sheds additional, indirect light on these dark problems. Hesiod, of course, is an archaic, mythological thinker. As such, he personifies Justice, or *Dikē*, like Gaia, as a woman (*Op.* 220 and 256). Yet Justice is portrayed in his work not so much as a deity, inherent moral quality, or abstract entity as it is a *process* – the process of arbitrating disputes and coming to settlements. Thus, *dikai* in the plural can refer, sometimes simultaneously, to a whole continuum of action: litigation, decisions (i.e. 'judgements'), pleas, and even penalties.[27] Inasmuch as they are processes and imply interrelationships, *dikai*, like paths, or 'courses of action', are described by Hesiod metaphorically as either 'crooked' or 'straight' (e.g. *Theog.* 85–6; *Op.* 36, 219, 221, 224–6, 230). In fact, in those instances where Hesiod personifies Justice, he uses the imagery of paths and byways: She is dragged off the road – the word used in the Greek, *helkomenēs*, implies rape – by 'bribe-swallowing judges' who literally pervert her course. Wherever Justice is given right of way, on the other hand, the land yields prodigious bounty and the people flourish (*Op.* 225–37); where she is impeded or contravened, the people perish (222–4; 238–47). Given the interconnectedness of right behaviour, righteous judgements, and economic prosperity in an agriculture-based economy like the one reflected in the *Works and Days* (and Hesiod himself was a farmer), it is not an exaggeration to say that *Dikē* – Justice – is the poet's word for a sustainable system. That is, Hesiod's *Dikē* describes what we might call in Latour's terms a complex, embedded social and ontological network of co-dependent, interrelated parts operating in a steady state.

Gaia Pandora

The way Hesiod depicts the creation of the first human being at *Works and Days* 53–105 – incidentally and quite unlike the biblical account, not a man, but a woman – aligns her closely with Gaia, both the ancient one and Latour's.[28] Pandora ('All-gift') is formed from earth and water by Hephaestus. She is at one and the same time a life-sized vase (*pithos*) and a vase-shaped woman with an abdominal cavity and a 'mouth' with 'lips'. Pandora is specially adorned with jewellery by Athena and Hephaestus, male and female deities respectively of handicraft. She is, in a very literal sense, like Latour's Gaia, an undifferentiated amalgam of Nature and Culture both. Jane Harrison suggested long ago that the name Pandora is simply a cult epithet of *Ge/Gaia* and that Hesiod's account of her opening the lid of her jar to release all the evils of the world (*Op.* 94–5) is a vestige of an old belief in ghosts emanating from the Earth.[29] That same belief, Harrison believed, was preserved in historical times in the jar-opening ritual (*Pithoigia*) at the Athenian wine festival of the *Anthesteria* and may lie behind the supposed mode of the Pythia's inspiration at Delphi by vapours emanating from below.

Be that as it may, Hesiod's Pandora, although she is in origin an aspect of Earth herself, is portrayed chauvinistically as a human harbinger of toil and bane, insofar as she is created at Zeus' behest to punish Man for Prometheus' theft of fire. Harrison's explanation of her transformation from the Giver of All Gifts to the originator of evils is not so dated as her views on ghosts, and well worth quoting for its apposite sarcasm. 'Why then does the πίθος of Pandora contain evil only?' she asks:

> The worshippers of Zeus were the natural enemies of the All-Mother Pandora. What was to become of monotheism, of the omnipotence of Zeus, if Gaia Pandora was the source of all good things? But monotheism is always tolerant of a duly subordinate devil, and Pandora was welcome to keep a *pithos* of evils only, provided always it was duly recognized that Zeus had two *pithoi* [alluding to *Il.* 24.524-33] on his Olympian threshold. It is a quaint conflict of theological systems; and forasmuch as Zeus is omnipotent, he takes over even the creation of the Earth-Mother, who was from the beginning. And patriarchal bourgeois as he is, the making of the first woman becomes a huge Olympian jest: ἐκ δ' ἐγέλασσε πατὴρ ἀνδρῶν τε θεῶν τε ['And the father of gods and men roared with laughter,' quoting Hes. *Op.* 59].[30]

Nothing in excess?

Aeschylus invokes Hesiod's Succession Myth, in which the mothers Gaia and Rhea play such important roles, in both the opening chorus and closing arguments of the *Oresteia*.

In the latter passage (*Eum.* 640–743), Athena, the motherless daughter of Zeus,[31] justifies the reign of the new Olympian gods over the older, chthonic forces represented by the *Erinyes*, arbiters and avengers of blood-feuds amongst kin – themselves divine beings born of blood from Ouranos' genitals, severed by the scheming Cronos according to the myth (*Theog.* 174–87). The 'new god' Apollo defends Orestes in that scene. Orestes is on trial for killing his mother, Clytemnestra – at Apollo's behest – in the aftermath of Agamemnon's perilous homecoming: his sacrifice of their daughter Iphigeneia provoked Clytemnestra, his wife, to murder him in retaliation.

In the *Oresteia* Aeschylus' solution to intergenerational and interfamilial strife involves Athena offering shared benefits and privileges to reconcile the opposing old and new gods: The Erinyes, primordial blood-goddesses of vengeance and retribution, are transfigured into Eumenides, 'Kindly Ones', agents of fertility and plenty, to be protectresses of the historical human community – Aeschylus' own Athens (*Eum.* 777–1047) – under the aegis of Persuasion, Social Contract and the Rule of Law, for which the *Oresteia* provides a charter myth. At Delphi a similar accommodation was struck between two male successor deities to Gaia, Apollo and – a less well-known patron of Delphi – Dionysus, whose divine attributes co-existed in productive tension: where Apollo represents civilized limit and individuation, Dionysus stands for wild exuberance and primal Oneness (*das Ur-Eine*). As Nietzsche was so keen to observe in *The Birth of Tragedy* (1872), the ancient Greeks deemed the domains of both deities as complementary, and essential to their social and psychic survival.[32]

The historical origins and cultic associations of Apollo are complicated and complex. Many of his various attributes and functions are non- or pre-Greek.[33] But for Greeks of the Archaic period and later, Apollo came to represent Order, as opposed to Chaos; Restraint, as opposed to Excess; and Reason, as opposed to ecstatic Abandon. At Delphi, two now famous phrases were inscribed at the entrance to his temple – *mēden agan* ('nothing in excess') and *gnōthi seauton* ('know thyself') (cf. Plut. *De E* 386d). Both sayings were attributed variously to one or more of the so-called Seven Sages of ancient Greece, proto-philosophers, statesmen and/or leading citizens, like the Athenian Solon and Thales of Miletus, noted for their exemplary wisdom. Indeed, the origin and attribution of these Delphic maxims were topics much discussed in Antiquity, and the nature of those discussions and the conflicting attributions of authorship suggest that the Greeks themselves did not know the source or exact import of these laconic sayings. Most likely, as H. W. Parke and D. E. W. Wormell once surmised, the maxims represent traditional folk wisdom later ascribed to celebrated individuals.[34] I would suggest even more specifically that the wisdom these maxims encode speaks to the need to live within socio-ecological bounds, and that they are made from the same notional stock as the myths of, e.g. Actaeon, a hunter who intrudes upon Artemis (who, as a 'Mistress of the Animals' figure, is an avatar of Gaia) in her sacred grove and is punished by being torn apart by his own dogs, and Erysichthon, who chops down an oak tree sacred to the grain goddess Demeter – yet another avatar of Gaia – is afflicted with perpetual hunger, forced to serially prostitute his daughter in exchange for food, and, ultimately, to eat his own flesh.[35] Only later did they become philosophical catchphrases with existential and ethical colouring. In fact, a third, less well-known maxim inscribed at Delphi, *engua para d'ata* – 'stand bail [or 'make a pledge'] and ruin is nigh' – is even more strongly suggestive of the traditional, folk quality of these sentiments. George Thomson, from a Marxist perspective, once observed something similar about the quintessentially philosophical 'Doctrine of the Mean', as elaborated ultimately by Aristotle, even if his assessment of the historical origin of the idea is tinged somewhat by his political commitments:

> The toiling serf was constrained to believe that 'measure is best in all things' [quoting Hes. *Op.* 694]. The proverbial doctrine of measure or restraint (μέτρον, καιρός), which does not appear in Homer, was developed under the landed aristocracy, to whose rule it lent an apparently external authority.[36]

Whatever the doctrine's social origins or designs, Greek writers at all periods prized Moderation, or Restraint (*sōphrosunē*) as a rule of life. But they also understood the Irrational, the Unlimited, the Ecstatic, the Uncanny. Long before Nietzsche employed his scheme, Plutarch, in his essay on the meaning of the E at Delphi (Plut. *De E* 384d-394c), had theorized a complementary link between the rivals Apollo and Dionysus, as he observed it in cult practice: Apollo was celebrated at Delphi by his musical form, the paean, Dionysus by his, the dithyramb, each sung in praise of the god during his respective tenure at the shrine – Apollo for nine months of summer 'plenty' (*koros*), Dionysus for three months of winter's 'lack' (*chrēsmosunē*). The local tradition was that Apollo wintered three months of the year with the Hyperboreans, a mythological people in the far North, during which time Dionysus held the Delphic seat. Some sort of alternating tenure as Plutarch describes is confirmed by the monuments and archaeological evidence, though it is difficult to know for certain how far back it goes. We know it was in full swing by at least the fourth century BCE, but is probably much older.[37] Jenny Strauss Clay has formulated the remarkable argument that Philodamus' paean from this period, found inscribed on a stone buried under the Sacred Way in Delphi and first published in 1895, blends Apolline and Dionysiac motifs in such a way as to vindicate the thrust of Nietzsche's speculations over twenty year earlier about the birth of tragedy – namely, the aesthetic, cultural fusion of Dionysiac and Apolline impulses – 'Out of the Spirit of Music' (the subtitle of his treatise).[38]

Plutarch was a priest at Delphi in the Roman era. His comments on the alternating tenure there are clearly interpretive, bordering on allegorical, even if based on historical fact. But Chaos and Order, Wildness and Civilization, Nature and Culture, are themselves, in essence, interpretive acts (i.e. social constructs and ideas) in the first place, as Latour highlights again and again. A now canonical collection of essays curated by William Cronon, *Uncommon Ground: Rethinking the Human Place in Nature*, brought the problems and ambivalences of our relationship to wilderness uniquely to the fore in 1996. In Cronon's own contribution to that volume, 'The Trouble with Wilderness; or, Getting Back to the Wrong Nature',[39] he criticizes a false and self-defeating dualism in American culture that pits the construct of a pristine wilderness against human communities, the one deemed pure and unspoiled, the other an inevitable perpetrator of environmental destruction and demise. His conclusion is that 'We mistake ourselves when we suppose that wilderness can be the solution to our culture's problematic relationships with the nonhuman world',[40] a view that Latour endorses, with the added *caveat*: 'What happened to the landscape, for earlier generations, is now happening to the whole Earth: its gradual artificialization is making the notion of "nature" as obsolete as that of "wilderness".[41] For its part, Dionysiac myth and cult, as it flourished not only at Delphi cheek-by-jowl with Apollo, but in the wider context of Greek Antiquity generally, represents, I suggest, for lack of a better phrase, a self-conscious 'wilderness ethos' – not an absolutist or fundamentalist dogma, oblivious to inherent entanglements and contradictions, but a balanced response of the sort that Cronon recommends, which institutionalized the sanctity of wilderness through the cultural prism of ritual and myth.[42]

In Euripides' last and perhaps most powerful play, the *Bacchae*, produced posthumously sometime after 405, we find a similar reconciliation – *not* a dualism of Nature pitted against Culture, or, if you will, of the Dionysiac versus the Apolline, but rather, as at Delphi, an underlying unity of opposites. Bacchic revel is repeatedly presented by Euripides as *sōphrosunē* ('moderation'), a trait associated more typically with Apollo. At the beginning of the play, the maenad chorus heeds the ritual cry to leave behind their distaffs and looms and head for the mountains – *eis oros, eis oros!* ('to the mountain, to the mountain!') they exclaim (Eur. *Bacch.* 116) – where honey, milk and wine gush from the rock of its own accord – nature miracles wrought from their righteous participation in Dionysiac frenzy (143–4; 704–11).[43] At line 686, exhausted from their revel, the worshippers fall asleep on the mountain, the Messenger reports, casting their heads upon the ground amidst soft leaves, 'in disarray' (*eikēi*), but 'modestly' (*sōphronōs*), not in intoxication or sexual trysts as Pentheus expects. Indeed, at line 940 Dionysus himself predicts that Pentheus, the antagonist in the play, will be surprised to find his devotees 'self-controlled' (*sōphronas*) 'against all expectation' (*para logon*). Even after Dionysus has exacted his revenge upon Pentheus for rejecting his rites, his body torn apart like his cousin Actaeon's, his severed head bobbling on his mother Agave's Bacchic wand, the chorus declares its ultimate credo (1150–2):

To be moderate (*to sōphronein*) and to revere the rites of gods
is best. This is also the wisest, I think,
acquisition for mortals to avail themselves of.[44]

Of this passage Richard Seaford writes: 'This elevation of σωφροσύνη is not a mere platitude.' Like Dionysiac cult itself, 'it is an agent of social and political cohesion.'[45] That the chorus has in mind not only the rites of Dionysus, but a larger reverence for life that the earliest forms of Greek religion associated with the Mother of All, is clear from the first song they sing in the play, to 'Sanctity, Queen of the Gods' (*Hosia potna theōn*; 370). Her epithet, *potna*, recalls the goddesses Cybele, Artemis and Demeter, who also bear this honorific title,[46] and who is contrasted *verbatim* with Pentheus' expressly 'sacrilegious hybris' (*ouch hosian hubrin*).

So, is the Delphic injunction really, absolutely, 'nothing in excess'?[47] At the most basic level the *Bacchae* presents an object lesson of what at Delphi, the navel of the Earth, was established cult practice: a prudent balance struck between Wilderness and Civilization, Nature and Culture, exuberance and restraint, or, as Plutarch put it, 'plenty' and 'lack', as represented by Apollo in good seasons, Dionysus in winter. The cycles of the year and the intersecting arcs of human thought about our place in the world – our *environment* – come full circle in the totalizing worldview of Greek ritual and myth. Like the observations of Plutarch, that verdict is perhaps an allegory, or, like the modern Gaia hypothesis, a metaphor. If indeed it is, one might agree with Latour that it is one for our time. But it is also more than that. In our globalized, resource-depleting pursuit of endless economic growth sprung from an excess of Apolline civilizing impulses dithyrambic strains like, e.g. the last stanza of Gerard Manley Hopkins' 'Inversnaid' (1881) capture the essence of what is, I think, a modest, reasonable, Dionysiac appeal:

What would the world be, once bereft
Of wet and of wildness? Let them be left,
O let them be left, wildness and wet;
Long live the weeds and the wilderness yet.

Gaia herself is presented by the Greeks as exactly this synthesis of prodigality and prudence, or, shall we say, of Nature and Culture, of wilderness and cultivated landscapes. It is as if the Olympians Dionysus and Apollo took up Earth's mantle and were simply resuming her duties at Delphi between them. *Homeric Hymn* no. 30, for example, 'To Earth, Mother of All', celebrates Earth's preeminence and patronage in the domestic sphere, guaranteeing peace and prosperity to those who revere her, while her older, wilder side – that of the *potnia thērōn*, or 'Mistress of the Animals'[48] – is captured in *Hymn* no. 14, 'To the Mother of the Gods'. In both of her guises, the poet sings of Gaia, Ge, the Mother of All: 'To give life or to take it away rests with you' (*Hom. Hymn.* 30.6).

Humility

In many respects, the discovery of systems in the modern age represents an unlearning of reductionism in both the sciences and the humanities that the early Greeks never quite possessed. The view of Culture, for example, as being set apart from or in opposition to Nature is one of those reductions. This, I take it, is part of Latour's objection to the concept of an 'Anthropocene'.[49] The origin of the idea that there is a sharp dichotomy between Nature and Culture stretches back quite a way, to be sure: it was the Sophists' stock-in-trade, and the notion raises its ugly head continuously in the history of Western thought in various ways. But in another very real sense, as Latour articulates with such *élan* elsewhere, in practice we have never really been 'Modern'; that is, in the way we actually behave there never has been, nor can there ever be any clear, objective distinctions between direct, sensory experience and recursive thought, fact and interpretation, observed phenomena, cultural values and social discourse.[50] The world is *bricolage* and we are imbricated in it.

If there is a call to action in *Facing Gaia* beyond its elaborate analyses and critiques, if there is any plan proposed to remediate human beings' environmental impact on the planet, it is a plea for what Latour calls 'sensitivity', defined in terms of systems science as 'detecting and reacting rapidly to small changes, influences, signals'. Organisms that lack sensitivity to Gaia's changes, influences and signals, Latour asserts, are doomed, whoever they may be.[51] To repeat what I said earlier, the ancients necessarily lived closer to the perils and prospects of their environments. Ancient Greeks like Hesiod, in other words, possessed a knowing sensitivity, both practical and poetic, whereas our age of technological, commercial and industrial excess (some call it success) seems to have blunted and bludgeoned us senseless. What is *themis* for our world, I suggest, invoking the Oracle and with Hesiod the farmer in mind, corresponds to an ancient word and concept: *humility*, from Latin *humus*, meaning 'the quality or condition of being close to the ground'. In other words, *facing Gaia*. The alternative posture is conveyed by that other Delphic injunction – GNŌTHI SAUTON ('know thyself') – as depicted on a tessellated Roman mosaic from the once opulent, now dilapidated, Baths of Diocletian. The image is of a skeletal corpse, reclining in repose and destined for putrefaction.[52]

Notes

1. *Metroac*, from the Greek adjective *mētrōios*, is Borgeaud's more neutral, non-emotive term, substituting for 'maternal', or 'of or pertaining to a mother'. See Borgeaud 2004.

2. Finley 1978: 79.

3. Ibid.: 83.

4. Ibid.: 78 (note) and 82.

5. The main sources are the Pythian portion of the *Homeric Hymn to Apollo* (300–69) and Ov. *Met.* 1.438-52.

6. Bachofen 1861.

7. Graves 1948.

8. Borgeaud 2004: xi–xix, Roller 1999: 9–26.

9. Latour 2017. See Bucchi 2021.

10. Latour 2017: 81–3.

11. Lovelock 2000.

12. 'Seeking "Man's place in Nature"—to fall back on an outmoded form of expression—is not at all the same task as learning to participate in the geohistory of the planet' (Latour 2017: 107).

13. Latour 2017: 86.

14. Ibid.: 213 (italics in the original).

15. Ibid.: 86 (italics in the original).

16. Ibid.: 106.

17. Ibid.: 219 (italics in the original).

18. Ibid.: 106 (italics in the original).

19. Ibid.: 219 (italics in the original).

20. Ibid.: 98.

21. Ibid.: 245.

22. I am grateful to have had lunch with him in Paris a few months before he died.

23. Now Hughes (2014). Studies that take a similar approach include, e.g. Harper 2017 and Walsh 2013.

24. For this line of thought see Usher 2020.

25. Latour 2017: 85–6.

26. Popper 1962: 38.

27. See Tandy and Neale 1996: 43.

28. Latour (1999) invokes Pandora as a metaphor to describe his philosophy of 'realistic realism', a position intermediate between the extremes of postmodern constructivism and traditional scientific realism.

29. Harrison 1900.

30. Ibid.: 108.

31. Athena was born from the head of Zeus after Zeus swallowed his pregnant consort Metis ('Cunning') to prevent any further dynastic succession (*Theog.* 886–99). As Aeschylus has her argue, Athena acquits Orestes based on a general inclination toward males over mothers that springs from the circumstances of her birth (*Eum.* 734–43).

32. In tracing his proposed transition from Matriarchy to Patriarchy, Bachofen coined the terms *Dionysian* to describe an intervening phase and *Apollonian* to characterize the full progression. Nietzsche, Bachofen's compatriot at Basel, later employed the terms in *Birth of Tragedy* (without acknowledgment). See Silk and Stern 1981: 212–14.

33. See West 1999: 55 and Burkert 1985: 144–5.

34. Parke and Wormell 1956: 389.

35. Ovid gives the fullest narrative account for both stories. Actaeon: *Met.* 3.138-253, Erysichthon: *Met.* 8.725-884. See my discussion in Usher 2020: 32–5.

36. Thomson 1938: 3.

37. Scott 2014: 153.

38. Strauss Clay 1996.

39. The essay was originally published in *Environmental History*, 1 (1) (1996): 7–28.

40. Cronon 1996: 69–90.

41. Latour 2017: 120–1.

42. The narrative logic of verisimilitude in Greek myths like those of Actaeon and Erysichthon mentioned briefly above implies that the antagonists' violations were perpetrated within the goddess's *temenos*, a kind of 'green belt' around Greek sanctuaries that was sequestered from surrounding land and off-limits to encroachment by humans. In the historical period, taking anything from inside the *temenos* of a god was considered stealing (*sulaō*) and punishable by law. Anything within the precinct – human, plant, animal or object – was considered to be in a state of sacrosanctity, *a-sulia* ('un-stealableness'), hence the word and institution of *asylum*. For a good general description of Greek sanctuaries, including the *temenos*, see Mikalson 2010: 1–30.

43. That this is the vocabulary of cult practice is confirmed by an inscription from Miletus that contains the exact phrase. See Henrichs 1978: 121 n. 2, 148–9.

44. Other passages that extoll *sōphrosunē* in Eur. *Bacch.* 329: *timōn te Bromion sōroneis* (Chorus to Tiresias: 'honoring [Dionysus] the Thunderer, you show good sense'), 641: *pros sophou gar andros askein sōphron' euorgēsian* (Dionysus to the Chorus about Pentheus: 'for it falls to a wise man to practice a restrained, balanced temper'). Dionysus appears as a *deus ex machina* at the end of the play (1341) and says to Cadmus and his house 'If you had known sensible restraint (*sōphronein*), even when you did not want to, you would now be happy.' At line 504 Dionysus declares that he is 'showing moderation' (*sōphrōnōn*) in the face of 'reckless' Pentheus (*ou sōphrosin*) who tries to bind him.

45. Seaford 1995: 405.

46. *Potnia* meaning 'Lady', or 'Queen', however, is an old, Mycenaean royal term predicated of goddesses in the Linear B tablets, suggestive of the buxom, bare-breasted effigies and figurines that have been discovered on the Peloponnese and on Crete. The epithet was used liberally in early Greek poetry to describe, e.g. Demeter, Athena, Aphrodite, Hera, and a host of other female deities, including Earth herself.

47. As to the other storied maxim from Delphi, 'know thyself': This command was not, if we consider it in its historical, social context, a call to existential introspection – (that is a view sprung from the saying's association with modern interpretations of the myth of Oedipus) – but rather an exhortation to consider one's proper role and destiny in the natural scheme of things. As such, it, too, resonates with concerns raised by contemporary environmental ethics.

48. The epithet is first ascribed to 'Wild' Artemis (*Agroterē*) in Homer (*Il.* 21.470).

49. Cf. Latour 2017: 109–10. Cronon makes a similar observation in critique of Bill McKibbon's landmark *The End of Nature* (1989): 'To think ourselves capable of causing "the end of nature" is an act of great hubris, for it means forgetting the wildness that dwells everywhere within and around us ... The absurdity of this proposition flows from the underlying dualism it expresses. Not only does it ascribe greater power to humanity than we in fact possess – physical and biological nature will surely survive in some form or another long after we ourselves have gone the way of all flesh – but in the end it offers us little more than a self-defeating counsel of despair' (Cronon [1996]: 19, 13).

50. Latour 1993.

51. Latour 2017: 141.

52. For the image, see https://en.m.wikipedia.org/wiki/File:Roman-mosaic-know-thyself.jpg.

BIBLIOGRAPHY

Introduction

Abram, D. (1996), *The Spell of the Sensuous*, New York: Vintage Books.

Armbruster, K. (2016), 'Nature Writing', in J. Adamson, W. A. Gleason and D. N. Pellow (eds), *Keywords for Environmental Studies*, 156–8, New York, NY: New York University Press.

Bladow, K. and J. Ladino (2018), 'Towards an Affective Ecocriticism: Placing Feeling in the Anthropocene', in K. Bladow and J. Ladino (eds), *Affective Ecocriticism: Emotion, Embodiment, Environment*, 1–22, Lincoln, NE: University of Nebraska Press.

Bosak-Schroeder, C. (2020), *Other Natures: Environmental Encounters with Ancient Greek Ethnography*, Oakland, CA: University of California Press.

Bubandt, N., ed. (2018), *A Non-secular Anthropocene: Spirits, Specters and Other Nonhumans in a Time of Environmental Change*. More-than-Human: AURA Working Papers 3, Aarhus: Aarhus University.

Buell, L. (1995), *The Environmental Imagination: Thoreau, Nature Writing and the Formation of American Culture*, Cambridge, MA: Harvard University Press.

Clark, T. (2019), *The Value of Ecocriticism*, Cambridge: Cambridge University Press.

Derrida, J. (1997), *Of Grammatology*, Baltimore: John Hopkins University Press.

Estok, S. (2013), 'The Ecophobia Hypothesis: Re-membering the Feminist Body of Ecocriticism', in G. Gaard, S. Estok, S., and S. Oppermann (eds), *International Perspectives in Feminist Ecocriticism,* 70–83, New York, NY: Routledge.

Felton, D. (2018), *Landscapes of Dread in Classical Antiquity: Negative Emotion in Natural and Constructed Spaces*, London: Routledge.

Gaard, G. (2010), 'New Directions for Ecofeminism: Toward a More Feminist Ecocriticism', *ISLE: Interdisciplinary Studies in Literature and Environment*, 17 (4): 643–65. https://doi.org/10.1093/isle/isq108

Garrard, G. (2012), *Ecocriticism*, 2nd edition, New York, NY: Routledge.

Garrard, G., ed. (2014), *The Oxford Handbook of Ecocriticism*, Oxford: Oxford University Press.

Gibson, J. J. (1979), *The Ecological Approach to Visual Perception*, Boston, MA: Houghton Mifflin and Company.

Gleick, J. (1987), *Chaos: Making a New Science*, New York, NY: Viking.

Glotfelty, C. and H. Fromm, eds (1996), *The Ecocriticism Reader: Landmarks in Literary Ecology*, Athens, GA: University of Georgia Press.

Haraway, D. (2007), *When Species Meet*, Minneapolis: University of Minnesota Press.

Hawes, G. (2017), *Myths on the Map: The Storied Landscapes of Ancient Greece*, Oxford: Oxford University Press.

Hollis, D. and König, J. (2022), *Mountain Dialogues from Antiquity to Modernity*, London: Bloomsbury.

Hunt, A. (2016), *Reviving Roman Religion: Sacred Trees in the Roman World*, Cambridge: Cambridge University Press.

Iovino, S. (2016), 'Afterword: Revealing Roots – Ecocriticism and the Cultures of Antiquity', in C. Schliephake (ed.), *Ecocriticism, Ecology, and the Cultures of Antiquity*, 309–16, Lanham, MD: Lexington.

Bibliography

Iovino, S. and S. Oppermann (2014), 'Introduction: Stories Come to Matter', in S. Iovino and S. Oppermann (eds), *Material Ecocriticism*, 1–17, Bloomington, IN: Indiana University Press.

Iovino, S. and S. Oppermann (2014), *Material Ecocriticism*, Bloomington, IN: Indiana University Press.

Latour, B. (1993), *We Have Never Been Modern*, Cambridge, MA: Harvard University Press.

Jones, A. and N. Strigul (2021), 'Is Spread of COVID-19 a Chaotic Epidemic?', *Chaos, Solitons & Fractals* 142: 110376. ISSN 0960-0779, https://doi.org/10.1016/j.chaos.2020.110376

Korhonen, T. and E. Ruonakoski (2017), *Human and Animal in Ancient Greece: Empathy and Encounter in Classical Literature*, London: I.B. Tauris.

Platt, V. (2018), 'Ecology, Ethics and Aesthetics in Pliny the Elder's *Natural History*', *Journal of the Clark Art Institute* 17: 219–42.

Rigby, K. (2004), *Topographies of the Sacred: The Poetics of Place in European Romanticism*, Charlottesville, VA: University of Virginia Press.

Rigby, K. (2015), 'Writing after Nature', in K. Hiltner (ed.), *Ecocriticism: The Essential Reader*, 357–67, London: Routledge.

Schiller, F. (1985), 'On Naive and Sentimental Poetry', in H. B. Nisbet (ed.), *German Aesthetic and Literary Criticism*, 177–232, Cambridge: Cambridge University Press.

Schliephake, C. (2020), 'From Storied to Porous Landscapes: Antiquity, the Environmental Humanities and the Case for Long-Term Histories', *GAIA* 29 (4): 230–4.

Schliephake, C. (2022), 'Profile: Ecocriticism and Ancient Environments', *The Classical Review* 72 (2): 393–6.

Scott, H. (2014), *Chaos and Cosmos: Literary Roots of Modern Ecology in the British Nineteenth Century*, Philadelphia: Pennsylvania University Press.

Sissa, G. and F. Martelli, eds (2023), *Ovid's* Metamorphoses *and the Environmental Imagination*, London: Bloomsbury.

Thornber, K. L. (2012), *Ecoambiguity: Environmental Crises and East Asian Literatures*, Ann Arbor, MI: University of Michigan Press.

von Humboldt, A. (1847), *Kosmos: Entwurf einer physischen Weltbeschreibung. Zweiter Band*, Stuttgart/Augsburg: Cotta.

Walls, L. D. (2017), 'Natural History in the Anthropocene', in J. Parham and L. Westling (eds) *A Global History of Literature and the Environment*, 187–200, Cambridge: Cambridge University Press.

Westling, L. (2014), 'Introduction', in L. Westling (ed.), *The Cambridge Companion to Literature and the Environment*, 1–13, Cambridge: Cambridge University Press.

Westling, L. and J. Parham (2017), 'Introduction', in in J. Parham and L. Westling (eds), *A Global History of Literature and the Environment*, 1–17.

Zapf, H. (2016a), 'Introduction', in H. Zapf (ed.), *Handbook of Ecocriticism and Cultural Ecology*, 1–16, Berlin: de Gruyter.

Zapf, H. (2016b), *Literature as Cultural Ecology: Sustainable Texts*, London: Bloomsbury.

Zapf, H. (2017), 'Ecological Thought and Literature in Europe and Germany', in J. Parham and L. Westling (eds), *A Global History of Literature and the Environment*, 269–85, Cambridge: Cambridge University Press.

Žižek, S. (1991), *Looking Awry: An Introduction to Jacques Lacan through Popular Culture*, Cambridge, MA: MIT Press.

Chapter 1

Barbara, S. (2015), 'L'origine mythique des venimeux chez Nicandre (*Ther.* 8–12)', in P. L. De Bellefonds, É. Prioux and A. Rouveret (eds), *D'Alexandre à Auguste: Dynamiques de la création dans les arts visuels et la poésie,* 151–66, Rennes: PUR.

Böhme, G. (2013), *Atmosphäre: Essays zur neuen Ästhetik*, Berlin: Suhrkamp (first edition 1995).

Bremmer, J. N. (2008), *Greek Religion and Culture, the Bible and the Ancient Near East*, Leiden: Brill.

Buell, L. (1995), *Thoreau, Nature Writing, and the Formation of American Culture*, Harvard: Harvard University Press.

Clausing-Lage, V. (2019), *Aratos Phainomena: Astronomische und meteorologische Phänomene als Bilder der Umwelt*, Tübingen (doctoral dissertation).

Clauss, J. J. (2006), 'Theriaca: Nicander's Poem of the Earth', *Studi Italiani di Filologia Classica*, 4 (2): 160–82.

Cusset, Ch. (1999), 'Nature et poésie dans les Idylles de Théocrite', in C. Cusset (ed.), *La nature et ses représentations dans l'Antiquité*, 147–55, Paris: Centre national de documentation pédagogique.

Cusset, Ch. (2011), 'Aratos et le stoïcisme', *Aitia*, 1. Available online: https://doi.org/10.4000/aitia.131 (accessed August 25, 2022).

Du Sablon, V. (2014), *Le système conceptuel de l'ordre du monde dans la pensée grecque à l'époque archaïque: Τιμή, μοῖρα, κόσμος, θέμις et δίκη chez Homère et Hésiode*, Louvain: Éditions Peeters.

Fakas, Ch. (2001), *Der Hellenistische Hesiod: Arats Phainomena und die Tradition der antiken Lehrepik*, Wiesbaden: L. Reichert.

Gee, E. (2000), *Ovid, Aratus and Augustus: Astronomy in Ovid's* Fasti, Cambridge: Cambridge University Press.

Gee, E. (2013), *Aratus and the Astronomical Tradition*, Oxford: Oxford University Press.

Golz, J., ed. (2005), *Friedrich Schiller: Sämtliche Werke*, 10 vols, Berlin: Aufbau.

Gow, A. S. F. and A. F. Scholfield (1953), *The Poems and Poetical Fragments*, Cambridge: University Press.

Harder, A. (2011), 'More Facts from Fragments?', in D. O. Obbink and R. B. Rutherford (eds), *Culture in Pieces: Essays on Ancient Texts in Honour of Peter Parsons*, 174–87, Oxford: Oxford University Press.

Horky, P. S., ed. (2019), *Cosmos in the Ancient World*, Cambridge: Cambridge University Press.

Hunter, R. (2014), *Hesiodic Voices: Studies in the Ancient Reception of Hesiod's* Works and Days, Cambridge: Cambridge University Press.

Jacques, J.-M. (2002), *Nicandre. Oeuvre. Tome II. Les Thériaques. Fragments iologiques antérieurs à Nicandre*, Paris: Les Belles Lettres.

Kidd, D. (1997), *Aratus.* Phaenomena: *Edited with Introduction, Translation, and Commentary*, Cambridge: Cambridge University Press.

Lincoln, B. (2009), 'In Praise of the Chaotic', in U. Dill and C. Walde (eds), *Antike Mythen: Medien, Transformationen und Konstruktionen*, 372–88, Berlin: De Gruyter.

Magnelli, E. (2006), 'Nicander's Chronology: A Literary Approach', in A. Harder, R. F. Regtuit and G. C. Wakker (eds), *Beyond the Canon*, 185–204, Leuven: Peeters.

Overduin, F. (2013), 'A Note on Alcibius and the Structure of Nicander's *Theriaca*', *Classical World*, 107 (1): 105–9.

Overduin, F. (2014), 'The Anti-Bucolic World of Nicander's *Theriaca*', *Classical Quarterly*, 64 (2): 623–41.

Overduin, F. (2015), *Nicander of Colophon's Theriaca: A Literary Commentary*, Leiden: Brill.

Overduin, F. (2019), 'The Didactic Callimachus and the Homeric Nicander: Reading the Aetia Through the Theriaca?', in J. Klooster, A. Harder, R. F. Regtuit and G. C. Wakker (eds), *Callimachus Revisited: New Perspectives in Callimachean Scholarship*, 265–83, Leuven: Peeters.

Payne, M. (2007), *Theocritus and the Invention of Fiction*, Cambridge: Cambridge University Press.

Payne, M. (2014a), 'The One Absolute Didactic Poem, and Its Opposite: Schelling on Ancient Didactic Poetry and the Scienticity of Contemporary Lyric', *Classical Receptions Journal*, 6 (2): 245–69.

Bibliography

Payne, M. (2014b), 'The Natural World in Greek Literature and Philosophy', *Oxford Handbook Topics in Classical Studies*. Available online: https://doi.org/10.1093/oxfordhb/9780199935390.013.001 (accessed May 24, 2022).

Payne, M. (2016), 'Aetna and Aetnaism: Schiller, Vibrant Matter, and the Phenomenal Regimes of Ancient Poetry', *Helios*, 43 (2): 89–108.

Payne, M. (2019), 'Shared Life as Chorality in Schiller, Hölderlin, and Hellenistic Poetry', in E. Bianchi, S. Brill and B. Holmes (eds), *Antiquities Beyond Humanism*, 141–57, Oxford: Oxford University Press.

Reitz, Ch. and A. Walter, eds (2014), *Von Ursachen sprechen. Eine aitiologische Spurensuche. Telling Origins. On the Lookout for Aetiology*, Hildesheim: Georg Olms.

Sider, D. and C. W. Brunschön, eds (2007), *Theophrastus of Eresus: On Weather Signs*, Leiden: Brill.

Sistakou, E. (2012), T*he Aesthetics of Darkness: A Study in Hellenistic Romanticism in Apollonius, Lycophron, and Nicander*, Leuven: Peeters.

Strauss Clay, J. (2009), *Hesiod's Cosmos*, Cambridge: Cambridge University Press.

Vesperini, P. (2015), 'La poésie didactique dans l'Antiquité: une invention des Modernes', *Anabases*, 21: 25–38.

Volk, K. (2005), 'Lehrgedicht oder Naturgedicht? Naturwissenschaft und Naturphilosophie in der Lehrdichtung von Hesiod bis zur Aetna', in M. Horster and Ch. Reitz (eds), *Wissensvermittlung in dichterischer Gestalt*, 155–73, Stuttgart: F. Steiner.

Volk, K. (2012), 'Letters in the Sky: Reading the Signs in Aratus' Phaenomena', *American Journal of Philology*, 133 (2): 209–40.

Weik von Mossner, A. (2017), *Affective Ecologies: Empathy, Emotion, and Environmental Narrative*, Columbus, OH: The Ohio State University Press.

West, M. L., ed. (1966), Hesiod. *Theogony*, Oxford: Clarendon Press.

Wohl, V. (2019), 'Afterword', in P. S. Horky (ed.), *Cosmos in the Ancient World*, 295–303, Cambridge: Cambridge University Press.

Zimmermann, B. and A. Rengakos, eds (2014), *Handbuch der Griechischen Literatur der Antike: Die Literatur der klassischen und hellenistischen Zeit*, München: Beck.

Chapter 2

Armstrong, R. (2019), *Vergil's Green Thoughts: Plants, Humans, and the Divine*, Oxford: Oxford University Press.

Barchiesi, A. (1995), 'Rappresentazioni del Dolore e Interpretazione nell'*Eneide*', *Antike und Abendland*, 40: 109–24.

Berlin, N. (1998), 'War and Remembrance: Aeneid 12.554–60 and Aeneas' Memory of Troy', *American Journal of Philology*, 119: 11–41.

Casey, E. S. (2011), 'The Edge(s) of Landscape: A Study in Liminology', in J. Malpas (ed.), *The Place of Landscape: Concepts, Contexts, Studies*, 91–110, Cambridge, MA: MIT Press.

Cohen, J. J. (2014), 'Ecology's Rainbow', in J. J. Cohen (ed.), *Prismatic Ecology: Ecotheory beyond Green*, xv–xxxv, Minneapolis, MN: Minnesota University Press.

Coo, L. (2008), 'Polydorus and the *Georgics*, Virgil *Aeneid* 3.13-68', *Materiali e Discussioni per l'Analisi dei Testi Classici*, 59: 193–9.

Cooley, A. (2009), *Res Gestae Divi Augusti: Text, Translation, and Commentary*, Cambridge: Cambridge University Press.

Felton, D., ed. (2018), *Landscapes of Dread in Classical Antiquity: Negative Emotion in Natural and Constructed Spaces*, New York, NY: Routledge.

Felton, D. and K. Gilhuly (2018), 'Introduction: Dread and the Landscape,' in D. Felton (ed.), *Landscapes of Dread in Classical Antiquity: Negative Emotion in Natural and Constructed Spaces*, 1–12, New York, NY: Routledge.

Fitzgerald, W. and E. Spentzou, eds (2018), *The Production of Space in Latin Literature*, Oxford: Oxford University Press.

Fratantuono, L. (2007), *Madness Unchained: A Reading of Virgil's* Aeneid, Lanham, MD: Lexington Books.

Gardner, H. (2019), *Pestilence and the Body Politic in Latin Literature*, Oxford: Oxford University Press.

Glare, P. G. W., ed. (1996), *Oxford Latin Dictionary*, Oxford: Clarendon Press.

Gramps, A. (2018), 'Living in Fear: Affect and Dwelling Space in Horace's Roman Odes,' in D. Felton (ed.), *Landscapes of Dread in Classical Antiquity: Negative Emotion in Natural and Constructed Spaces*, 97–118, New York, NY: Routledge.

Hardie, P. (1994), *Virgil Aeneid Book IX*, Cambridge: Cambridge University Press.

Hardie, P. (2007), 'Review of Horsfall 2006', *Bryn Mawr Classical Review*. Available online: https://bmcr.brynmawr.edu/2007/2007.08.47/ (accessed 24 September 2022).

Häussler, R. and G. F. Chiai (2020), *Sacred Landscapes in Antiquity: Creation, Manipulation, Transformation*, Havertown, PA: Oxbow Books.

Horsfall, N. (2006), *Virgil, Aeneid 3: A Commentary*, Leiden: Brill.

Hughes, J. D. (2015), *What Is Environmental History*, 2nd edition, Cambridge: Polity.

Huskey, S. J. (1999), 'Turnus and Terminus in *Aeneid* 12', *Mnemosyne*, 52: 77–82.

Iovino, S. and S. Oppermann (2014), 'Introduction: Stories Come to Matter', in S. Iovino and S. Oppermann (eds), *Material Ecocriticism*, 1–20, Bloomington, IN: Indiana University Press.

James, S. (1995), 'Establishing Rome with the Sword: *Condere* in the *Aeneid*', *American Journal of Philology*, 116: 623–37.

Mader, G. (2015), 'The Final Simile in the *Aeneid*: Mechanics of Warfare and Textual Mechanisms', *Mnemosyne*, 68: 588–604.

Maran, T. (2014), 'Semiotization of Matter: A Hybrid Zone between Biosemiotics and Material Ecocriticism,' in S. Iovino and S. Oppermann (eds), *Material Ecocriticism*, 141–56, Bloomington, IN: Indiana University Press.

McInerney, J. and I. Sluiter, eds (2016), *Valuing Landscape in Classical Antiquity*, Leiden: Brill.

Perkell, C. (2007), *Vergil Aeneid 3*, Newburyport, MA: Focus Publishing.

Phillips, C. R. III (1978–9), 'Landscape in Vergil's *Aeneid*: Theory and Practice', *Helios*, 6: 63–74.

Schliephake, C. (2020), *The Environmental Humanities and the Ancient World*, Cambridge: Cambridge University Press.

Seider, A. M. (2013), *Memory in Vergil's* Aeneid: *Creating the Past*, Cambridge: Cambridge University Press.

Seider, A. M. (2021), 'A Landscape of Control? *Aeneid* 8 and Environmental Agency', *Vita Latina*, 201: 142–63.

Tarrant, R. (2012), *Virgil: Aeneid Book XII*, Cambridge: Cambridge University Press.

Thaniel, G. (1971), 'Turnus' Fatal Stone', *Echoes du Monde Classique: Classical News and Views*, 15: 20–2.

Thomas, R. F. (1988), 'Tree Violation and Ambivalence in Virgil', *Transactions of the American Philological Association*, 118: 261–73.

Tueller, M. A. (2010), 'Palinurus and Polydorus: Two Epigrammatic Passages in Vergil's *Aeneid*', *Latomus*, 69: 344–58.

Vuković, K. (2020), 'Silvia's Stag on the Tiber: The Setting of the *Aeneid*'s *Casus Belli*,' *Mnemosyne*, 73: 464–82.

Wills, J. (1996), *Repetition in Latin Poetry: Figures of Allusion*, Oxford: Clarendon Press.

Bibliography

Chapter 3

Alaimo, S. (2010), *Bodily Natures: Science, Environment, and the Material Self*, Bloomington, IN: Indiana University Press.

Aygon, J.-P. (2003), 'Le banquet tragique: Le renouvellement du thème dans le *Thyeste* de Sénèque', *Pallas*, 61: 271–84.

Bonandini, A. (2022), '*Nox missa ab ortu*: Variazioni del motivo astronomico nel mito di Tieste e Atreo', *ClassicoContemporaneo*, 8: 50–77.

Boyle, A. J. (1985), 'In Nature's Bonds: A Study of Seneca's *Phaedra*', *Aufstieg und Niedergang der römischen Welt*, 2 (32.2): 1284–347.

Boyle, A. J., ed. (2017), *Seneca: Thyestes*, Oxford: Oxford University Press.

Braidotti, R. (2002), *Metamorphoses: Towards a Materialist Theory of Becoming*, Cambridge: Polity Press.

Braidotti, R. (2013), *The Posthuman*, Cambridge: Polity Press.

Cohen, J. J. (2015), *Stone: An Ecology of the Inhuman*, Minneapolis, MN/London: University of Minnesota Press.

Cordovana, O. D. and G. F. Chiai, eds (2017), *Pollution and the Environment in Ancient Life and Thought*, Stuttgart: Steiner.

Davis, P. J. (1989), 'The Chorus in Seneca's *Thyestes*', *Classical Quarterly*, 39: 421–35.

Fedeli, P. (2000), 'Seneca e la natura', in P. Parroni (ed.), *Seneca e il suo tempo: Atti del Convegno internazionale di Roma-Cassino (11–14 novembre 1998)*, 25–45, Roma: Salerno Editrice.

Fitch, J. G. (2000), 'Playing Seneca?', in G. W. M. Harrison (ed.), *Seneca in Performance*, 1–12, London: Duckworth.

Fitch, J. G., ed. (2004), *Seneca: Tragedies. Volume II*, Cambridge, MA: Harvard University Press.

Garrard, G. (2012), *Ecocriticism*, 2nd edition, London/New York, NY: Routledge.

Gunderson, E. (2015), *The Sublime Seneca: Ethics, Literature, Metaphysics*, Cambridge: Cambridge University Press.

Haley, M. (2018), 'Teknophagy and Tragicomedy: The Mythic Burlesques of *Tereus* and *Thyestes*', *Ramus*, 47: 152–73.

Haraway, D. (2003), *The Companion Species Manifesto*, Chicago, IL: Prickly Paradigm Press.

Harper, K. (2017), *The Fate of Rome: Climate, Disease, and the End of an Empire*, Princeton, NJ: Princeton University Press.

Hine, H. M. (2004), '*Interpretatio stoica* of Senecan Tragedy', *Entretiens sur l'Antiquité Classique*, 50: 173–220.

Holmes, B. (2019), 'On Stoic Sympathy. Cosmobiology and the Life of Nature', in E. Bianchi, S. Brill and B. Holmes (eds), *Antiquities Beyond Humanism*, 239–70, Oxford: Oxford University Press.

Hunt, A. and H. Marlow, eds (2019), *Ecology and Theology in the Ancient World: Cross-Disciplinary Perspectives*, London: Bloomsbury.

Inwood, B. (2005), *Reading Seneca: Stoic Philosophy at Rome*, Oxford: Clarendon Press.

Lane, M. (2011), *Eco-Republic: Ancient Thinking for a Green Age*, Witney: Peter Lang.

Latour, B. (2017), *Facing Gaia: Eight Lectures on the New Climatic Regime*, trans. C. Porter, Cambridge: Polity Press.

Littlewood, C. A. J. (2004), *Self-Representation and Illusion in Senecan Tragedy*, Oxford: Oxford University Press.

Littlewood, C. A. J. (2008), 'Gender and Power in Seneca's *Thyestes*', in J. G. Fitch (ed.), *Oxford Readings in Classical Studies: Seneca*, 244–63, Oxford: Oxford University Press.

Long, A. A. and D. N. Sedley, eds (1987), *The Hellenistic Philosophers. Volume 1: Translation of the Principal Sources with Philosophical Commentary*, Cambridge: Cambridge University Press.

Martorana, S. (2022), '*Tantalus Poeta*: The Catalogue of the Great Sinners in *Thyestes* 1–13,' *Classical Quarterly*, 72: 269–84.

Matias, M. M. (2009), *Paisagens naturais e paisagens da alma no drama senequiano: Troades e Thyestes*, Coimbra: Imprensa da Universidade de Coimbra.

Mazzoli, G. (2014), 'The Chorus: Seneca as Lyric Poet', in G. Damschen and A. Heil (eds), *Brill's Companion to Seneca: Philosopher and Dramatist*, 561–74, Leiden/Boston: Brill.

Mazzoli, G. (2016), *Il chaos e le sue architetture: Trenta studi su Seneca tragico*, Palermo: Palumbo.

Merleau-Ponty, M. (1964), 'Eye and Mind', trans. C. Dallery, in J. M. Edie (ed.), *The Primacy of Perception and Other Essays on Phenomenological Psychology, the Philosophy of Art, History and Politics*, 159–90, Evanston, IL: Northwestern University Press.

Nenci, F., ed. (2002), *Seneca: Tieste*, Milano: Mondadori.

Picone, G. (1984), *La fabula e il regno: Studi sul Thyestes di Seneca*, Palermo: Palumbo.

Pociña, A. (2003), 'Virtualités dramatiques d'un banquet effroyable: Thyeste dans la tragédie romaine', *Pallas*, 61: 251–70.

Rosenmeyer, T. G. (1989), *Senecan Drama and Stoic Cosmology*, Berkeley/Los Angeles, CA: University of California Press.

Rosenmeyer, T. G. (2000), 'Seneca and Nature', *Arethusa*, 33: 99–119.

Schiesaro, A. (1997), 'Passion, Reason and Knowledge in Seneca's Tragedies', in S. Morton Braund and C. Gill (eds), *The Passions in Roman Thought and Literature*, 89–111, Cambridge: Cambridge University Press.

Schiesaro, A. (2003), *The Passions in Play: Thyestes and the Dynamics of Senecan Drama*, Cambridge: Cambridge University Press.

Schliephake, C., ed. (2016), *Ecocriticism, Ecology, and the Cultures of Antiquity*, Lanham, MD: Rowman and Littlefield.

Schliephake, C. (2020), *The Environmental Humanities and the Ancient World: Questions and Perspectives*, Cambridge: Cambridge University Press.

Segal, C. (1983), 'Boundary Violation and the Landscape of the Self in Senecan Tragedy', *Antike und Abendland*, 29: 172–87. [Reprinted in J. G. Fitch (ed.), *Oxford Readings in Classical Studies: Seneca*, 136–56, Oxford: Oxford University Press.]

Schmitz, C. (1993), *Die kosmische Dimension in den Tragödien Senecas*, Berlin/New York: De Gruyter.

Tarrant, R. J., ed. (1985), *Seneca's Thyestes*, Atlanta, GA: Scholar's Press.

Tarrant, R. J. (2002), 'Chaos in Ovid's *Metamorphoses* and Its Neronian Influence', *Arethusa*, 35: 349–60.

Torre, C. (2018), 'Le stelle dimenticate: Note "aratee" sulla quarta ode del *Tieste* di Seneca', *Rivista di Filologia e di Istruzione Classica*, 146: 440–88.

Viansino, G., ed. (1993), *Seneca: Teatro, Vol. 2*, Milano: Mondadori.

Volk, K. (2006), 'Cosmic Disruption in Seneca's *Thyestes*: Two Ways of Looking at an Eclipse', in K. Volk and G. D. Williams (eds), *Seeing Seneca Whole*, 183–200, Leiden/Boston: Brill.

Vottero, D. (1998), 'Seneca e la natura', in R. Uglione (ed.), *L'uomo antico e la natura: Atti del Convegno nazionale di studi, Torino, 28–30 aprile 1997*, 291–303, Torino: Celid.

Walde, C. (2012), 'Paesaggi, oracoli e sogni: Per un'interpretazione del prologo dell'*Oedipus* (vv. 1-109)', in L. Landolfi (ed.), *Ibo, ibo qua praerupta protendit iuga/meus Cithaeron: Paesaggi, luci e ombre nei prologhi tragici Senecani*, 71–94, Bologna: Pàtron.

Williams, G. D. (2006), 'Greco-Roman Seismology and Seneca on Earthquakes in *Natural Questions* 6', *Journal of Roman Studies*, 96: 124–46.

Zapf, H. (2016), *Literature as Cultural Ecology: Sustainable Texts*, London: Bloomsbury.

Zwierlein, O., ed. (1986), *L. Annaei Senecae Tragoediae*, Oxford: Oxford University Press.

Bibliography

Chapter 4

Alaimo, S. (2010), *Bodily Natures: Science, Environment, and the Material Self*, Bloomington, IN: Indiana University Press.

Alaimo, S. (2020), 'New Materialisms', in V. Sherryl (ed.), *After the Human: Culture, Theory, and Criticisms in the 21st Century*, 177–91, Cambridge: Cambridge University Press.

Alaimo, S. and S. Hekman, eds (2008), *Material Feminisms*, Bloomington, IN: Indiana University Press.

Allan, W. (2005), 'Tragedy and the Early Greek Philosophical Tradition', in J. Gregory (ed.), *A Companion to Greek Tragedy*, 71–82, Malden, MA: Blackwell Publishing.

Arthur, M. (1972), 'The Choral Odes of the *Bacchae* of Euripides', *Yale Classical Studies*, 22: 145–80.

Bakola, E. (2019), 'Reconsidering the Chthonic in Aeschylus' *Oresteia*: Erinyes, the Earth's Resources and the Cosmic Order', in A. Hunt and H. Marlow (eds), *Ecology and Theology in the Ancient World: Cross-Disciplinary Perspectives*, 103–18, London: Bloomsbury.

Barad, K. (2007), *Meeting the Universe Halfway: Quantum Physics and the Entanglement of Matter and Meaning*, Durham: Duke University Press.

Bednarek, B. (2019), 'Pelting Pentheus: on the Use of *OULAI* in Sacrificial Ritual', *Classical Philology*, 114 (1): 144–53.

Bianchi, E., S. Brill and B. Holmes (2019), *Antiquities beyond Humanism*, Oxford: Oxford University Press.

Bierl, A. (2013), 'Maenadism as Self-Referential Chorality in Euripides' *Bacchae*', in R. Gagné and M. Govers Hopman (eds), *Choral Mediations in Greek Tragedy*, 211–26, New York, NY: Cambridge University Press.

Billings, J. (2017), 'The Smiling Mask of *Bacchae*', *Classical Quarterly*, 67 (1): 19–26.

Bongers, B. (2002), 'Euripides' Bacchae 1064-9: Dionysus, the Wheel and the Lathe', *Mnemosyne*, 55: 83–7.

Burkert, W. (1966), 'Greek Tragedy and Sacrificial Ritual', *Greek, Roman and Byzantine Studies*, 7: 87–121.

Buxton, R. (2009), 'Feminized Males in *Bacchae*: The Importance of Discrimination', in S. Goldhill and E. Hall (eds), *Sophocles and the Greek Tragic Tradition*, 232–50, Cambridge: Cambridge University Press.

Castellani, V. (1976), 'That Troubled House of Pentheus in Euripides' *Bacchae*', *Transactions of the American Philological Association*, 106: 61–83.

Chaston, C. (2010), *Tragic Props and Cognitive Function: Aspects of the Function of Images in Thinking*, Leiden: Brill.

Chesi, G. M. and F. Spiegel (2020), *Classical Literature and Posthumanism*, London: Bloomsbury.

Cless, D. (2010), 'Greek Tragedy', in D. Cless (ed.), *Ecology and Environment in European Drama*, 17–29, New York, NY: Routledge.

Csapo, E. (1997), 'Riding the Phallus for Dionysus: Iconology, Ritual, and Gender-Role De/Construction', *Phoenix*, 51: 253–95.

Deleuze, G. and Guattari, F. (1987), *A Thousand Plateaus: Capitalism and Schizophrenia*, trans. B. Massumi, Minneapolis, MN: University of Minnesota Press.

Dodds, E. R. (1960), *Euripides Bacchae*, Oxford: Clarendon Press.

Dunning, A. and P. Woodrow (2005), 'Electric Flesh – the Electromagnetic Medium: The Einstein's Brain Project', *Technoetic Arts*, 3: 155–68.

Fisher, J. (1992), 'The Palace Miracles in Euripides' *Bacchae*: A Reconsideration', *The American Journal of Philology*, 113: 179–88.

Foley, H. (1980), 'The Masque of Dionysus', *Transactions of the American Philological Association*, 110: 107–33.

Foley, H. (1985), *Ritual Irony: Poetry and Sacrifice in Euripides*, Ithaca, NY: Cornell University Press.

Gaard, G., S. C. Estok, and S. Oppermann, eds (2013), *International Perspectives in Feminist Ecocriticism*, New York, NY: Routledge.

Grene, D. and R. Lattimore (2013), *Euripides V. The Bacchae. Iphigenia in Aulis. The Cyclops. Rhesus*, Chicago, IL: Chicago University Press.

Haraway, D. (2003), *The Companion Species Manifesto: Dogs, People, and Significant Otherness*, Chicago, IL: Chicago University Press.

Haraway, D. (2008), *When Species Meet*, Minneapolis, MN: University of Minnesota Press.

Henrichs, A. (2012), 'Animal Sacrifice in Greek Tragedy. Ritual, Metaphor, Problematizations', in C. Faraone and F. S. Naiden (eds), *Greek and Roman Animal Sacrifice: Ancient Victims, Modern Observers*, 180–94, Cambridge: Cambridge University Press.

Holmes, B. (2010), *The Symptom and The Subject: The Emergence of the Physical Body in Ancient Greece*, Princeton, NJ: Princeton University Press.

Holmes, B. (2018), 'The Body', in P. E. Pormann (ed.), *The Cambridge Companion to Hippocrates*, 63–88, Cambridge: Cambridge University Press.

Hughes, J. D. (2014), *Environmental Problems of the Greeks and Romans: Ecology in the Ancient Mediterranean*, Baltimore, MD: John Hopkins University Press.

Kalke, C. (1985), 'The Making of a Thyrsus: The Transformation of Pentheus in Euripides' *Bacchae*', *American Journal of Philology*, 106: 409–26.

Konstantinou, A. (2018), *Female Mobility and Gendered Space in Ancient Greek Myth*, London: Bloomsbury Academic.

Kovacs, D. (2003), *Bacchae. Iphigenia at Aulis. Rhesus*, Cambridge, MA: Harvard University Press.

Merleau-Ponty, M. (1968), *The Visible and the Invisible*, Evanston, IL: Northwestern University Press.

Mimidou, E. (2013), 'In Looks You Resemble Exactly One of the Daughters of Cadmus (Euripides, *Bacchae*, 917): The Disguise of Pentheus in *Bacchae* and in Visual Elements', *L'Antiquité Classique*, 82: 1–10.

Morton, T. (2010), 'Thinking Ecology: The Mesh, the Strange Stranger and the Beautiful Soul', *Collapse*, VI: 265–93.

Morton, T. (2011), 'The Mesh', in S. LeMenager, T. Shewry and K. Hiltner (eds), *Environmental Criticism for the Twenty-First Century*, 19–30, New York, NY: Routledge.

Mueller, M. (2016a), 'Dressing for Dionysus: Statues and Material Mimesis in Euripides' *Bacchae*', in A. Coppola, C. Barone, and M. Salvadori (eds), *Gli oggetti sulla scena teatrale ateniese: Funzione, rappresentazione, comunicazione*. Giornate Internazionali di Studio, 57–70, Univeisà degli Studi di Padova.

Mueller, M. (2016b), *Objects as Actors: Props and the Poetics Performance in Greek Tragedy*, Chicago, IL: Chicago University Press.

Murnaghan, S. (2006), 'The Daughters of Cadmus: Chorus and Characters in Euripides' *Bacchae* and *Ion*', *Bulletin of the Institute of Classical Studies*, Suppl 87: 99–112.

Otto, W. F. (1965), *Dionysus: Myth and Cult*, trans. Robert B. Palmer, Bloomington: Indiana University Press.

Rehm, R. (2002), *The Play of Space: Spatial Transformation in Greek Tragedy*, Princeton, NJ: Princeton University Press.

Reitzammer, L. (2017), 'Bacchae', in L. K. McClure (ed.), *A Companion to Euripides*, Chichester, 61–79, West Sussex: Wiley Blackwell.

Schliephake, C. (2017). *Ecocriticism, Ecology, and the Cultures of Antiquity*, Lanham, MD: Lexington Books.

Schliephake, C. (2020), *The Environmental Humanities and the Ancient World: Questions and Perspectives*, Cambridge: Cambridge University Press.

Bibliography

Seaford, R. (1981), 'Dionysiac Drama and the Dionysiac Mysteries', *Classical Quarterly*, 31 (2): 252–75.

Seaford, R. (2018), 'Thunder, Lightning and Earthquake in the *Bacchae* and the *Acts of the Apostles*,' in R. Bostock (ed.), *Tragedy, Ritual and Money in Ancient Greece*, 330–42, New York, NY: Cambridge University Press.

Segal, C. (1978), 'The Menace of Dionysus: Sex Roles and Reversals in Euripides' *Bacchae*', *Arethusa*, 11: 185–202.

Segal, C. (1982), 'Etymologies and Double Meanings in Euripides' *Bacchae*', *Glotta*, 60: 81–93.

Segal, C. (1985), 'The *Bacchae* as Meta-Tragedy', in P. Burian (ed.), *Directions in Euripidean Criticism*, 156–73, Durham, NC: Duke University Press.

Segal, C. (1987), *Dionysiac Poetics and Euripides' Bacchae*, Princeton: Princeton University Press.

Seidensticker, B. (1979), 'Sacrificial Ritual in the *Bacchae*,' in G. W. Bowersock, W. Burkert, and M. C. J. Putnam (eds), *Arktouros: Hellenic Studies Presented to Bernard M. W. Knox*, 181–90, Berlin: W. De Gruyter.

Stieber, M. (2006), 'The Wheel Simile in *Bacchae*, Another Turn', *Mnemosyne*, 59: 585–92.

Thumiger, C. (2006), 'Animal World, Animal Representation, and the Hunting Model: Between Literal and Figurative in Euripides' *Bacchae*', *Phoenix*, 60: 191–210.

Thumiger, C (2008), 'Ἀνάγκης ζεύγματ' ἐμπεπτώκαμεν: Greek Tragedy between Human and Animal,' *Leeds International Classical Studies*, 7: 1–20.

Vernant, J. P. (1988), 'The Masked Dionysus of Euripides' *Bacchae*,' in J. P. Vernant and P. Vidal-Naquet (eds), trans. J. Lloyd, *Myth and Tragedy in Ancient Greece*, 381–419, New York, NY: Zone Books.

Wohl, V. (2005), 'Beyond Sexual Difference: Becoming-Woman in Euripides' *Bacchae*', in V. Pedrick and S. M. Oberhelman (eds), *The Soul of Tragedy: Essays on Athenian Drama*, 137–54, Chicago, IL: University of Chicago Press.

Warren, E. W., trans. (1975), *Porphyry the Phoenician*, Isagoge, Toronto: Pontifical Institute of Medieval Studies.

Worman, N. (2021), *Tragic Bodies: Edges of the Human in Greek Drama*, London: Bloomsbury.

Zatta, C. (2018), *Interconnectedness: The Living World of the Early Greek Philosophers*, Sankt Augustin: Academia Verlag.

Zeitlin, F. (1985), 'Playing the Other: Theater, Theatricality, and the Feminine in Greek Drama', *Representations*, 11: 63–94.

Chapter 5

Aguirre, M. (2010), 'Erinyes as Creatures of Darkness', in M. Christopoulos, E. D. Karakantza and O. Levaniouk (eds), *Light and Darkness in Ancient Greek Myth and Religion*, 133–41, Lanham, MD: Rowman and Littlefield.

Amsel, B. D., T. P. Urbach and M. Kutas (2014), 'Empirically Grounding Grounded Cognition: The Case of Color', *NeuroImage*, 99: 149–57.

Barsalou, L. W. (2016), 'Situated Conceptualization: Theory and Applications', in Y. Coello and M. H. Fischer (eds), *Foundations of Embodied Cognition: Volume 1: Perceptual and Emotional Embodiment*, 11–37, London: Routledge.

Bradley, M. (2013), 'Colour as Synaesthetic Experience in Antiquity', in S. Butler and A. Purvis (eds), *Synaesthesia and the Ancient Senses*, 127–40, Cambridge: Cambridge University Press.

Bubandt, N., ed. (2018), *A Non-secular Anthropocene: Spirits, Specters and Other Nonhumans in a Time of Environmental Change*. More-than-Human: AURA Working Papers 3, Aarhus: Aarhus University.

Buber, M. (2020), *I and Thou*. Translated by Ronald Gregor Smith, London: Bloomsbury Academic. [Authorised Translation, 1923, Berlin: Schocken Verlag].

Bury, R. G. trans. (1926), *Plato. Laws, Vol. 1 (Books 1-6)*, Loeb Classical Library 187, Cambridge, MA: Harvard University Press.

Carne-Ross, D. S. (1985), *Pindar*, New Haven, CT: Yale University Press.

Clarke, M. (2004), 'The Semantics of Colour in the Early Greek Word-hoard', in L. Cleland, K. Stears, and G. Davies (eds), *Colour in the Ancient Mediterranean World*, BAR International Series 1267, 74–90, Oxford: BAR Publishing.

Cohen, J. J. (2013), 'Introduction: Ecology's Rainbow', in J. J. Cohen (ed.), *Prismatic Ecology: Ecotheory beyond Green*, xv–xxxvi, Minneapolis, MN: University of Minnesota Press.

Conca, F., V. M. Borsa, S. F. Cappa and E. Catricalà (2021), 'The Multidimensionality of Abstract Concepts: A Systematic Review', *Neuroscience & Biobehavioral Reviews*, 127: 474–91.

Cowley, S. J. (2011), 'Taking a Language Stance', *Ecological Psychology*, 23 (3): 185–209.

Dowden, K. (2010), 'Trojan Night', in M. Christopoulos, E. D. Karakantza, and O. Levaniouk (eds), *Light and Darkness in Ancient Greek Myth and Religion*, 110–20, Lanham, MD: Rowman and Littlefield.

Eidinow, E. (2022), 'Ancient Greek Smellscapes and Divine Fragrances: Anthropomorphizing the Gods in Ancient Greek Culture', in E. Eidinow, A. Geertz, and J. North (eds), *Cognitive Approaches to Ancient Religious Experience* (Ancient Religion and Cognition), 69–95, Cambridge: Cambridge University Press.

Eidinow, E. (2023), 'I-Thou-Nymph: A Relational Approach to Ancient Greek Religious Devotion', *Religion*, 53 (1): 24–42.

Emlyn-Jones, C. and W. Preddy, eds. and trans. (2013), *Plato. Republic. Vol. II: Books 6-10*. Cambridge, MA: Harvard University Press.

Epstein, R. (2016), 'The Empty Brain', *Aeon*, 2016-05-18. https://aeon.co/essays/your-brain-does-not-process-information-and-it-is-not-a-computer

Fowler, H. N., trans. (1921), *Plato. Theaetetus. Sophist*. Cambridge, MA: Harvard University Press.

Gallagher, S. and M. Allen (2018), 'Active Inference, Enactivism and the Hermeneutics of Social Cognition', *Synthese*, 195: 2627–48.

Gibson, J. J. (1979), *The Ecological Approach to Visual Perception*, Boston, MA: Houghton Mifflin and Company.

Grand-Clément, A. (2020), '"What color is the sacred?" Couleurs et émotions dans les rituels grecs, de l'époque archaïque à l'époque hellénistique', in K. Ierodiakonou (ed.), *Psychologie de la couleur dans le monde gréco-romain: huit exposés suivis de discussion' etrunoquilogue*. Entretiens sur l'Antiquité classique, 66, 227–69, Geneva: Fondation Hardt pour l'étud' de l'Antiquité classique.

Hammond, M. (2009), *Thucydides: The Peloponnesian War*, Oxford: Oxford University Press.

Harvey, M. I. (2015), 'Content in Languaging: Why Radical Enactivism Is Incompatible with Representational Theories of Language', *Language Sciences*, 48: 90–129.

Hornblower, S. (2008), *A Commentary on Thucydides: Volume III: Books 5.25–8.109*, Oxford: Oxford University Press.

Kiverstein, J. D. and E. Rietveld (2018), 'Reconceiving Representation-hungry Cognition: An Ecological-enactive Proposal', *Adaptive Behavior*, 26 (4): 147–63.

Kovacs, D., ed. and trans. (1994), *Euripides. Cyclops. Alcestis. Medea*, Cambridge, MA: Harvard University Press.

Kovacs, D., ed. and trans. (1998), *Euripides. Suppliant Women. Electra. Heracles*. Loeb Classical Library 9, Cambridge, MA: Harvard University Press.

Kovacs, D., ed. and trans. (2002), *Euripides. Helen. Phoenician Women. Orestes*. Loeb Classical Library 11, Cambridge, MA: Harvard University Press.

Kovacs, D., ed. and trans. (2003), *Euripides. Bacchae. Iphigenia at Aulis. Rhesus*. Loeb Classical Library 495, Cambridge, MA: Harvard University Press.

Bibliography

Kyle Simmons, W., V. Ramjee, M. S. Beauchamp, K. McRae, A. Martin and L. W. Barsalou (2007), 'A Common Neural Substrate for Perceiving and Knowing about Color', *Neuropsychologia*, 45 (12): 2802–10.

Latour, B. (2013), 'Facing Gaia. Six Lectures on the Political Theology of Nature', *The Gifford Lectures on Natural Religion*, Edinburgh 18th–28th of February 2013. http://www.bruno-latour.fr/

Latour, B. (2014), 'Agency at the Time of the Anthropocene', *New Literary History*, 45 (1): 1–18.

Lloyd-Jones, H. (1994), *Ajax. Electra. Oedipus Tyrannus*, Loeb Classical Library 20, Cambridge, MA: Harvard University Press.

MacDowell, A. T., ed. and trans. (1990), *Demosthenes. Against Meidias (Oration 21)*, Oxford: Oxford University Press.

Malafouris, L. (2019), 'Mind and Material Engagement', *Phenomenology and the Cognitive Sciences* 18: 1–17. doi:10.1007/s11097-018-9606-7

Murray, A. T. trans. (rev. G. E. Dimock) (1919), *Homer. Odyssey, Volume II*, Loeb Classical Library 105, Cambridge, MA: Harvard University Press.

Murray, A. T. trans. (rev. W. F. Wyatt) (1924), *Homer. Iliad. Volume 1*, Loeb Classical Library 170, Cambridge, MA: Harvard University Press.

Pelling, C., ed. (2022), *Thucydides. The Peloponnesian War. Book VII*, Cambridge: Cambridge University Press.

Raab, M. and D. Araújo (2019), 'Embodied Cognition With and Without Mental Representations: The Case of Embodied Choices in Sports', *Frontiers in Psychology* 10:1825. doi: 10.3389/fpsyg.2019.01825

Race, W. H. (1997), *Nemean Odes. Isthmian Odes. Fragments*, Loeb Classical Library 485, Cambridge, MA: Harvard University Press.

Read, C. and A. Szokolszky (2020), 'Ecological Psychology and Enactivism: Perceptually-Guided Action vs. Sensation-Based Enaction', *Frontiers in Psychology* 11:1270. doi: 10.3389/fpsyg.2020.01270.

Sommerstein, A. 2009. *Oresteia: Agamemnon. Libation-Bearers. Eumenides*, Loeb Classical Library 146, Cambridge, MA: Harvard University Press.

Still, A. and A. Costall (1991), 'The Mutual Elimination of Dualism in Vygotsky and Gibson', in A. Still and A. Costall (eds), *Against Cognitivism: Alternative Foundations for Cognitive Psychology*, 225–36, Hemel Hempstead: Harvester Wheatsheaf.

Szokolszky, A. (2019), 'Perceiving Metaphors: An Approach from Developmental Ecological Psychology', *Metaphor and Symbol*, 3 (1): 17–32.

Vince, C. A. and J. H. Vince, trans. (1926), *Demosthenes, Orations 18-19: De Corona, De Falsa Legatione*, Loeb Classical Library 155, Cambridge, MA: Harvard University Press.

Waterfield, R. (1998), *Herodotus. The Histories*, Oxford: Oxford University Press.

Whitehead, D. (2003), *Aeneas the Tactician: How to Survive Under Siege*, London: BCP Classical Studies.

Witzel, C. (2019), 'Misconceptions About Colour Categories', *Rev. Phil. Psych.* 10: 499–540. doi. org/10.1007/s13164-018-0404-5.

Chapter 6

Alcock, S. E. (1993), *Graecia Capta: The Landscapes of Roman Greece*, Cambridge: Cambridge University Press.

Allen, J. (2010), 'Greek Philosophy and Signs', in A. Annus (ed.), *Divination and Interpretation of Signs in the Ancient World*, 29–42, Chicago, IL: The Oriental Institute.

Arènes, A., B. Latour and J. Gaillardet (2017), '"Giving Depth to the Surface" – An Exercise in the Gaia-Graphy of Critical Zones', *The Anthropocene Review*, 5 (2): 120–35.

Beck, M., ed. (2014), *A Companion to Plutarch*, Malden, MA: Blackwell.

Bendlin, A. (2011), 'On the Uses and Disadvantages of Divination: Oracles and their Literary Representation in the Time of the Second Sophistic', in J. A. North and S. R. F. Price (eds), *The Religious History of the Roman Empire: Pagans, Jews, and Christians*, 175–250, Oxford: Oxford UP.

Borgeaud, P. (1983), 'La mort du grand Pan. Problèmes d'interprétation', *Revue de l'Histoire des Religions*, 200: 3–39.

Bowden, H. (2013), 'Seeking Certainty and Claiming Authority: The Consultation of Greek Oracles from the Classical to the Roman Imperial Period', in V. Rosenberger (ed.), *Divination in the Ancient World: Religious Options and the Individual*, 42–59, Stuttgart: Steiner.

Brenk, F. E. (1977), *In Mist Apparelled: Religious Themes in Plutarch's* Moralia and Lives, Leiden: Brill.

Brenk, F. E. (2005), 'Plutarch's Middle-Platonic God: About to Enter (or Remake) the Academy', in R. Hirsch-Luipold (ed.), *Gott und die Götter bei Plutarch: Götterbilder – Gottesbilder – Weltbilder*, 27–49, Berlin: de Gruyter.

Brouillette, X. (2014), *La philosophie delphique de Plutarque*, Paris: Les Belles Lettres.

Dörrie, H. (1983), '"Der Weise vom Roten Meere". Eine okkulte Offenbarung durch Plutarch als Plagiat entlarvt', in P. Haendel and W. Meid (eds), *Festschrift für Robert Muth*, 95–110, Innsbruck: Institut für Sprachwissenschaft der Universität Innsbruck.

Eidinow, E. (2013), 'Oracular Consultation, Fate and the Concept of the Individual', in V. Rosenberger (ed.), *Divination in the Ancient World: Religious Options and the Individual*, 21–39, Stuttgart: Steiner.

Frazier, F. (2005), 'Göttlichkeit und Glaube: Persönliche Gottesbeziehung im Spätwerk Plutarchs', in R. Hirsch-Luipold (ed.), *Gott und die Götter bei Plutarch: Götterbilder – Gottesbilder – Weltbilder*, 111–39, Berlin: de Gruyter.

Iovino, S. and S. Oppermann (2014), 'Introduction: Stories Come to Matter', in S. Iovino and S. Oppermann (eds), *Material Ecocriticism*, 1–17, Bloomington, IN: Indiana University Press.

König, J. (2009), *Greek Literature in the Roman Empire*, Bristol: Bristol Classical Press.

Latour, B. (2016), *Facing Gaia: Eight Lectures on the New Climatic Regime*, Cambridge: Polity.

Latour, B. (2020), 'Seven Objections Against Landing on Earth', in B. Latour and P. Weibel (eds), *Critical Zones – The Science and Politics of Landing on Earth*, 12–19, Cambridge, MA: MIT Press.

Maurizio, L. (1995), 'Anthropology and Spirit Possession: The Pythia's Role at Delphi', *The Journal of Hellenic Studies*, 115: 69–86.

Miller, Dana R. (1997), 'Plutarch's Argument for a Plurality of Worlds in De defectu oraculorum 424c10-425e7', *Ancient Philosophy*, 17 (2): 375–95.

Roskam, G. (2021), *Plutarch*, Cambridge: Cambridge University Press.

Scott, M. (2014), *Delphi: A History of the Center of the Ancient World*, Princeton: Princeton University Press.

Simonetti, E. G. (2017), *A Perfect Medium? Oracular Divination in the Thought of Plutarch*, Leuven: Leuven University Press.

Simonetti, E. G. (2021), 'The Pythia as Matter: Plutarch's Scientific Account of Divination', in C. Addey (ed.), *Divination and Knowledge in Greco-Roman Antiquity*, 174–93, London: Routledge.

Sirinelli, J. (2000), *Plutarque de Chéronée: Un philosophe dans le siècle*, Paris: Fayard.

Timotin, A. (2022), *Trois théories antiques de la divination: Plutarque, Jamblique, Augustin*, Leiden: Brill.

Wheeler, W. (2006), *The Whole Creature: Complexity, Biosemiotics and the Evolution of Culture*, London: Larence and Wishart.

Ziegler, K. (1964), *Plutarchos von Chaironeia*, 2nd edition, Stuttgart: Druckenmüller.

Bibliography

Chapter 7

Baladie, R. (1980), *Le Péloponnèse de Strabon: Étude de géographie historique*, Paris: Les Belles Lettres.

Barrett, J. L. (2000), 'Exploring the Natural Foundations of Religion', *Trends in Cognitive Sciences*, 4 (1): 29–34.

Barrett, J. L. (2011), 'Cognitive Science of Religion: Looking back, Looking forward', *Journal for the Scientific Study of Religion*, 50 (2): 229–39.

Borsch, J. and L. Carrara eds (2016), *Erdbeben in Der Antike: Deutungen – Folgen – Repräsentationen*, Tübingen: Mohr Siebeck.

Boyer, P. (2001), *Religion Explained: The Evolutionary Origins of Religious Thought*, New York, NY: Basic Books.

Bremmer, J. (2006), 'Poseidon', in H. Cancik, H. Schneider, and C. F. Salazar (eds), *Brill's New Pauly*, http://dx.doi.org/10.1163/1574-9347_bnp_e1006030

Burkert, W. (1985), *Greek Religion*, trans. P. Bing, Cambridge: Harvard University Press.

Burkert, W. (1996), *Creation of the Sacred: Tracks of Biology in Early Religions*, Cambridge: Harvard University Press.

Cashman, K. V. and S. J. Cronin (2008), 'Welcoming a Monster to the World: Myths, Oral Tradition, and Modern Societal Response to Volcanic Disasters', *Journal of Volcanology and Geothermal Research*, 176: 407–18.

Chaniotis, A. (1998), 'Willkommene Erdbeben', in E. Olshausen and H. Sonnabend (eds), *Naturkatastrophen in der antiken Welt*, 404–16, Stuttgart: Steiner.

Curry, P. and A. Voss (2007), *Seeing with Different Eyes: Essays in Astrology and Divination*, Newcastle: Cambridge Scholars Publishing.

Detienne, M. (2008), *Comparing the Incomparable*, trans. J. Lloyd, Stanford: Stanford University Press.

Dumézil, G. (1966), *La Religion romaine archaïque*, Paris: Payot.

Dumézil, G. (1973), *Mythe et épopée, III, Histoires romaines*, Paris: Gallimard.

Ehmig, U. (2016), 'Der "Erdbebengott Neptun" und die "unbestimmten Erdbebengötter" in lateinischen Inschriften', in J. Borsch and L. Carrara (eds), *Erdbeben in Der Antike: Deutungen – Folgen – Repräsentationen*, 37–59, Tübingen: Mohr Siebeck.

Eidinow, E. (2022), 'Ancient Greek Smellscapes and Divine Fragrances: Anthropomorphizing the Gods in Ancient Greek Culture', in E. Eidinow, A. W. Geertz and J. North (eds), *Cognitive Approaches to Ancient Religious Experiences*, 69–95, Cambridge: Cambridge University Press.

Eidinow, E., A. W. Geertz and J. North, eds (2022), *Cognitive Approaches to Ancient Religious Experiences*, Cambridge: Cambridge University Press.

Gerten, D. and S. Bergmann, eds (2012), *Religion in Environmental and Climate Change: Suffering, Values, Lifestyles*, London: Bloomsbury.

Guthrie, S. E. (1993), *Faces in the Clouds: A New Theory of Religion*, New York: Oxford University Press.

Katsonopoulou, D. (2016), 'Natural Catastrophes in the Gulf of Corinth, Northwestern Peloponnese, from Prehistory to Late Antiquity: the Example of Helike', in J. Borsch and L. Carrara (eds), *Erdbeben in Der Antike: Deutungen – Folgen – Repräsentationen*, 137–52, Tübingen: Mohr Siebeck.

Katsonopoulou, D. (2021), 'The Cult of Poseidon Helikonios: From Helike of Achaea to Asia Minor and the Black Sea', *História*, 69 (1): 121–35.

Kohn, E. (2007), 'How Dogs Dream: Amazonian Natures and the Politics of Transspecies Engagement', *American Ethnologist*, 34 (1): 3–24.

Kohn, E. (2013), *How Forests Think: Toward an Anthropology Beyond the Human*, Berkeley, CA: University of California Press.

Larson, J. (2016), *Understanding Greek Religion: A Cognitive Approach*, London: Routledge.

Mackey, J. L. (2022), *Belief and Cult: Rethinking Roman Religion*, Princeton, NJ: Princeton University Press.

Manetti, G. (1993), *Theories of the Sign in Classical Antiquity*, Bloomington, IN: Indiana University Press.

Muellner, L. (1996), *The Anger of Achilles: Mēnis in Greek Epic*, Ithaca, NY: Cornell University Press.

Olshausen, E. and H. Sonnabend, eds (1998), *Naturkatastrophen in der antiken Welt*, Stuttgart: Steiner.

Peirce, C. S. (1965–6), *Collected Papers*, eds C. Hartsthrone, P. Weiss, and A. W. Bruks (8 vols), Cambridge, MA: Harvard University Press.

Pongratz-Leisten, B. and K. Sonik, eds (2015), *The Materiality of Divine Agency*, Boston, MA/Berlin: De Gruyter.

Schliephake, C., ed. (2016), *Ecocriticism, Ecology, and the Cultures of Antiquity*, Lanham, MD: Lexington Books.

Simon, E. (1969), *Die Götter der Griechen*, München: Hirmer.

Sonnabend, H. (2012), 'Environment, Climate and Religion in Ancient European History', in D. Gerten and S. Bergmann (eds), *Religion in Environmental and Climate Change: Suffering, Values, Lifestyles*, 261–6, London: Bloomsbury.

Steinberg, T. (2006), *Acts of God: The Unnatural History of Natural Disaster in America*, Oxford: Oxford University Press.

Stubblefield, T. (2015), *9/11 and the Visual Culture of Disaster*, Bloomington, IN: Indiana University Press.

Struck, P. (2007), 'A World Full of Signs: Understanding Divination in Ancient Stoicism', in P. Curry and A. Voss (eds), *Seeing with Different Eyes: Essays in Astrology and Divination*, 3–20, Newcastle: Cambridge Scholars Publishing.

Stylianou, P. J. (1998), *A Historical Commentary on Diodorus Siculus, Book 15*, New York, NY: Oxford University Press.

Thély, L. (2016), *Les Grecs Face aux Catastrophes Naturelles*, Athens: École française d'Athènes.

Tremlin, T. (2006), *Minds and Gods: The Cognitive Foundations of Religion*, New York, NY: Oxford University Press.

Vernant, J.-P. (1990), *Myth and Society in Ancient Greece*, trans. J. Lloyd, New York, NY: Zone Books.

Waldherr, G. H. (1997), *Erdbeben: Das aussergewöhnliche Normale*, Stuttgart: Steiner.

Walter, J. (2016), 'Poseidon's Wrath and the End of Helike: Notions about the Anthropogenic Character of Disasters in Antiquity', in C. Schliephake (ed.), *Ecocriticism, Ecology, and the Cultures of Antiquity*, 31–43, Lanham, MD: Lexington Books.

Chapter 8

Aldrete, G. S. (2007), *Floods of the Tiber in Ancient Rome*, Baltimore, MD: John Hopkins University Press.

Ammerman, A. J. (2018), 'The East Bank of The Tiber Below The Island: Two Recent Advances in The Study of Early Rome', *Antiquity*, 92: 398–409.

Armstrong, R. (2019), *Vergil's Green Thoughts: Plants, Humans, and The Divine*, Oxford: Oxford University Press.

Beard, M. et al., eds (1998), *Religions of Rome*, Cambridge: Cambridge University Press.

Bettini, M. (2015), *Il dio elegante: Vertumno e la religione romana*, Torino: Giulio Einaudi.

Bianchi, E. (2015), *La Cloaca Maxima e i sistemi fognari di Roma dall'antichità ad oggi*, Rome: Palombi Editori.

Bibliography

Blouin, K. (2019), 'Classics, Antiquity and the Anthropocene: Some Thoughts', *Everyday Orientalism* blog. Accessed on 22 November 2022.

Brock, A., L. Motta and N. Terrenato (2021), 'On the Banks of the Tiber: Opportunity and Transformation in Early Rome', *Journal of Roman Studies*, 111: 1–30.

Butler, J. (2011), *Gender Trouble*, London: Routledge.

Carlassare, E. (2000), 'Socialist and Cultural Ecofeminism: Allies in Resistance', *Ethics and the Environment*, 5 (1): 89–106.

Clark, R. J. (2010), 'Ilia's Excessive Complaint and The Flood In Horace, Odes 1.2', *The Classical Quarterly*, 60: 262–7.

Coarelli, F. (2012), *Palatium*, Rome: Quasar.

Corbeill, A. (2020), *Sexing the World*, Princeton, NJ: Princeton University Press.

Davies, J. P. (2007), *Rome's Religious History*, Cambridge: Cambridge University Press.

Descola, P. (2013), *Beyond nature and culture*, Chicago, IL: University of Chicago Press.

Devoto, G. (1940), 'Nomi di divinita etrusche, III: Vertumno', *Studi Etruschi*, 14: 275–80.

Dumézil, G. (1988), *Mitra-Varuna*, Chicago, IL: University of Chicago Press.

Eidinow, E. (2016), 'Telling Stories: Exploring The Relationship between Myths and Ecological Wisdom', *Landscape and Urban Planning*, 155: 47–52.

Giovannini, M. J. (1981), 'Woman: A Dominant Symbol Within the Cultural System of a Sicilian Town', *Man*, 16: 408.

Graham, E.-J. (2021), *Reassembling Religion in Roman Italy*, London: Routledge.

Hawes, G. (2017), 'Of Myths and Maps', in G. Hawes (ed.), *Myths on the Map: The Storied Landscapes of Ancient Greece*, 1–13, Oxford: Oxford University Press.

Jones, P. J. (2005), *Reading Rivers in Roman Literature and Culture*, Lanham, MD: Lexington Books.

Kaur, G. (2012), 'An Exegesis of Postcolonial Ecofeminism in Contemporary Literature', *International Journal of Law and Social Sciences*, 2: 188.

Keegan, P. (2008), 'Q(uando) St(ercus) D(elatum) F(as): What was Removed from the Temple of Vesta', *New England Classical Journal*, 35: 91–7.

Latour, B. (2005), *Reassembling the Social: An Introduction to Actor-network-theory*, Oxford: OUP.

La Rocca, E. (1984), *La riva a mezzaluna*, Rome: L'Erma di Bretschneider.

Lahiri-Dutt, K. and G. Samanta (2013), *Dancing with the River*, New Haven, CT: Yale University Press.

Le Gall, J. (1953a), *Le Tibre, fleuve de Rome dans l'antiquité*, Paris: Presses universitaires de France.

Le Gall, J. (1953b), *Recherches sur le culte du Tibre,* Paris: Institut d'Art et d'archéologie de l'université de Paris.

Levene, D. S. (1993), *Religion in Livy*, Leiden: Brill.

Marra, F. et al. (2018), 'Rome in its Setting: Post-glacial Aggradation History of the Tiber River Alluvial Deposits and Tectonic Origin of the Tiber Island', *PloS One*, 13.

Masterson, M. (2013), 'Studies of Ancient Masculinity', in T. K. Hubbard (ed.) *A Companion to Greek and Roman Sexualities*, 17–30, Chichester: Wiley.

Mommsen, T. (1864), *Römische Forschungen*, Berlin: Weidmannsche Buchhandlung.

Morton, T. (2010), 'Guest column: Queer Ecology', *Publications of the Modern Language Associations of America*, 125: 273–82.

Nečas Hraste, D. and K. Vuković (2015), 'Virgins and Prostitutes in Roman Mythology', *Latomus*, 74: 313–38.

Newlands, C. E. (1995), *Playing with Time*, Ithaca, NY: Cornell University Press.

Nisbet, R. G. M. and M. Hubbard (1989), *A Commentary on Horace: Odes, book 1*, Oxford: Clarendon Press.

Ogilvie, R. M. (1965), *A Commentary on Livy 1-5*, Oxford: Clarendon Press.

Perono Cacciafoco, F. (2013), 'Ancient Names Origins: Water Roots and Place-Names in the Prehistoric Ligurian', *Review of Historical Geography and Toponomastics*, 8 (15–16): 7–24.

Plant, J. (2008), *Healing the Wounds*, London: New Catalyst Books.

Prescendi Morresi, F. (2020), 'Une prostituée comme bienfaitrice du peuple romain: Acca Larentia et l'origine des Larentalia', in I. Becci and F. Prescendi Morresi (eds), *Imaginaires queers*, 63–76, Lausanne: BSN Press.

Saadi-Nejad, M. (2021), *Anahita: a History and Reception of the Iranian Water Goddess*, London: Bloomsbury Publishing.

Schliephake, C. (2020), *The Environmental Humanities and the Ancient World: Questions and Perspectives*, Cambridge: Cambridge University Press.

Seider, A. (2021), 'A Landscape of Control? *Aeneid* 8 and Environmental Agency', *Vita Latina*, 201: 142–63.

Sessa, K. (2019), 'The New Environmental Fall of Rome: a Methodological Consideration', *Journal of Late Antiquity*, 12: 211–55.

Simon, E. (1969), 'Altar des Mars' in W. Helbig (ed.), *Führer durch die öffentlichen Sammlungen klassischer Altertümer in Rom III. Die Staatlichen Sammlungen. Museo Nazionale Romano (Thermenmuseum). Museo Nazionale di Villa Giulia*, 222–4, Tübingen: Ernst Wasmuth.

Spivak, G. C. (1999), *A Critique of Postcolonial Reason*, Cambridge, MA: Harvard University Press.

Thomas, R. F. (2004), 'Torn between Jupiter and Saturn: Ideology, Rhetoric and Culture Wars in the "Aeneid"', *The Classical Journal*, 100: 121–47.

Vuković, K. (2020a), 'Silvia's Stag on the Tiber: The Setting of the *Aeneid*'s *Casus Belli*', *Mnemosyne*, 73: 464–82.

Vuković, K. (2020b), 'Review of David Leeming, *Sex in the World of Myth*. London: Reaktion Books Limited, 2018', *Bryn Mawr Classical Review*, 2020.10.51.

Williams, C. A. (2010), *Roman Homosexuality*, Oxford: Oxford University Press.

Woodman, A. J. (2003), *Rhetoric in Classical Historiography*, London: Routledge.

Chapter 9

Albrecht, G. (2005), '"Solastalgia:" A New Concept in Health and Identity', *Philosophy Activism, Nature*, 3: 41–55.

Al-Jallad, A. (2022a), 'Ancient North Arabian' in T. Kaizer (ed.), *A Companion to the Hellenistic and Roman Near East*, 99–104, Hoboken, NJ: Wiley Blackwell.

Al-Jallad, A. (2022b), *The Religion and Rituals of the Nomads of Pre-Islamic Arabia: A Reconstruction Based on the Safaitic Inscriptions*, Leiden: Brill.

Al-Jallad, A. and K. Jaworska (2019), *A Dictionary of the Safaitic Inscriptions*, Leiden: Brill.

Bennett, C. (2014), 'Geographic and Religious Trends in the Pre-Islamic Religious Beliefs of the North Arabian Nomadic and Semi-Nomadic Tribes', *Proceedings of the Seminar for Arabian Studies*, 44: 43–52.

Bosak-Schroeder, C. (2020), *Other Natures: Environmental Encounters with Ancient Greek Ethnography*, Berkeley, CA: University of California Press.

Butler, J. (2004), *Precarious Life: The Powers of Mourning and Violence*, New York, NY: Verso.

Cairns, D. and D. Nelis (2017), 'Introduction', in D. Cairns and D. Nelis (eds), *Emotions in the Classical World: Methods, Approaches, and Directions*, 7–30, Stuttgart: Steiner.

Chaniotis, A. (2012), 'Moving Stones: The Study of Emotions in Greek Inscriptions', in A. Chaniotis (ed.), *Unveiling Emotions: Sources and Methods for the Study of Emotions in the Greek World*, 91–129, Stuttgart: Steiner.

Chaniotis, A. (2016), 'Displaying Emotional Community: The Epigraphic Evidence', in E. Sanders and M. Johncock (eds), *Emotion and Persuasion in Classical Antiquity*, 93–111, Stuttgart: Steiner.

Bibliography

Chaniotis, A. and P. Ducrey (2013), 'Approaching Emotions in Greek and Roman History and Culture: Introduction', in A. Chaniotis and P. Ducrey (eds), *Unveiling Emotions II. Emotions in Greece and Rome: Texts, Images, Material Culture*, 9–14, Stuttgart: Steiner.

Craps, S. (2020), 'Introduction: Ecological Grief', *American Imago. Special issue: Ecological Grief*, 77 (1): 1–7.

Cunsolo, A. and N. R. Ellis (2018), 'Ecological Grief as a Mental Health Response to Climate Change-Related Loss', *Nature Climate Change*, 8: 275–81.

Cunsolo Willox, A. (2012), 'Climate Change as the Work of Mourning', *Ethics and the Environment*, 17 (2): 137–64.

Cunsolo Willox, A., S. L. Harper, J. D. Ford, et al. (2012), '"From This Place and of This Place:" Climate Change, Sense of Place, and Health in Nunatsiavut, Canada', *Social Science & Medicine*, 75: 538–47.

Cunsolo Willox, A., S. L. Harper, V. L. Edge, et al. (2013), 'The Land Enriches the Soul: On Climatic and Environmental Change, Affect, and Emotional Health and Well-Being in Rigolet, Nunatsiavut, Canada', *Emotion, Space and Society*, 6: 14–24.

Della Puppa, C. (2022), 'The Safaitic Scripts: Palaeography of An Ancient Nomadic Writing Culture', PhD diss., Leiden University.

Dentzer, J. (1979), 'A propos du temple dit de <<Dusarès>> à Sî', *Syria*, 56: 325–32.

Dentzer-Feydy, J. (2015), 'New Archaeological Research at the Sanctuary of Sî' in Southern Syria: The Graeco-Roman Divinities Invite Themselves to Baalshamîn', in M. Blömer, A. Lichtenberger and R. Raja (eds), *Religious Identities in the Levant from Alexander to Muhammed: Continuity and Change*, 312–25, Turnhout: Brepols.

Eksell, K. (2002), *Meaning in Ancient North Arabian Carvings*, Stockholm: Faculty of Humanities.

Eksell, K. (2005), 'The verb wǧm in Safaitic inscriptions', in T. Bauer and U. Stehli-Werbeck, with T. G. Schneiders (eds), *Alltagsleben und materielle Kultur in der arabischen Sprache und Literatur. Festschrift für Heinz Grotzfeld zum 70. Geburtstag*, 163–72, Wiesbaden: Harrassowitz.

Ellis, N. R. and G. A. Albrecht (2017), 'Climate Change Threats to Family Farmers' Sense of Place and Mental Wellbeing: A Case Study from the Western Australian Wheatbelt', *Social Science & Medicine*, 175: 161–8.

Gallegos-Riofrío, C. A., H. Arab, A. Carrasco-Torrontegui, et al. (2022), 'Chronic Deficiency of Diversity and Pluralism in Research on Nature's Mental Health Effects: A Planetary Health Problem', *Current Research in Environmental Sustainability*, 4: 100148. Available at https://doi.org/10.1016/j.crsust.2022.100148

Harper, K. (2017), *The Fate of Rome: Climate, Disease, and the End of Empire*, Princeton, NJ: Princeton University Press.

Head, L. (2016), *Hope and Grief in the Anthropocene: Re-conceptualising Human-Nature Relations*, London: Routledge.

Howe, C. and D. Boyer (2020), 'Death of a Glacier', *Anthropology News*, 22 April. Available online: https://www.anthropology-news.org/articles/death-of-a-glacier/ (last accessed 21 March 2024).

Keitel, E. and V. M. Closs, eds (2020), *Urban Disasters and the Roman Imagination*, Berlin: De Gruyter.

Khademi, F., M. Rassouli, F. Rafiei, et al. (2021), 'The Effect of Mandala Colouring on Anxiety in Hospitalized COVID-19 Patients: A Randomized Controlled Clinical Trial', *International Journal of Mental Health Nursing*, 30: 1437–44.

Lightfoot, J. L. (2005), 'Pilgrims and ethnographers: in search of the Syrian Goddess', in J. Elsner and I. Rutherford (eds), *Pilgrimage in Graeco-Roman and Early Christian Antiquity: Seeing the Gods*, 333–52, Oxford: Oxford University Press.

Macdonald, M. C. A. (1992), 'The Seasons and Transhumance in the Safaitic Inscriptions', *Journal of the Royal Asiatic Society*, 3 (2): 1–11.

Macdonald, M. C. A. (1993), 'Nomads and the Hawran in the Late Hellenistic and Roman Periods: A Reassessment of The Epigraphic Evidence', *Syria* 70 (3–4): 303–403.

Macdonald, M. C. A. (2003), 'References to Sīʿ in the Safaitic Inscriptions', in J. Dentzer-Feydy, J., Jean-Marie Dentzer and Pierre-Marie Blanc (eds), *Hauran II. Les Installations de Sīʿ 8. Du Sanctuaire a l'Etablissement Viticole. Volume 1*, 278–80, Beirut: Institut Francais D'archeologie Du Proche-Orient.

Macdonald, M. C. A. (2014), '"Romans Go Home"? Rome and Other "Outsiders" as Viewed from The Syro-Arabian Desert', in J. H. F. Dijkstra and G. Fisher (eds), *Inside and Out: Interactions between Rome and the Peoples on the Arabian and Egyptian Frontiers in Late Antiquity*, 145–63, Leuven: Peeters.

Macdonald, M. C. A. (2022a), 'The Desert and its Peoples', in Kaizer, T. (ed.), *A Companion to the Hellenistic and Roman Near East*, 327–33, Hoboken: Wiley Blackwell.

Macdonald, M. C. A. (2022b), 'The Arabs', in T. Kaizer (ed.), *A Companion to the Hellenistic and Roman Near East*, 397–401, Hoboken, NJ: Wiley Blackwell.

McConnell, J. R., M. Sigl, G. Plunkett, et al. (2020), 'Extreme Climate after Massive Eruption of Alaska's Okmok Volcano in 43 BCE and Effects on the Late Roman Republic and Ptolemaic Kingdom', *Proceedings of the National Academy of Sciences*, 27: 15443–9.

McCormick, M. K. Harper, A. M. More, et al. (2013), *Geodatabase of Historical Evidence on Roman and Post-Roman Climate*. Available online: https://doi.org/10.7910/DVN/TVXATE (last accessed: 21 March 2024).

Mitchell, E. (1946), *Soil and Civilization*, Sydney: Angus and Robertson Ltd.

Nixon, R. (2011), *Slow Violence and the Environmentalism of the Poor*, Cambridge, MA: Harvard UP.

Østerled Brusgaard, N. (2019), *Carving Interactions: Rock Art in the Nomadic Landscape of the Black Desert, North-Eastern Jordan*, Oxford: Archaeopress.

Sessa, K. (2019), 'The New Environmental Fall of Rome: A Methodological Consideration', *Journal of Late Antiquity*, 12 (1): 211–55.

Strabo (1930), *Geography, Volume VII: Books 15-16*, trans. Horace Leonard Jones. Loeb Classical Library 241, Cambridge, MA: Harvard University Press.

Chapter 10

Albrecht, G. A. (2005), 'Solastalgia: A New Concept in Human Health and Identity', *Philosophy, Activism, Nature*, 3: 44–59.

Albrecht, G. A. (2020), 'Negating Solastalgia: An Emotional Revolution from the Anthropocene to the Symbiocene', *American Imago*, 77: 9–30.

Behr, C. A. (1981), *P. Aelius Aristides, The Complete Works, Volume 2: Orations 17–53*, Leiden: Brill.

Borsch, J. (2018), *Erschütterte Welt: Soziale Bewältigung von Erdbeben im östlichen Mittelmeerraum der Antike*, Tübingen: Mohr Siebeck.

Borsch, J. (2021), 'Erdbeben im römischen Kleinasien und die Grenzen der Resilienz', *Historia*, 70: 206–41.

Bosak-Schroeder, C. (2020), *Other Natures: Environmental Encounters with Ancient Greek Ethnography*, Oakland, CA: University of California Press.

Bruns, C. J. (2021), 'Grieving Okjökull: Discourses of the Ok Glacier Funeral', in H. Bødker and H. E. Morris (eds), *Climate Change and Journalism: Negotiating Rifts of Time*, 121–35, Routledge: London.

Burton-Christie, D. (2011), 'The Gift of Tears: Loss, Mourning and the Work of Ecological Restoration', *Worldviews*, 15: 29–46.

Bibliography

Civiletti, M. (2002), *Filostrato*, Vite dei Sofisti, Milan: Bompiano.

Clark, T. (2019), *The Value of Ecocriticism*, Cambridge: Cambridge University Press.

Clark, T. (2020), 'Ecological Grief and Anthropocene Horror', *American Imago*, 77: 61–80.

Cunsolo, A. and K. Landman, eds (2017a), *Mourning Nature: Hope at the Heart of Ecological Loss and Grief*, Montreal: McGill-Queens University Press.

Cunsolo, A. and K. Landman (2017b), 'Introduction: To Mourn beyond the Human', in A. Cunsolo and K. Landman (eds), *Mourning Nature: Hope at the Heart of Ecological Loss and Grief*, 3–26, Montreal: McGill-Queens University Press.

Cunsolo, A. and N. R. Ellis (2018), 'Ecological Grief as a Mental Health Response to Climate Change Related Loss', *Nature Climate Change*, 8: 275–81.

Craps, S. (2020), 'Introduction: Ecological Grief', *American Imago*, 77: 1–7.

Craps, S. and I. M. Olsen (2020), 'Grief as a Doorway to Love: An Interview with Chris Jordan', *American Imago*, 77: 109–35.

Deeg, P. (2019), *Der Kaiser und die Katastrophe: Untersuchungen zum politischen Umgang mit Umweltkatastrophen im Prinzipat (31 v. Chr. bis 192 n. Chr.)*, Stuttgart: Franz Steiner Verlag.

Demoen, K. (2001), '"Où est ta beauté qu'admiraient tous les yeux?" La ville détruite dans les traditions poétique et rhétorique', in K. Demoen (ed.), *The Greek City from Antiquity to the Present: Historical Reality, Ideological Construction, Literary Representation*, 103–26, Leuven: Peeters.

Downie, J. (2013), *At the Limits of Art: A Literary Study of Aelius Aristides' Hieroi Logoi*, Oxford: Oxford University Press.

Downie, J. (2017), 'The Romance of Imperial Travel in Aelius Aristides's Smyrna Orations', in M. R. Niehoff (ed.), *Journeys in the Roman East: Imagined and Real*, 53–76, Tübingen: Mohr Siebeck.

Franco, C. (2005), *Elio Aristide e Smirne*, Rome: Accademia Nazionale dei Lincei.

Franco, C. (2008), 'Aelius Aristides and Rhodes: Concord and Consolation', in W. V. Harris, and B. Holmes (eds), *Aelius Aristides Between Greek, Rome, and the Gods*, 217–49, Leiden: Brill.

Garrard, G. (2012), *Ecocriticism*, 2nd edition, London: Routledge.

Ghosh, A. (2016), *The Great Derangement: Climate Change and the Unthinkable*, Chicago, IL: Chicago University Press.

Harris, W. V. and B. Holmes, eds (2008), *Aelius Aristides Between Greek, Rome, and the Gods*, Leiden: Brill.

Heise, U. (2008), *Sense of Place, Sense of Planet: The Environmental Imagination of the Global*, Oxford: Oxford University Press.

Holmes, B. (2008), 'Aelius Aristides' illegible body', in W. V. Harris and B. Holmes (eds), *Aelius Aristides Between Greek, Rome, and the Gods*, 81–113, Leiden: Brill.

Huggan, G. and H. Tiffin (2010), *Postcolonial Ecocriticism: Literature, Animals, Environment*, Abingdon: Routledge.

Jensen, T. (2019), *Ecologies of Guilt in Environmental Rhetorics*, London: Palgrave Macmillan.

Jones, C. P. (2012), 'Earthquakes and emperors', in A. Kolb (ed.), *Infrastruktur und Herrschaftsorganisation im Imperium Romanum*, 52–65, Berlin: De Gruyter.

Lertzman, R. (2015), *Environmental Melancholia: Psychoanalytic Dimensions of Engagement*, London: Routledge.

Lorimer, J. (2015), *Wildlife in the Anthropocene*, Minneapolis, MN: University of Minnesota Press.

Morton, T. (2013), *Hyperobjects: Philosophy and Ecology after the End of the World*, Minneapolis: University of Minnesota Press.

Newbold, R. F. (1982), 'The Reporting of Earthquakes, Fires and Floods by Ancient Historians', *The Proceedings of the African Classical Associations*, 16: 28–36.

Petsalis-Diomidis, A. (2008), 'The Body in the Landscape: Aristides' Corpus in Light of the Sacred Tales', in W. V. Harris and B. Holmes (eds), *Aelius Aristides Between Greek, Rome, and the Gods*, 131–50, Leiden: Brill.

Petsalis-Diomidis, A. (2010), *Truly Beyond Wonders: Aelius Aristides and the Cult of Asklepios*, Oxford: Oxford University Press.

Sideris, L. H. (2020), 'Grave Reminders: Grief and Vulnerability in the Anthropocene', *Religions*, 11 (6): 293.

Toner, J. (2013), *Roman Disasters*, Cambridge: Polity Press.

Walter, J. (2019), *Erdbeben im antiken Mittelmeerraum und im frühen China: Vergleichende Analyse der gesellschaftlichen Konstruktion von Naturkatastrophen bis zum 3. Jahrhundert n. Chr.*, Berlin: Logos Verlag.

Watts, E. (2014), 'The Historical Context: The Rhetoric of Suffering in Libanius' Monodies, Letters and Autobiography', in L. Van Hoof (ed.), *Libanius: A Critical Introduction*, 39–58, Cambridge: Cambridge University Press.

Webb, R. (1997), 'Imagination and the Arousal of the Emotions in Greco-Roman rhetoric', in S. Braund and C. Gill (eds), *The Passions in Roman Thought and Literature*, 112–27, Cambridge: Cambridge University Press.

Webb, R. (2009), *Ekphrasis, Imagination, and Persuasion in Ancient Rhetorical Theory and Practice*, Farnham: Ashgate.

Woolf, G. (2020), *The Life and Death of Ancient Cities: A Natural History*, New York, NY: Oxford University Press.

Yatromanolakis, Y. (2005), 'Poleos Erastes: The Greek City as the Beloved', in E. Stafford and J. Herrin (eds), *Personification in the Greek World: From Antiquity to Byzantium*, 267–83, Farnham: Ashgate.

Chapter 11

Benjamin, W. (1998), *The Origin of German Tragic Drama*, trans. J. Osborne, London: Verso.

Butler, S. (2011), *The Matter of the Page: Essays in Search of Ancient and Medieval Authors*, Madison, WI: Wisconsin University Press.

Cameron, A. (1970), *Claudian: Poetry and Propaganda at the Court of Honorius*, Oxford: Oxford University Press.

Chakrabarty, D. (2009), 'The Climate of History: Four Theses', *Critical Inquiry*, 35 (2): 197–222.

Charlet, J.-L. (2000), 'Comment lire le *de raptu Proserpinae* de Claudien', *Révue des Études Latines*, 78: 180–94.

Charlet, J.-L. (2002), *Claudien, OEuvres, tome I, Le rapt de Proserpine*, Paris: Les Belles Lettres.

Danowski, D. and E. Viveiros de Castro (2017), *The End of the World*, trans. R. Guimaraes Nunes, Malden, MA: Polity.

DeLoughrey, E. (2019), *Allegories of the Anthropocene*, Durham, NC: Duke University Press.

Deleuze, G. (1988), *Le pli: Leibniz et le baroque*, Paris: Les Éditions du Minuit.

Deleuze, G. and F. Guattari, eds (1987), *A Thousand Plateaus: Capitalism and Schizofrenia*, trans. B. Massumi, Minneapolis, MN: University of Minnesota Press.

Fauth, W. (1988), '*Concussio terrae*: Das Thema der seismischen Erschütterung und der vulkanischen Eruption in Claudians *De raptu Proserpinae*', *Antike & Abendland,* 34 (1): 63–78.

Feder, H., ed. (2021), *Close Reading the Anthropocene*, London: Routledge.

Formisano, M. (2018), 'Fragments, Allegory, and Anachronicity: Walter Benjamin and Claudian', in S. Schottenius-Cullhed and M. Malm (eds), *Reading Late Antiquity*, 33–50, Heidelberg: Universitätsverlag Winter.

Formisano, M. (2021a), '*Legens*: Ambiguity, Syllepsis and Allegory in Claudian's *De Raptu Proserpinae*', in M. Vöhler, T. Fuhrer and S. Frangoulidis (eds), *Strategies of Ambiguity in Ancient Literature,* 219–33, Berlin/Boston: De Gruyter.

Bibliography

Formisano, M. (2021b), '*Land und Meer*: La Praefatio al De raptu Proserpinae di Claudiano', in A. Bruzzone, A. Fo and L. Piacente (eds), *Metamorfosi del classico in età romanobarbarica*, 23–42, Florence: SISMEL Edizioni del Galluzzo.

Gruzelier, C. (1993), *Claudian*, De Raptu Proserpinae, Oxford: Oxford University Press.

Hamilton, J. (2015), 'Rahmen, Küsten und Nachhaltigkeit in Theodor Storms *Der Schimmelreiter*', in *Weimarer Beiträge*, 2: 165–80.

Hartman, J. (2021), 'Creative Destruction: Metaliterary Tree Violation in Claudian's *De Raptu Proserpinae*', Arethusa, 54 (1): 93–120.

Heintges, E. (2021), 'What Is Dead May Never Die: Sicilian Regeneration in Claudian's *De Raptu Proserpinae*', Arethusa, 54 (3): 425–54.

Huggan, G. (2021), 'Going Underground: In Defense of Deep Reading', in H. Feder (ed.), *Close Reading the Anthropocene*, 131–43, London: Routledge.

Joyce, J. (1961 [1922]), *Ulysses*, New York, NY: Random House.

Jameson, F. (2019), *Allegory and Ideology*, London: Verso Books.

Jansen, L., ed. (2014), *The Roman Paratext: Frame, Texts, Readers*, Cambridge: Cambridge University Press.

Lysen, F. and P. Pisters (2012), 'Introduction: The Smooth and The Striated', *Deleuze Studies*, 6 (1): 1–5.

Moinot, P. (1979), *Le Guetteur d'ombre*, Paris: Gallimard.

Morton, T. (2013), *Hyperobjects: Philosophy and Ecology after the End of the World*, Minneapolis, MN: University of Minneapolis Press.

Oppermann, S. (2018), 'Storied Matter', in R. Braidotti and M. Hlavajova (eds), *Posthuman Glossary*, 411–14, London: Bloomsbury.

Roberts, M. (1989), *The Jeweled Style: Poetry and Poetics in Late Antiquity*, Ithaca, NY: Cornell University Press.

Ruddiman, W. F. (2003), 'The Anthropogenic Greenhouse Era Began Thousands of Years Ago', *Climatic Change*, 61: 261–93.

Schoentjes, P. (2015), *Ce qui a lieu: Essai d'écopoétique*, Marseille: Wildproject.

Westphal, B. (2011), *Geocriticism: Real and Fictional Spaces*, trans. R. T. Tally Jr., New York, NY: Palgrave MacMillan.

Zapf, H. (2016), 'Cultural Ecology of Literature – Literature as Cultural Ecology', in H. Zapf (ed.), *Handbook of Ecocriticism and Cultural Ecology*, 135–53, Berlin: De Gruyter.

Chapter 12

Bachofen, J. J. (1861), *Das Mutterrecht: Eine Untersuchung über die Gynaikokratie der alten Welt nach ihrer religiösen und rechtlichen Natur*, Stuttgart: Krais & Hoffmann.

Borgeaud, Ph. (2004), *Mother of the Gods: From Cybele to the Virgin Mary*, trans. L. Hochroth, Baltimore, MD: Johns Hopkins University Press.

Bucchi, D. (2021), 'Gaia face à Gaïa: Figurations de la terre chez Eschyle et Bruno Latour', in F. Aït-Touati and E. Coccia (eds), *Le Cri de Gaïa: Penser la Terre avec Bruno Latour*, Paris: La Découverte.

Burkert, W. (1985), *Greek Religion*, Cambridge, MA: Harvard University Press.

Cronon, W. (1996), *Uncommon Ground: Rethinking the Human Place in Nature*, New York, NY: W. W. Norton & Co.

Finley, M. (1978), *The World of Odysseus*, revised edition, New York, NY: Viking Press.

Graves, R. (1948), *The White Goddess: A Historical Grammar of Poetic Myth*, London: Faber & Faber.

Harper, K. (2017) *The Fate of Rome: Climate, Disease, and the End of an Empire*, Princeton, NJ: Princeton University Press.

Harrison, J. (1900), 'Pandora's Box', *Journal of Hellenic Studies,* 20: 99–114.

Henrichs, A. (1978), 'Greek Maenadism from Olympias to Messalina', *Harvard Studies in Classical Philology,* 82: 121–60.

Hughes, J. D. (2014), *Environmental Problems of the Greeks and Romans,* 2nd edition, Baltimore: Johns Hopkins University Press.

Latour, B. (1993), *We Have Never Been Modern,* trans. C. Porter, Cambridge, MA: Harvard University Press.

Latour, B. (1999), *Pandora's Hope: Essays on the Reality of Science Studies,* Cambridge, MA: Harvard University Press.

Latour, B. (2017), *Facing Gaia: Eight Lectures on the New Climatic Regime,* trans. C. Porter, Cambridge: Polity Press.

Lovelock, J. (2000), *Gaia: A New Look at Life on Earth,* 3rd edition, Oxford: Oxford University Press.

McKibbon, B. (1989), *The End of Nature,* New York, NY: Random House.

Mikalson, J. (2010), *Ancient Greek Religion,* Malden, MA: Wiley-Blackwell.

Parke, H. W. and D. E. W. Wormell (1956), *The Delphic Oracle, Volume 1: The History,* Oxford: Basil Blackwell.

Popper, K. (1962), *Conjectures and Refutations: The Growth of Scientific Knowledge,* New York: Basic Books.

Roller, L. E. (1999), *In Search of God the Mother: The Cult of Anatolian Cybele,* Berkeley, CA: University of California Press.

Scott, M. (2014), *Delphi: A History of the Center of the Ancient World,* Princeton, NJ: Princeton University Press.

Seaford, R. (1995), *Reciprocity and Ritual: Homer and Tragedy in the Developing City-State,* Oxford: Clarendon.

Silk, M. S. and J. P. Stern (1981), *Nietzsche on Tragedy,* Cambridge: Cambridge University Press.

Strauss Clay, J. (1996), 'Fusing the Boundaries: Apollo and Dionysus at Delphi', *Mètis: Anthropologie des mondes grecs anciens,* 11: 83–100.

Tandy, D. W. and W. C. Neale (1996), *Hesiod's* Works and Days: *A Translation and Commentary for the Social Sciences,* Berkeley, CA: University of California Press.

Thomson, George (1938), *The* Oresteia *of Aeschylus, edited with Introduction, Translation, and a Commentary in which is included the work of the late Walter G. Headlam,* Cambridge: Cambridge University Press.

Usher, M. D. (2020), *Plato's Pigs and Other Ruminations: Ancient Guides to Living with Nature,* Cambridge: Cambridge University Press.

Walsh, K. (2013), *The Archaeology of Mediterranean Landscapes,* Cambridge: Cambridge University Press.

West, M. L. (1999), *The East Face of Helicon: West Asiatic Elements in Greek Poetry and Myth,* Oxford: Clarendon Press.

INDEX

Index

Index